Programming for Adults

A Guide for Small- and Medium-Sized Libraries

Raymond Ranier

THE SCARECROW PRESS, INC.

Lanham, Maryland • Toronto • Oxford

2005

SCARECROW PRESS, INC.

Published in the United States of America
by Scarecrow Press, Inc.
A wholly owned subsidiary of
The Rowman & Littlefield Publishing Group, Inc.
4501 Forbes Boulevard, Suite 200, Lanham, Maryland 20706
www.scarecrowpress.com

PO Box 317
Oxford
OX2 9RU, UK

British Library Cataloguing in Publication Information Available

Library of Congress Cataloging-in-Publication Data

Ranier, Raymond, 1950–
  Programming for adults : a guide for small- and medium-sized libraries / Raymond
Ranier.
    p. cm.
  Includes bibliographical references and index.
  ISBN 0-8108-5155-5 (pbk. : alk. paper)
  1. Adult services in public libraries—United States. 2. Libraries and adult education—
United States. 3. Public libraries—Cultural programs—United States. I. Title.
  Z711.92.A32R36 2005
  027.6'2—dc22
                                                                    2005008277

⊗™ The paper used in this publication meets the minimum requirements of
American National Standard for Information Sciences—Permanence of Paper for
Printed Library Materials, ANSI/NISO Z39.48-1992.
Manufactured in the United States of America.

To Dave, the two Andys, and Steve:
After all those cheap beer nights at
library school, I'll bet you thought
I'd never have enough brain cells left to
write a book.

~

Contents

~

Introduction

While I was in library school, one of the livelier class discussions I remember concerned a now-famous article entitled "Give 'em What They Want." The author of the article contended that libraries, being in the public trust, are not only obliged to supply the materials that patrons want, as opposed to what we think they should have, it is also good business sense to do so. Because the majority of the class (a collection development course) were young, idealistic, and probably never faced wrath any more forceful than dad's for missing a curfew, they thought that plying our patrons with volume upon volume of schlock was worse than the most diabolical of Inquisition tortures. Those of us who had been around the real world a time or two (as a former bartender, I had seen what a normally docile person could become when deprived of what they think is theirs by right) thought that this article made a certain measure of sense: I always like to get something back for my tax dollars.

I often think about those young men and women and their indignation over the cultural preferences of the unwashed masses. Did these new librarians go on to academic libraries, where you still have to give them what they want; with "them" being the faculty? Did they dare to take a public library job and, if so, how long before cruel reality set in? Wherever they are, I wish them well; wherever they are, I am sure that it wasn't where they expected to be when they were sheltered in the halls of graduate school. I know that I am far from there, myself.

When I took the job of adult services librarian at a smallish library in rural Northern Indiana, one line of my job description read, "plans and conducts programs for adults." I had the job scoped out as being reference, collection development, and scheduling a few elderly ladies to work the circulation desk, so I asked the boss what the "plan and conduct" was all about. "Oh, we aren't doing that yet, but it's in the strategic plan" was her response. Because we were in an old, small building and there was no place to do programming anyway, it soon became a forgotten item on a list I already had come to view as too long.

That all changed when, after five years on the job, we built a new facility and acquired a new vision, not to mention about three times the space we had before. We not only had room for programs, we had made it one of our reasons for being. I, however, was content to stay on the old-fashioned course of reference and collection. Finally, the pressure for programming increased to the point where I had to decide which path I intended to take. I went so far as to update my resume and send it out, but what expectations can a forty-nine year old career-changer expect in the Twenty-First Century? Running away was not the answer, for I knew that change would catch up to me sooner or later. At one point, I had thrived on change, turning my life around to attend college and graduate school at midlife—so why was I now contemplating running? Looking at the options, I realized that few had yet traveled down the adult program path, and that no one had drawn a road map to guide us. I was suddenly an explorer in uncharted territory and I liked the idea very much. I would keep a record of success and failure, and perhaps guide others along the way. Or maybe not: I just wanted to do my job.

Some or all of this scenario might be familiar to you; none of us who decided to join the library world were trained—or even warned—that we would soon be functioning somewhere along the lines of Julie, the activity director on the *Love Boat*; if I had had a choice in the matter, I probably would have chosen to be Isaac, the bartender. At first, there was much floundering, as is typical when one has absolutely no idea what is going on. It didn't help matters that our patrons had no idea what we were trying to do, either. After a while, however, we began to figure some things out, either on our own (the sightless squirrel and the acorn scenario), or by engaging in information sharing and general commiseration with other library personnel forced into similar situations. As I slowly gained confidence (and carried my coworkers along with me), I took a gradual liking to the task and the challenge. Soon, the staff and I were gleefully booking programs of all sorts, and even discovered that we were looked up to by other small libraries in the area as "programming gurus."

Never finding a satisfactory manual for adult programming grated on me; why had this aspect of librarianship been ignored when so many people were engaging in it? Those that existed were geared mainly to children's programming—even if they claimed they weren't. I swore that if I were ever to write a book on the subject, it would contain discussion on a number of topics that had bamboozled me and held me back from success. Sometimes, just knowing that another person has or is facing similar difficulties is stimulus enough to find answers or at least to buoy the spirit. Therefore, what you will find in this book are the problems we faced, the ideas we had, and the mistakes we made on the way to what we and, most importantly, our patrons see as programming success. You will find what I feel are justifications for adult programs (if anyone still needs them), budgetary considerations, and program planning. I literally emptied my head when it came to program ideas, and the chapters on crafts, cultural, and educational programs have many ideas that we have not even tried. I plan on willing the whole bunch to my successor because I will probably never have time to undertake them all.

While writing about programs in various subject areas, I found myself compelled to step out of my role as programmer and into my other identity as reference librarian. What good is my telling you about a program idea if you have no idea what that program is and, consequently, whether it would be something you want in your library? Not all people come to programming from reference, so they might not have the deep wells of trivial information at their fingertips that will tell them the difference between bop and cool jazz, or between a country and a Nantucket basket. If you do possess such arcane facts, please forgive my seeming pedantry; I have simply attempted to aid you in making informed decisions about programs and whether you want to do further research into some of the ideas that interest you.

Almost as important as ideas are finding the right people to present your programs, scheduling for optimum results, and the fine art of advertising what you are offering. I am certain that I have left something out because this topic is so large and grows larger every day. Indeed, I had no idea I would have this much to say on the topic and went into the project initially thinking of ways to pad the text with diagrams and photographs. I had no such need, obviously. It might be in part my natural verbosity, but I really do believe that adult programming is an immense new field of possibilities that will serve librarians in their work far into the future. We are indeed giving them what they want.

CHAPTER ONE

~

Adult Programming
and the New Public Library

One of the fun games library science educators used to play back in the late 1980s and early 1990s was something they referred to as "library of the future," which they used to force students into envisioning their given profession in five or ten years. The library world was rapidly changing then, with card catalogs disappearing, databases on CD-ROM appearing, the Internet fascinating everyone, and something called the *World Wide Web* getting a lot of attention. Students would use what mental powers they had—most were bewildered enough by the Dewey Decimal System—and dream up things that you would find in a near-future library, if indeed there was even a library to consider in the near future. Most imaginings include computers—lots and lots of computers—total access to materials and their contents via the online catalog, document delivery on demand, and a "virtual" library that existed without walls. Although I would guess that your library has at least four very real walls, most of these things have indeed come to pass.

The purpose of these exercises was to point out the unmissable fact that libraries were rapidly changing in the wired, bottom-line world and we would need to justify our institutions and ourselves if we wished to avoid becoming relics—of the unemployed variety—in the near future. No more hiding in a corner of a dark building tucked into a dark corner of town, catering to a few semi-washed people who liked to read dusty old books and nap in our easy chairs. In a society that holds little value for the esoteric, we had to show the taxpayers the potential of libraries to give some sort of real return on their involuntary investment. We needed to be of the utmost

1

use to the greatest number of people, not just a few bookworms seen as outside the mainstream.

What we managed to miss in all of this farseeing—in the computers, the video collections, and the virtual reference—was the library as a total community center, a place for leisure, entertainment, hobbies, artistic endeavors, and a place to meet. In other words, we never gave a thought to the idea of programs for the people who paid for the library: adults.

Adults have long been, so to speak, the neglected stepchild of public libraries, despite being responsible for two-thirds of the circulation and a majority of the funding. Instead, they were viewed as chauffeurs for the real patrons: their kids. Get the children early, the reasoning went, and you had them for life. Not in the age of two-minute sound bites, instant gratification, and short attention spans, you don't. Offer them the same old stuff you gave mom and dad, grandpa and grandma, and they might be lost for life, at least after they get out of school. Even if they do grow into adult library users, what of all the "lost souls" who view the library as a place to avoid? Do we give up? How do we convince them that the library is an asset if they won't buy into the "book thing"? When we began our video collection at the Peabody Public Library, we deliberately placed it in the back of the building, much as a supermarket puts its bread, milk, and other staples in back so that you have to pass by the other stuff. When we began programming, our thoughts were much the same: if we can just get them here inside the door, they will see what a treasure they have in their community.

The Case for Adult Programming

When looking for statistics and studies on adult programming, we are faced with several displeasing choices: no information, old information, or partial information. It is also somewhat difficult to analyze trends because, up until a few years ago, states did not even collect statistics on adult programs at public libraries—some still do not. Two studies exist that do measure some aspects of programming, but they are not really specific enough and one is rather old, at least by today's standards of change in libraries and in patron expectations.

The ALA commissioned a study of cultural programming for adults, which was conducted by the University of Illinois School of Library and Information Science in 1997. The statistics are derived from a survey sent to 1500 (1229 responses) public libraries of all sizes.[1] The study's main modifier—"cultural"—is focused on several categories of programs, some specific and others more broadly defined. Those of a more focused nature include book discussions, creative writing workshops, author visits, and reading incentive programs (grown-up versions of summer reading clubs). More nebulous are programs simply labeled *music, dance, drama,* and *lectures.* There are also some rather odd choices: local exhibits and readers' advisory. Any library with a glass case full of a patron's Barbie doll collection could have marked that box, and unless you are helping your book discussion group with title selection, how is readers' advisory a program (table 1.1)?

The chart holds few surprises, given that the study is from the mid-1990s. Book discussion groups and author visits are by far the most commonly held programs for adults, which fit in with the library's traditional role as a center for books and reading. Lecture series also scored high, as did musical performances, although we are not told anything more about them: did librarians schedule mostly classical music, or were they more daring? Film showing, one of the easiest of all program ideas, fared poorly, but this was at a time when many libraries were still debating whether or not videos even belonged in their collections. There were also performance rights problems, which no longer exist (the problems, not the rights). Finally, it would be interesting to see what percentage of these libraries now offer reading incentive programs to adults, as opposed to the 20% in 1997. This sort of low-investment/high-return program has gained in popularity (table 1.2).

As seen in table 1.2, the mix of libraries by size is equitable, with about 36% falling into the under-25,000 population category. Depending upon your definition of medium-sized, as many as 56% of reporting libraries could fit into this size range.

Table 1.1.   Adult Programs Offered in Public Libraries

Does Your Library Offer:	Yes %	No %
Book discussion groups	61.4	38.6
Creative writing workshops	18.2	81.8
Author presentations	59.3	40.7
Reading incentive programs	20.1	79.9
Local cultural exhibits	70.2	29.8
Traveling exhibits	38.2	61.8
Lecture series	42.7	57.3
Musical performances	41.6	58.4
Dance performances	14.2	85.8
Drama performances	22.9	77.1
Film series	19.8	80.2
Readers' advisory	26.5	73.5
Other	17.5	82.5

Source: American Library Association. 1999. *Survey of Cultural Programs for Adults in Public Libraries 1998* [computer file] Urbana-Champaign, IL: American Library Association/University of Illinois at Urbana-Champaign [producer and distributor].

Table 1.2.   Size by Population Served
of Libraries Surveyed

Population	# of Libraries
Over 1 million	18
500,000 to 999,999	43
250,000 to 499,999	72
100,000 to 249,999	238
50,000 to 99,999	162
25,000 to 49,999	250
10,000 to 24,999	337
5,000 to 9,999	109

Source: American Library Association. 1999. *Survey of Cultural Programs for Adults in Public Libraries 1998* [computer file]. Urbana-Champaign, IL: American Library Association/University of Illinois at Urbana-Champaign [producer and distributor].

ALA's main purpose for this study might have been geared toward studying the effectiveness of and continued need for some of the program options it offered at the time, such as *Let's Talk About It* and *Authors@Your Library*, both of which are covered in detail.[2] The study is available online, and I encourage you to check it out.

The National Center for Educational Statistics (NCES) did a more recent (2002) study that included such subjects as hobbies and computer instruction, as well as cultural programs.[3] Part of the study is dedicated to adult literacy classes in libraries, while the rest is defined as "Adult Lifelong Learning," which we will take to mean adult programming.

The NCES surveyed 1011 public libraries of all sizes in the spring of 2000. For the purposes of the survey, size was determined by the number of patron visits per day, rather than collection size or population served, freeing it from those traditional instruments of measurement, neither of which might be practical for programming. Libraries with less than 300 visits per day were deemed small, while those registering between 300–1500 were medium, etc. Distinction between rural, urban, and suburban facilities was also made (fig. 1.1), under the assumption that different types of programs would prevail in each of these environments.[4]

Literacy programs existed in only 17% of all libraries surveyed, and were most common in larger facilities. Lack of staff training and the existence of an outside literacy group were the most common reasons for such sparseness.[5] Computer instruction programs were very popular, most likely because staffs needed to do something other than help individuals at the terminals every few minutes. Most staffers can probably do at least a basic introduction to the

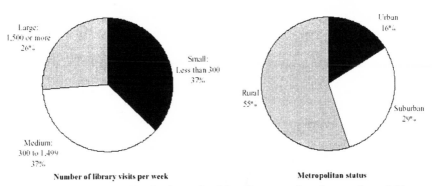

Figure 1.1. Percentage Distributions of Public Library Outlets, by Number of Library Visits per Week and Metropolitan Status: 2000

Source: U.S. Department of Education, National Center for Education Statistics, Fast Response Survey System, *Survey on Programs for Adults in Public Library Outlets,* 2000.

machine. We also find further confirmation of the popularity of book discussion groups. For some reason beyond my ken, the study also includes Internet access as a program. It is doubtful that any libraries would consider it to be such and would never total it into their year-end statistics. If it were, the Peabody Public Library could lay claim to about five thousand annual programs, and I would be looking for a large salary increase.

The NCES study is lacking in several respects. The survey simply asks if any of these types of programs have been scheduled over the preceding twelve months. Libraries could have offered a computer-instruction program once or a thousand times; it would not have made any difference. Neither is there any indication of attendance, budgeting, or staff and time involvement (table 1.3).

Although most state statistics are quite general about adult programming or just ignore it altogether, they remain the best way to actually document the rise in adult programming over the years. Edythe Huffman of the Indiana State Library Development Office sent me a copy of all the statistics they had on adult programming in Indiana since 1992. At one point, separate attendance figures for senior adults had been kept, but that was curtailed because of an increase in other reported statistics—library directors just did not want to be burdened with all these year-end extras.[6] The figures show a substantial increase in programming over the period recorded, with a growth of 64% in programs and 130% in attendance over the years covered in the table (table 1.4).

Perhaps the best indication of adult programming growth is the Wisconsin Public Library Statistics from the state Library Development Team. They

Table 1.3. Percentage of Public Library Outlets that Offered Specific Types of Adult Lifelong Learning Programs during the Last 12 Months, by Number of Library Visits per Week and Metropolitan Status: 2000

Library Characteristic	Computer Internet Instruction	Book/film Discussions or Presentations	Cultural Performances	Recreational Activities (Hobbies, Crafts)	Parenting Skills	Financial/ Investment Planning	Employment & Career Guidance	College & Educational Guidance	Citizenship Classes
All outlets	56	43	41	39	20	18	17	15	5
Number of Visits/week									
Small	36	22	11	24	6	4	8	9	5
Medium	59	45	48	40	22	19	20	18	4
Large	77	69	71	59	38	38	24	18	3
Metropolitan Status									
Urban	68	56	60	52	28	30	31	21	7
Suburban	59	50	51	50	24	26	18	14	6
Rural	49	34	28	29	15	11	12	13	3

Source: U.S. Department of Education, National Center for Education Statistics, Fast Response Survey System, *Survey on Programs for Adults in Public Library Outlets*, 2000.

Table 1.4.   Statistics of Indiana Public Library Programs for Adults

Year	Programs	% Change from First Year	Attendance	% Change from First Year
1993	11,809		218,311	
1994	10,864	-8.0%	225,619	3.3%
1995	8,935	-24.3%	228,311	4.6%
1996	9,851	-16.6%	205,374	-5.9%
1997	9,393	-20.5%	248,070	13.6%
1998	13,581	15.0%	220,225	0.9%
1999	15,665	32.7%	240,765	10.3%
2000	16,790	42.2%	319,069	46.2%
2001	14,421	22.1%	320,760	46.9%
2002	19,388	64.2%	502,925	130.4%

Source: Indiana State Library, Library Development Office. Statistics of Indiana Public Libraries. http://www.statelib.lib.in.us/www/isl/ldo/plstatsmenu.html

have records of both numbers of programs and attendance for children's and adult programs since 1991. You will note that although children's programs basically doubled, adult programs tripled. Attendance for both types of programs more or less doubled. It is impossible to draw any inferences from this data, however: all programs vary in their capacity to attract patrons. Craft classes cannot fill up the way a concert, lecture, or play can, and computer classes (which obviously grew in popularity during this period) are naturally limited by the number of available terminals. We simply might have gotten more intimate with our programs over the years (table 1.5).

Table 1.5.   Programming Statistics, State of Wisconsin

	Adult Programs	Attendance	Growth in Attendance	Child Programs	Child Attendance	Growth in Attendance
1991	3,317	84,065		22,108	773,491	
1992	3,885	98,956	17.7%	31,372	957,900	23.8%
1993	3,694	89,207	6.1%	30,794	999,168	29.2%
1994	4,319	98,016	16.6%	32,792	1,023,391	32.3%
1995	4,403	105,788	25.8%	33,653	1,087,949	40.7%
1996	4,711	119,924	42.7%	34,248	1,075,317	39.0%
1997	5,746	124,762	48.4%	35,671	1,079,714	39.6%
1998	5,631	128,980	53.4%	36,258	1,120,092	44.8%
1999	6,409	130,480	55.2%	39,173	1,146,275	48.2%
2000	8,510	147,446	75.4%	40,327	1,170,649	51.3%
2001	9,284	163,938	95.0%	43,146	1,220,324	57.8%
2002	9,909	175,418	108.7%	46,482	1,267,934	63.9%
Totals	69,818	1,466,980		426,024	12,922,204	

Source: Wisconsin Department of Public Instruction, Public Library Development, Wisconsin Public Library Statistics, 2002. [computer file] http://www.dpi.state.wi.us/dltcl/pld/xls/02state.xls

Programming and the Library's Mission

The number of programs and potential attendance should not be the sole factor in program determination. Just as your material collection is not judged by the number of titles and total circulation, you need to look at quality and, most importantly, how a program helps to fulfill your library's mission. This was something I did not pay close attention to when the programming bug first got me. I would schedule just about anything, and then wonder why my director was not impressed (not that she ever is). "Booking a large number of programs is good to help bring attention to the fact that we offer them now," she explained, "but just having a program to fill in the schedule and look impressive is like buying books to fill up the shelves: they may be of use to someone by accident, but if they sit there being ignored, they are worthless." What we do when programming is decide what is a "classic" and what is a "condensed book." We do that by examining our mission statement. Is the program going to fit our intentions for the community, or does it belong in someone else's repertoire? There are many program ideas in this book, but it is doubtful you would want to use all of them. If your library does not collect entertainment videos, you are unlikely to offer a film series of Hollywood blockbusters. Your mission and, to a great extent, your goals, were written to reflect the needs of your patrons, and so, too, should those needs be reflected in your programming.

Notes

1. American Library Association. 1999. *Survey of Cultural Programs for Adults in Public Libraries 1998* [computer file]. Urbana-Champaign, IL: American Library Association/University of Illinois at Urbana-Champaign [producer and distributor].

2. *Survey of Cultural Programs for Adults in Public Libraries 1998.*

3. U.S. Department of Education, National Center for Education Statistics. *Programs for Adults in Public Library Outlets*, NCES 2003-010, by Laurie Lewis and Elizabeth Farris. Project Officer: Bernard Greene. Washington, DC: 2002.

4. Ibid., 8.

5. Ibid., 11–12.

6. Edythe Huffman, Indiana State Library Development Office. Personal communication, February 13, 2004.

~

CHAPTER TWO

Programming for Patrons:
Design, Budgets, and Networking

Researching Your Community

Before you commit your library's staff, time, and budget to a course of programming, you will need to do some serious study of what your patrons do with their time, both in the library and outside of it. Researching various aspects of patron preferences is not difficult—in fact, it might have been done for you—but you must take the time to do this analysis of your community.

Local Demographics

The first and best place to get a feel for the community via figures and data is in the city and county housing and population statistics from the U.S. Census Bureau. Going to the state census sites from the federal census homepage, you can work your way down to county and city level and, for some things, even to township. Race, gender, and ethnicity are the most obvious figures, but others can help you in your programming. What percentage of the community are homeowners? If it is a large number, domestic programs, such as gardening, DIY, and decorating, could be just right. Family demographics can also suggest certain types of programs: a plethora of families with school-aged children could mean an interest in child rearing, financing college, and certain health and social topics. Education levels could determine the nature of concerts, plays, and films, while income and job categories can also speak to you of programs.

Patterns of Commercialism

Business and industry do a stellar job of researching a community before moving into it. Take a long, close look at local business, especially retail and service. Look, too, on supermarket shelves to see what is offered and perhaps more tellingly, what is missing. My wife works for a regional food chain, and I had the opportunity to look closely at several of their outlets when she was working at them. One of their newer stores, built in conjunction with several upscale housing developments, has a sushi bar; in our local store, you can't even find fresh fish. Situations such as this say more about people than their eating habits (you are what you eat, after all). Durable goods are another area you can study. Do a variety of stores offer many categories of items, or is the community dominated by a chain mega store? Look in the phone book: are there interior designers, massage therapists, farm supply stores, or anything else that would indicate dominance of a particular lifestyle? Are there more bail bondsmen in town than police officers? If so, you might consider a move.

Seriously, none of these businesses would exist in your area if there was no one to patronize them. You might also learn a great deal from taking the opposite view: what of the businesses that fail? Columbia City (home of the Peabody) does not seem to be able to keep a coffee shop in business because about four of them have come and gone in as many years. I probably won't be holding any coffee tastings in the near future. There is also a lack of bars—the type whose main business is alcohol, not food—which certainly suggests a lot.

Whenever I think of business, I think chamber of commerce. A good chamber will have its finger on the pulse of community business patterns, and might even have done some studies for its members. If your library belongs to the chamber, you should have no problem finding out what they have done.

Collection Statistics

Whatever your overall opinion of library technology, one thing must be freely admitted: it has given us statistical detail we never dreamed possible in the old ink-and-stamp days. Where once we were happy to know how much fiction circulated as opposed to nonfiction, we can now look to the fourth decimal place and beyond for our usage patterns, and tie them into patron ages and geographic data. If you or someone in the library has made a study of these circulation statistics, it will help you in your determination of program direction. If you have a large readership in Civil War history, you might want to book that lecturer on Gettysburg, or avoid that Ben Franklin impersonator if none of old Ben's biographies get checked out.

In-House Studies and Surveys

Anyone who has taken sociology or psychology 101 knows of the apparent pitfalls of surveys. Our problem as librarians is that 101 is probably the extent of our training in designing surveys. It is too easy to get only the complainers or the praisers, or have the thing ignored completely. Questions that seem neutral or self-explanatory to you might appear loaded or obscure to the patron. Nevertheless, we use them all the time and there really isn't a better way directly into our patrons' thoughts and feelings. Using surveys to find out what sort of programs our patrons would like to see does not translate into programs they will actually come to see. Faced with a survey, a person will often feel it is expected to put something down. If we give them a list, they will choose some items and leave others unmarked; if we just give them a blank space to write in their own list, we might only get back a blank space.

At the Peabody Public Library, we place surveys on the seats at programs (along with golf pencils) and ask attendees what other sorts of programs they would like to see at the library. Of course, there is a tendency to mark programs similar to what they are attending, but we still get a good input of other ideas. We also use the form for other information, such as best times and days, and the effectiveness of our advertising. See the appendixes for samples of such surveys.

Focus Groups

Unlike surveys, focus groups put you face-to-face with your patrons and their opinions. Choosing your groups and their participants carefully will ensure a variety of input from a cross-section of the community. Although people at focus groups often share their ideas and feelings openly, they can be influenced by others and perhaps intimidated if a librarian or other staff member sits in with the group. Often, a group will contain people who do not actually use the library, but are there because they are community leaders or are known for their ideas. As a result, focus groups should be used in conjunction with other methods. The point of focus groups should be to obtain ideas and criticism from another perspective, one that you, as a person with a vested interest, might not be able to see.

Program Policies

Oh no, not another written policy! Your policy manual is overflowing, no one reads it anyway, and now you should create yet another one for programming? If you are serious about your job, and the place of programs in the library: yes. Having already compared programs to collections, I feel strongly about working with some guidelines. You don't collect books and videos on whims, and neither should you do so with programs. A policy is not only a roadmap for you, it is also insurance against those who would say the library needs to do certain programs that do not fit your mission, just as a collection policy guards against demands for inappropriate materials. Several policy samples are in the appendix, and you might be able to find more through your state library. You already know how to write policies, and just how detailed they need to be in your library, but at the very least the policy should state what kind of programs you will schedule and the reasons for doing so. As you can see from the policy I wrote for the Peabody, we have added additional details such as publicity, cleanup, and financing. The section I feel strongest about is the one entitled "parameters," which has probably been used more by me than any other portion of the policy. The line between pure commercialism and acceptable program is very fine, as is the one between legitimate debate and iconoclastic rant.

A Tale of Two Budgets

Whenever I get together with other program librarians—and we do that quite often—the most persistent topic is the matter of budgets. I have been blessed with a relatively large amount of money for programming, but many libraries, some larger than Peabody, have absolutely no budget for programs, yet are expected to do them. I am reminded of the poor Israelites ordered to make twice the number of bricks but given no straw. Such are the pharaohs of some library boards making it difficult for many of us to do the jobs for which we were hired.

Working without a Budget

Programming without a budget might be difficult, but it is not impossible. Just as a guess, I would say that 50–60% of our programming at the Peabody either does not cost anything or could be done totally free by making a few adjustments, such as eliminating refreshments. Several program people I have talked to have no budget, yet still manage to schedule a lot of programs. This is why speaking to others in the same predicament is so essential: it is the best way to obtain the most ideas from those working to conquer the impractical.

Dina Ferree of the Steuben County (Indiana) Public Library has been planning and promoting programs for several years, and her budget is zero. Nevertheless, she always manages to do at least two programs each month, including visits from authors. One type of programming that Dina books is the bus trip. As a bus trip sponsor, the library will make arrangements with a bus company to take patrons to a certain event such as an important art exhibit or to a cultural or historical destination. Sometimes the trip is as mundane as holiday shopping (no parking hassles), or it could be an extended sightseeing tour of several days. Theoretically, the library should incur no expense by doing such sponsorships, except perhaps to pay for a staff member to go along. There are some snags to this arrangement, depending on circumstances. Depending upon the bus company, you might be required to place a down payment to hold the bus, and it might not be refundable should you have to cancel for some reason. Another problem is that buses tend to be large, and if you cannot fill all the seats, you might end up paying the difference because the per-person price quoted is usually for a full vehicle.

Other no-budget programs are craft and art workshops, in which the patron pays for the materials and the instructor donates her time. Dina also schedules gardening programs, which can be presented by local amateurs or by the cooperative extension office. Local persons often have interesting stories to tell or a skill to share, and they can be the main source for your programs.

One step up from absolutely free are those government and organization speakers who do not charge for their services, but are expected to be reimbursed for travel expenses, most often mileage. There are several ways to try and get around this barrier: you can beg and, as a public institution, they might waive your fees; or, there might be some money in the budget somewhere that can take care of the expense.

The Advantages of a Budget

If we can do so many programs without a budget, then why should we even try to get one? Asking for money is an aggravation and we have all heard the same old reasons for saying no. If you really want to do programming that will encompass everything the library stands for, you will profit from the freedom and flexibility of a budget behind you and your program policy. When you are limited by what you can get for free or by what will willingly come your way, you will find your schedule suffering from an unevenness that manifests itself in one or two types of programs. You will not be able to fulfill the library's mission if all you can do is craft programs; you really need the ability to "shop" for the people and events that will give you a complete schedule. Once again, let's think of it in terms of your collection: what sort of library would you have if the only books you could put on the shelves were donations? If your patrons are like ours, you would have no trouble putting out a steady offering of old encyclopedias, coffee table books, outdated textbooks, and paperback romances. Not really anyone's idea of a well-balanced collection. So, no matter how many basket classes you have to schedule, keep begging for that budget.

What's Available?

With a budget, you will be able to contract cultural programs and artists, such as musicians and actors. Dina has said that if she were ever to have a budget, she would want to schedule more music. You can move beyond the local self-published author to regional and perhaps even national names. You can mount plays and show films, all the while not having to worry about breaking copyright laws. You can hire lecturers and re-enactors, health professionals, and historians. You will be able to stock your library with the tools needed to do real programming, put out food and drink for attendees, and even offer prizes for contests and competitions. In short, you, too, will become a program guru.

Working with a Budget

Once you are given a budget, you will have to figure out how not to spend it all the first month. In other words, you will need to budget your budget. You should learn the average prices charged by authors, performers, lecturers, and others, decide how much of each you want, and divide it up. If there is an author you really want who is over your self-imposed limit, you will have to sacrifice and cut some lectures or concerts. It's just like your household budget, only without the credit cards for binge spending.

At the Peabody Public Library, I actually have two budgets for programming: one for professional services and one for everything else, called *programming supplies* (this actually grew out of mimicry of the children's department budget, where program supplies mean paper and glue). Professional services are, of course, fees for performers and speakers (not their expenses). This is the budget that gets divided up, à la the preceding paragraph. The supply budget supports programming by paying for refreshments, prizes, play scripts and royalties, and other program essentials. The burners for our cooking classes were purchased through this fund and for our first library mystery play, we used it to cover costume rental.

Cost-Benefit Analysis

One way to see if you are using your budget wisely—and to convince the board that you are—is to evaluate your programs by a method known as *cost-benefit*. Although I am not a business person, I do know a simple formula when I see it. You simply attach a (reasonable) per-person price to your programs, add up your expenses, and subtract one from the other. Because we aren't a for-profit organization, if you break even, you are doing something right. Our last jazz concert drew seventy-three people. I figure five dollars a person is not unreasonable for a local band that, if playing in a club, would probably generate a five-dollar cover charge. Multiply 73 × $5 = $365. The band charged $250, and we spent about twenty dollars for refreshments, so $250 + $20 = $270. Subtract this from the spurious $365 gate and you are left with a $95 dollar profit. Birdland has risen from the ashes! If you are interested in pursuing the cost-benefit aspect of evaluation for this and other library functions, check out the study from the St. Louis Public Library at http://www.slpl.lib.mo.us/libsrc/resurp.htm, which put the entire library under the analysis.[1]

Putting it all Together

Finding programs is not as difficult a task as the ones we have just discussed. The World Wide Web is one of the best tools a programmer could wish for and relatively simple searches often provide fruitful, if time-consuming, results. Networking with your peers is also an obvious choice for ideas, and actual program and expense sharing. If two or more libraries decide they would like to book a particular speaker or performer, they might receive a discount on individual fees—or at the very least, will save money by sharing travel and lodging expense. Another similar tool is program exchange. This involves using locally developed programs and sending them "on the road" in trade. Recently, I learned that a staff member of an area library was teaching an interesting class to her patrons. When I inquired into the possibility of having her do the class at Peabody, her director said, "What have you got to trade?" As it turned out, we had just what she wanted: two staffers who had been doing a class on buying and selling online.

As you progress in your work as program procurer, you will discover many methods of finding and developing programs. Our *Jeopardy* tournament came about after I had watched an episode of the television program one evening in a "program frame of mind." Other librarians have told me that ideas will just "pop" into their heads, and they will then explore those ideas for program possibilities. Local online discussion groups and listservs probably exist in your area; they do in Indiana, even though they do not seem to be used much. Perhaps we are too busy devising new programs to think about such things.

I have actually attended some recent conferences that featured workshops on adult programming—stuff I could actually use—but they are still few and far between. You will continue to rely upon your wits and creative nature for some time to come.

A time will come in your career as event meister when two things will happen: you will have people come to you wanting to do programs, and you will begin to reach out to the community to partner with you in your programming. Once it has been established in your community that the library is at the forefront of event programming, those who feel they have something to contribute will offer their services. If so, don't be afraid to ask for their credentials and a sample of what they say or do, and don't hesitate to politely turn down their offer if it does not fit your policies. You will soon find that some programs just naturally belong in partnership with other community organizations. If you schedule a speaker on animal welfare, it would be smart to involve the local humane society in the project, in advertising, helping with setup, and providing attendance. When we organized our *Jeopardy* tournament, we partnered with the local Kiwanis chapter, which helped with promotion, canvassed local businesses for prizes, and even scheduled local "celebrity" hosts. When you connect your library and its programs to the community, you make them an essential part of local life.

Little Things Mean a Lot

Programs are missions, policies, planning budgets, sharing, booking, and advertising. Yet they are also a lot of small things that need to be thought about, delegated, worked on, and dispensed with in order to have it all fall into place and be a success. Some of these things are obvious and some are not; some require advanced decision making while others may occur unexpectedly during the course of planning and scheduling. However and whenever they happen, you may need to address these concerns at some point.

Travel Expenses and Lodging

Many presenters who travel more than an hour or two in order to give a program might require reimbursement of their travel expenses. In the vast majority of cases, this will mean payment of a flat mileage rate for the round trip. Government officials have a set rate, but private presenters will have their own, based on what they bring with them. A traveling theater troupe might fit into a single van, but might need to pull a large trailer filled with props, costumes, and sets. You need to know average rates for such things and how far the actual trip will be: thirty cents a mile might sound like a small amount until you multiply it a few hundred times. If the person or persons also require lodging for the night, it should be for one of three reasons: they could have driven too far to go back after an evening program, the program was scheduled too early for them to have conveniently driven that day (this is more likely with children's programs), or they may be continuing on to another venue farther from their home base. If the latter is the reason, you should find out what that next venue is, contact them, and arrange to share some expenses (some caring presenters will actually do this for you or at least suggest it). Also check with your local hotels to see if any would consider offering a reduced rate in exchange for some free publicity in your flyers and at the event. Our local Amerihost Inn will sometimes waive the charge entirely for a simple promotion. I have also had presenters tell me that they would not be averse to staying at the home of a library staff member.

Refreshments

To feed or not to feed is quite often the question. The goodwill incurred by offering food and drink can be very positive, both for the image of the library and for attendance at your programs. Once you start, however, be prepared to continue because it will be expected. Popcorn at a movie is a tradition and very inexpensive, but more substantial spreads for all your programs could add up over the course of the year. You might want to limit your offerings to certain types of events, such as those with intermissions (plays, concerts, etc.). This will help to keep people from leaving during the break, a common occurrence with free entertainment. Refreshments offered after a program will give patrons a chance to mingle and talk to the presenter, maybe asking questions they did not feel comfortable positing during the program itself. It also affords you and the staff an opportunity to discover what people thought of the event, and what they would enjoy seeing in the future.

Keeping Things Organized

Because many people will be working on your programs, you will need some way to keep them all advised of the progress being made. Some sort of schedule can be made accessible to everyone so that they can use it for publicity, date planning, statistics, and other essentials. This will not only help ensure that all work is done; it will help keep work from being repeated needlessly. I have included a couple of examples in the appendix: one a simple word-processing table, the other a spreadsheet file.

Targeted Programs

You need to think in terms of the groups that you serve in your library. "Adult" is as nebulous a term as "young" or "old." Most adults have other agendas besides being over eighteen. Younger adults might be concerned about careers, job searching, or starting a family; senior adults might be more interested in leisure activities, travel, and retirement income, among other things. Ethnic and racial groups, people with various disabilities, chronic illnesses, and special social needs must be addressed as well. Remember, programming is about fulfilling your mission and attending to patron needs and wants, not about attendance figures.

Thinking Programming

One way to be sure that you have a steady flow of program ideas is to think of everything you do—yes, even that—in terms of potential programs. I mentioned our *Jeopardy* tournament being birthed during a couch potato session; you can have ideas like that spring into your head at any time, in any situation. If you see someone with a tattoo, that should suggest a program; when taking trash out to the curb, something besides your olfactory senses should be sparked. Everything has potential; it is up to you to find it and determine, as the ad execs say, if it will fly.

Programs and the Calendar Year

At times you might be devoid of ideas. Blockage is part of the creative process. At such times, try turning to the calendar for inspiration. What is going on in the world? Current events can be tapped and, if scheduled in a timely manner, might bring a large audience to your event. Holidays and festivals large and small can also inspire programs. Keep a copy of *Chase's Calendar of Events* close at hand; no one says that only Maine is allowed to celebrate the Potato Blossom Fest.

You will never run out of ideas as long as you can think, see, or hear. It is all out there waiting for you to grasp, shape, and mold into an event. As Mickey and Judy used to say in those old movies, "Let's put on a show!"

Note

1. Holt, Glen E., Donald Elliott, and Amonia Moore. *Placing a Value on Public Library Service.* http://www.slpl.lib.mo.us/libsrc/resurp.htm

~

CHAPTER THREE

Bringing Speakers to Your Library

People are out there waiting for you. They have something important to say, but they can't say it until you call. Some of these people work for the government, some for nonprofit organizations, some for businesses that have a stake in the common good of the community, and others are representatives of business and industry who are trying to get the word out about their products, services, and good intentions. Some of these speakers come to you at no extra charge; some for mileage fees, if they apply. Some are individuals interested in profit, and will charge you according to what they think they are worth; and it will amaze you at times to find out just how highly some people value themselves. All of these people want to be found and, despite what you might think when you are desperate for a program, truly make it easy to find them. There are even ways for them to find you and occasionally they will do so. Several have found us at the Peabody Public Library, and if they can find a small library in rural Indiana, they can find you.

These are the speakers, both amateur and professional, whose job it is—at least in part—to disseminate their special knowledge to the public. In the daytime, they might take on the secret identity of an engineer, a banker, a clergyman, or even a mild-mannered reporter. For many in academia, government, business, and other areas, part of their job is that of public speaker. Not only do they fulfill their job descriptions through the work for which they were trained or schooled, they also are expected to go out into the world and talk about it. Such a task might also be part of your job. Many librarians, especially those who work at the public desks, are expected to speak at schools, service clubs, community organizations, and other functions. Too bad we can't book each other at our libraries; we work cheap and certainly know a lot. We just can't get anyone to listen to us.

Many businesses and organizations hire people whose full time job it is to speak to the public. They don't work in IT, they aren't part of research and design, and they certainly aren't driving rivets down on the assembly line floor. Although these speakers can give you the overall message the company wants to get across, they really don't work inside the organization and, therefore, will not have all the interesting little things that people want to hear. When we had a NASA engineer at the library, he told us some of the "unusual" things they used to do to the astronauts during training, just for fun. You won't hear that from the PR people, who are little more than walking commercials. There are also businesses whose business is speakers. They are clearing houses for people who think they have something to say and that someone will pay them to say it. It seems that anything a person has done in life can be turned into a lucrative enterprise if the right spin is put on it, from shooting drugs to shooting people. A few jokes, lots of slides, an upbeat attitude and a smile, and you have sold yourself. There are speakers' bureaus out there representing people who have successfully (or even unsuccessfully, if they have suffered enough) climbed Mount Everest. It seems Sir Edmund Hillary's retort, "Because it is there" has been replaced by, "Because it pays big."

Authors also have something to say to anyone who will listen. Unlike the Everest guys, however, authors are very different in their focus and their accomplishments. Not all writers are equal in the eyes of your patrons; if they haven't read their books, or seen them on Oprah, why bother listening to what they have to say? Some authors are out of your reach both financially and physically, and the ones who aren't, well, ask your patrons about them. Authors are also seasonal; when they are busy writing, they do not emerge from their cocoons, but when their new book is ready and the tour begins, they seem to be everywhere.

With all of these speakers out there, just waiting to help you fulfill your mission while fulfilling their own, you need to start finding and evaluating them. You will be able to fill your schedule for the next year. They are busy, so you, too, need to get busy.

Speakers' Bureaus

Most government agencies and offices, nonprofit organizations, and some businesses have organized speakers' bureaus that will put you in contact with or arrange a date with one of their people. As mentioned earlier, these people are usually employees who have duties beyond speaking, but are encouraged to engage the public in discourse. To this end, they are given a prede-termined amount of time to travel and give speeches. Speakers' bureaus will often list their speakers by name, their area(s) of expertise, and the topics on which they will speak or have spoken in the past. If you don't see exactly what you want, these bureaus will often work with you to find a speaker who can address the subject in which you are interested, as long as it is directly related to the organization's purpose. With so much cooperation available, you cannot fail to find what you want.

Organizations and Outreach

Some organizations, both nonprofit and for-profit, are viewed by the general populace as somehow being in the public trust, above the petty concerns of profit and loss, working first and foremost for the welfare of the individual and the good of society as a whole. These organizations are well aware of this man-date that has been conferred upon them de facto, take it very seriously, and might even have written it into their mission and goals. They generally have several forms of outreach in place to perpetuate this mission, such as classes, literature, public service announcements and, of course, speakers. This speaker availability might not be quite as evident to you as some of these other forms of information dissemination, mainly because it is of limited use to the general public—not to say that the public is not the end beneficiary, but rather that they themselves do not seek it from the organization. These bureaus are most often contacted by service clubs, such as Kiwanis or Optimists, by social or-ganizations like the Moose or Eagles, or by businesses planning training semi-nars for employees. Service clubs and social groups usually have an outside speaker as a normal part of their regular meetings, which can be held as often as once a week. That adds up to a lot of speakers over a year. Businesses with a large number of employees often hold in-house training several times a year, and if they can find a speaker that even remotely touches on the theme of that particular session, someone who can address the same sort of problem from a different perspective, that business will grab her up. Quite often these busi-nesses are looking for presentations on motivation and teamwork, topics that transcend individual business activity. Sometimes, though, people just want to hear what the speaker has to say, without having to tie it into some greater whole. This is when they should be coming to the library to hear them.

Hospitals and Health Care Providers
The hospital is the quintessential organization that has been placed on a pedestal and held to a higher standard of operation than most businesses. Of

course, not all hospitals are private or even run for profit, but for some reason, the more commercial the institution, the more it is revered. We have all heard horror stories about county hospitals, or feared having elective surgery at a teaching hospital (remember the television program *St. Elsewhere?*). On the other hand, just mention that you have had tests at the Cleveland Clinic, or treatment at Mayo, and you will see awe in the faces of your friends. They will not feel badly for you or worry for your future, for they know you will be fine in the long run. Because these institutions want to retain this image in the public's eye, they will have large publicity departments in place that work very hard and most likely have speakers at the ready.

Hospital speakers will address the most popular of today's health topics, including diseases, prevention, nutrition, and insurance concerns. Among the subjects on a typical hospital's list:

- Diabetes
- Smoking and its implications
- Affordable health care
- Cancer
- Heart health
- Choosing a doctor
- Second opinions
- Pediatric and neonatal health
- Stress, hypertension, and stroke

Depending upon the staff of the hospital and its particular specialty, if any, there will be a number of other topics available. The small hospital in Columbia City has a two-page list of subjects covered by its speakers, so even the smallest community hospital is going to provide you with plenty of material. Like most speakers' bureaus, it will try to custom fit a topic for you if you don't find it on the list.

Nonprofit health organizations and associations are another source of speakers. These groups raise money for research and also educate the public about the particular health issue for which they exist. Groups like the American Heart Association, the American Cancer Society, and the Muscular Dystrophy Association not only have national offices, but also are active with local chapters, and this is where you will find your speakers.

Nursing homes and assisted living centers are also a fertile ground for speakers that will be of interest to your patrons. The Peabody Public Library had a series of talks using speakers from or procured by one of the local homes. The topics included long-term care insurance, choosing a nursing home, working with Medicare, and even alternatives to nursing homes. A good home will not go around shopping for business; they are first and foremost a health-care facility, designed to help those with needs when and if the needs arise, but they are not ghouls, hoping for the worst for grandma and grandpa. What they will do is explain all of the options to families, and if they can do that in a large public forum—especially for people who are not under immediate pressure to do something—the less stressful it will be for all when it comes time to make a decision.

Many nursing homes have assisted living centers associated with them, and this can open up some alternative program ideas, plus a chance to partner with these community health givers. Such centers will usually have communal rooms for eating, meeting, and socializing. You can arrange for some of your library programs to be repeated at their facility. We take books and other materials to the people who live there, so why not take our programming there as well?

Home health-care and wellness centers will also have speakers available for you. Large doctors' clinics, veterinarian clinics, and even private practice physicians might offer some form of outreach. It pays to check with all of them because the emphasis for all health-care providers today is on prevention rather than treatment, and the best way to treat is to educate.

Historical Societies
The historical society is a prime source of speakers on local and regional history, and people are definitely interested in history. Surprisingly, many people are more knowledgeable about national and world history than they are about the past events in their own town or state. This is, in part, a result of the extremely mobile nature of our society. A lot of people were not raised in the area in which they presently live; those who want to belong to their new communities will be glad to learn of its history. Another problem contributing to our lack of historical perspective is the overwhelming influence of pop culture society to live in the present or, more commercially, in the future. As we lose a lot of our personal history, we will begin to look for another past to claim.

If you start with the local historical society or museum, you will probably find someone who knows the history of local events, people, structures, and businesses. These organizations may or may not have organized speakers' bureaus, but they most certainly will know everyone in the area who has any amount of expertise on local history and, more importantly, if they would be willing and capable of speaking on their favorite topic. As an added bonus, the society might be able to direct you to people who have probably lived some history themselves, and can give some first-hand accounts. At the Peabody, we have had area speakers who have been a part of some of the most momentous events of the Twentieth Century. A retired local photographer was assigned to the Army Air Force photographic corps during World War II; it was his job to fly over Hiroshima and Nagasaki to record the devastation of the two atomic blasts that ended the conflict. What he showed the audience and told them was beyond any imaginings of their own. A former county historian, an expert on pioneer life on the early frontier, is also a veteran whose division helped to liberate concentration camps in Germany. Obviously, veterans of the armed services are very good candidates for insights into important events from the personal perspective.

State historical societies are the real gold mines for library programmers. State societies will have speakers' bureaus, programs on selected topics (usually tied into their current themes) and traveling displays. By using both displays and speakers, you can build a theme for your programming that can work for you over several months. A few years ago, the Peabody hosted a celebration of automobile transportation in Indiana (home at one time to several classic makers of automobiles). We had someone speak about the Studebaker Company, coupled with a display from the Indiana Historical Society featuring the history of auto plants in the state. We also brought in another speaker who was an expert on the Lincoln Highway, which ran through Indiana near Columbia City. Finally, the Historical Society loaned us an author who spoke about Carl Fisher, the founder of the Indianapolis 500 and a major backer of the Lincoln Highway.

Most traveling displays offered by historical societies and museums are essentially free, with only shipping costs involved (which, unfortunately, can be somewhat high, depending upon the size of the display, and the value of what it contains). Recently, the Indiana Historical Society stopped charging for shipping, choosing instead to deliver and pick up the display themselves. Located in the middle of the state, they are only a few hours from virtually any point, and their munificent gesture has made the displays available to small libraries and historical museums that would otherwise have no budget for such things. Authors who publish through our historical society are also available to speak at no charge save their expenses. You will need to check with your state's society to see if their policies are as generous. Even if they are not, they will be able to provide you with quality at a reasonable price.

Other historical organizations might be regional or topical. A great deal of interrelated events might have occurred in a certain area, such as a part of a state, part of several states, or even encompassed several whole states (such as history of the Old West); if so, a society or societies might be devoted to that regional history. The previously mentioned speaker on the Lincoln Highway is a member of the Lincoln Highway Association, which covers states from New York to California. Other examples of such societies deal with Lewis and Clark, the Great Lakes maritime history, or the Erie Canal. Even if the Lincoln Highway had not threaded its way through the state near the Peabody Public Library, we would still have found the topic interesting enough to book the speaker. Check with such societies for topics of interest. Even the local historical society in the next town over might have some speakers on an interesting subject from their history.

Some of these speakers will ask for a donation to their organization as a fee for their lecture, essentially leaving the amount up to you (don't be too cheap; you might want to work with them in the future). In Indiana, such a direct approach—one nonprofit giving money to another—is not allowed; the check can, however, be made out to the speaker, who can endorse it over to his organization. Other than that, the only fees you incur are for travel and lodging, if the speaker comes from a fair distance.

The state or county historical museum is another place to look for speakers and programs. These could be separate entities from the historical society; if they are, they might be able to help. A museum, by its very nature, is a place of education and information, so it probably has its own programs to go along with its exhibits. However, as a government-sponsored organization, they might also have an outreach program that can take some of their lectures on the road. The Indiana State Museum does programs at its facility in Indianapolis, sends some of them to other locations if requested, and also makes them available through video conferencing.

Arts and Humanities Councils

Humanities councils usually work in the same way as historical societies do, at least at the state level. They provide cultural education and leadership for the public through support of the arts. They also offer grants to local institutions to develop cultural programs in those localities. They will also act as coordinators of the cultural activities in their state, making available contacts to musical groups, artists, theater troupes, and individuals involved in the humanities. In Indiana, the council has a service called *History Alive!*, which has information on and contacts for a number of people who perform or speak, usually in the persona of a famous literary figure, such as Hoosier poet James Whitcomb Riley. Like the historical society, they also have traveling exhibits available. To libraries and other groups, the Indiana council also makes available multiple copies of fiction titles often used in book discussion groups.

The Peabody Public Library has booked several very successful programs through the council—especially the first-person portrayals, such as Riley and Henry David Thoreau (an Indianapolis attorney and a college professor in real life). People seem to be drawn to the theatricality of such presentations, which afford learning opportunities in a comfortable, entertaining atmosphere.

Ethnic, Religious, and National Groups

Ethnic and national organizations can be political associations, educational museums and libraries furthering the knowledge and understanding of the ethnic or national group, or even social clubs, such as the Sons of Italy. Native American, Hispanic, and African American organizations can be contacted for speakers, exhibits, and themed programs. Religious organizations—not individual churches—are also a source. Non-Christian or out-of-the-mainstream religious groups will be happy to explain their beliefs and rituals to nonmembers. Islamic groups such as ING (Islamic Networks Group) are very active at this time, trying to dispel misconceptions and miseducation about their religion and culture. Nationalist organizations, representing just about every conceivable nationality that has ever settled in the United States, can send you speakers who can give your patrons some insight into their cultural background, their immigration to the New World, and their place in our society.

Don't be afraid to contact one of these groups if their headquarters are far outside your area; quite often, they will be able to direct you to speakers in your area. Although not all of these groups will be able to help you, they are a natural starting point for locating speakers on these topics.

The Federal Government Speaker

As this is being written, we have just passed the April 15th deadline for filing income tax, so the following statement might seem just a bit strange: the federal government is your friend. When you really need a speaker, they have them; every agency, every department, all the cabinet offices, services, and all the branches of the government are chock-full of speechifiers. Even if you aren't looking for a speaker, they will make it so tempting that you will want to book several. You know that government documents and information are the best out there, that our depository libraries are filled to overflowing with everything from proceedings to patents, and government web sites are endless links to data and statistics. With these credentials, do you think the United States government would send you second-rate speakers?

You will face a bit more paperwork and regulations with a government speaker than your anarchic self is used to, but it is a small price to pay. Speaking of pay, because our taxes pay for these fellows, the only fees you are likely to incur are for travel. Granted, some speakers might be based some distance from your facility, making those fees a bit steep, but plenty of speakers will be in your area (the government is everywhere, don't you know), which will keep the bill down. You will also have to do a good deal of waiting for your speaker; waiting for a reply, waiting for speaker confirmation, waiting for the date and the speaker's time off to be okayed, and even at times, waiting for a bill. A three- to four-month lead-time is the minimum, but realistically you should plan at least six months in advance. Depending upon the time of year, the organization, and the amount of public interest in its operations, you might not get the date, the speaker, or even the topic that you want. You will be safest if you give them several alternatives for each date so that they can have enough leeway to put something together for you. Because they are doing most of the work here, you should make it as easy as possible for them. Often, there will be a follow-up to the visit, usually in the form of a short survey; these people are very serious about maintaining the quality of their service.

NASA, the Librarian's Best Friend

If you have never had a speaker from NASA at your library, what are you waiting for? Your reference department knows about the NASA web site and its seemingly endless resources for homework assignments and answers to all manner of questions astronomical, geological, and meteorological. Their mission runs both deep and wide.

Basically, about twelve individual NASA research and space centers are placed conveniently across the country. Each facility specializes in a specific area of space research, and has its own experts in certain fields. They also have people who can address more general and popular topics. You cannot pick and choose between these facilities and their speakers; you must work with the one assigned to your area. This should not be a problem because each center has many speakers on many diverse topics. Here is a list of the facilities that offer speakers and the states they cover:

- Marshall Space Flight Center (Alabama, Arkansas, Iowa, Louisiana, Missouri, Tennessee).
- Ames Research Center (Alaska, Arizona, California, Hawaii, Idaho, Montana, Nevada, Oregon, Utah, Washington, Wyoming).
- Dryden Flight Research Center (south/central California, Arizona, Nevada).

- Jet Propulsion Laboratory (all states, provided that all travel expenses are paid).
- Lyndon B. Johnson Space Center (Colorado, Kansas, Nebraska, New Mexico, North Dakota, Oklahoma, South Dakota, Texas).
- Goddard Space Flight Center (New England, Mid-Atlantic states, District of Columbia).
- Glenn Research Center (Illinois, Indiana, Michigan, Minnesota, Ohio, Wisconsin).
- Langley Research Center (Kentucky, North & South Carolina, Virginia, West Virginia).
- Stennis Space Center (Louisiana, Mississippi).
- John F. Kennedy Space Center (Florida, Georgia, Puerto Rico, Virgin Islands).

These facilities are not all centrally located within the geographic areas they serve, so for some libraries the simple mileage fee can become quite a burden. This is especially true in the Western states.

The speakers of NASA are very polished and professional, and they often bring many bits of space-related items. One of the speakers from the Glenn Research Center brought with him to the Peabody Public Library an actual Apollo spacesuit, which a fortunate young man got to model. Models, space food, clothing, shuttle tiles, clothing, and tools are also pieces they might bring along when talking about the manned space program.

Like any organization, NASA is fond of telling us about past glories and future dreams, so a lot of topics center on the space race, moon landings, the Saturn V rocket, and the Pioneer and Voyager probes. Some programs feature present missions to Mars, comets, and asteroids. The future is represented by terraforming, space colonies, and new forms of propulsion. A partial list of the topics available from the Glenn Research Center includes:

- The Wright Brothers—Inventing the Airplane
- Planets, Comets, Stars, and Galaxies
- Seeing our Earth from Space
- The Galileo Mission to Jupiter
- Communication via Satellites
- Long-Term Effects of Space Travel on Humans
- Alternative Energy Sources
- Columbia Accident Investigation Report
- NASA Careers
- Women in Science and Engineering

As you can see, quite a wide range is covered, although you might not get your first choice, as stated earlier. NASA requires a ten-week advance notice, plus a signed letter agreeing to the terms of the visit (i.e., to provide lodging if needed, and to pay the speaker's mileage at the present government rate).

The space agency also makes astronauts available for public appearances, but don't expect Neil Armstrong or Buzz Aldrin. There is also no guarantee that your request will be accepted; astronauts are much in demand and your potential event must compete with many others. The size of the venue and the number and make-up of the audience are among the factors in NASA's decision. The astronauts' extensive training and on-call status for missions could also interfere with your plans. Be aware also that you would be paying travel expenses from and to Houston, Texas, rather than from your local NASA facility.

Finally, NASA has available for your library traveling exhibits, displays, models, and even a moon rock exhibit. Like traveling displays from other organizations, there is no charge, per se; the shipping costs and insurance for some of the costly technical items and irreplaceable artifacts can run the costs up substantially. With the moon rocks, you will even have to provide 24-hour security.

Other Government Science Speakers
Even though NASA is into a lot more science than astronautics and astronomy, they might still not have the topic you want for your presentation. Luckily, the government is responsible for much of the physical and biological research done in this country, with many agencies running laboratories and other facilities that provide cutting-edge science—and also speakers.

One of the most scientifically active—and geographically widespread—agencies is the Department of Energy, which has dozens of laboratories around the country. Their main focus is energy in many forms. They also oversee the nation's atomic energy programs, both nuclear energy production and weapons technology and production. As petroleum prices continue their astronomical rise, and the public interest is piqued by such alternative fuel sources as hydrogen, people will be very aware of what the government is doing and where they think we are headed. Atomic power, particle physics, and quantum mechanics are very dense subjects for the majority of us, but are still topics of fascination. DOE speakers can provide your inquiring patrons with insights into these and many more energy-related issues. Some of the labs and field offices that operate speakers' bureaus include:

- Argonne National Laboratory, Argonne, Illinois
- Brookhaven National Laboratory, Upton, New York
- Fermi National Accelerator Laboratory, Batavia, Illinois

- Lawrence Berkeley National Laboratory, Berkeley, California
- Los Alamos National Laboratory, Los Alamos, New Mexico
- Nevada Test Site
- Oak Ridge National Laboratory, Oak Ridge, Tennessee
- Ohio Field Office, with facilities in Ashtabula, Columbus, Fernold, Miamisburg, and West Valley
- Pacific Northwest National Laboratory, Richmond, Washington
- Savannah River Field Office, Aiken, South Carolina

A number of other labs and offices are scattered around the country, dealing with a wide variety of issues, from renewable energy resources and sustainability to pollution control and energy security. Some of these named facilities are well known from the era of the Manhattan Project, and still deal in nuclear energy; some of the more secure facilities do not publicize themselves as do most government departments, for obvious reasons.

Another science-centered agency is the Department of Agriculture. The USDA is deeply rooted in many areas besides farming: soil conservation, meat inspection, and the Forest Service (rather disturbing because our national forests appear to be just another harvestable crop). The Farm Services Agency and the Agricultural Research Facility are among the USDA divisions that have speakers available. Many USDA divisions operate local offices, such as the Natural Resources Conservation Service (NRCS) and the Forest Service; you can contact these organizations for speakers.

The Department of Commerce has jurisdiction over several areas of science, such as the National Oceanographic and Atmospheric Agency (NOAA) and the National Weather Service (NWS). Interior runs the National Park Service and the Bureau of Land Management, and oversees archaeological digs on federal lands. The Environmental Protection Agency has many regulatory and research offices, with many speakers available. The best way to research any federal agency is to go to the FirstGov web site (www.firstgov.gov), which lists every federal department and agency you could possibly want to find.

Speakers on Health and Medicine

Unlike the departments just mentioned, the medical arms of the government— The National Institutes for Health and the Center for Disease Control—are far more centralized. You won't find a lot of laboratories and offices spread across the country. Because of the interrelated nature of medical research and the cost of duplication of equipment and facilities, it makes more sense to keep all the research close together. The National Institutes of Health (NIH) are located in

Bethesda, Maryland, near Washington, D.C. Notice the operative word here: institutes. More than a dozen research facilities are on the NIH "campus," working on everything from brain tumors to toe fungus. All these separate institutes contribute speakers to the NIH bureau, so it is only necessary to access the main web page of the agency to find a list of speakers and their topics. Among the listings are such important and timely matters as aging, diabetes, medical ethics, infectious diseases, mental health, nutrition, pathology, science education, teaching, vaccines, and women's health. Many more topics are available, and if you are within driving distance of the metro Washington area, you will have access to many program speakers for little or no cost. The NIH speakers will travel, but you must pay the proverbial travel expenses piper.

The other large federal health agency is the Center for Disease Control in Atlanta, Georgia. Like its Bethesda counterpart, the CDC consists of many smaller units, each devoted to different types of diseases. The CDC, as its name implies, is engaged in the prevention of widespread outbreaks of communicable illnesses. They deal with immediate and potentially dangerous problems, rather than theoretical research. The CDC speakers' bureau is comprised of volunteers from the center's labor force. You simply send a request to the CDC for a speaker on a given topic, and if a speaker is available, your request will be passed on to her; from there, you and she will make all the arrangements. Like all government speakers, those of the CDC receive no honorarium for lecturing on a job-related topic, but can be reimbursed for transportation, lodging, and meals.

When you go in search of government speakers by way of FirstGov, you might be swept away by the sheer enormity of the government's structure and the availability of information. Be certain of what it is you seek or you could lose track of time in the library.

Local Government Sources

Local government—specifically county and city or town—can also be tapped for speakers, usually with a lot less red tape and time than the federal variety. Of course, the trade-off is that most every other organization in the area will have thought to use these same speakers. You will probably not find formal speakers' bureaus at these units—at least not at the smaller, rural ones. Direct contact, either by phone or e-mail is the standard. With smaller government units, you will need to get through to the proper person, namely the person in charge. Lower-level functionaries, such as receptionists and assistants, might not have the information you need or even be aware that their people will speak at public functions.

Because local government officials are within a few miles of your location, you will not need to be concerned about travel and lodging. When they speak at community affairs, such as banquets, these people usually receive a gratis meal, but that might consist of a veggie plate or a few peanuts at your library, if you even have refreshments. Whether or not an honorarium is paid is probably determined by the rules of the governmental unit. Because your library is supported by the very same taxes that support the local government, it would seem silly to be doing such fund juggling. At the Peabody Public Library, we always have gifts for the speakers who don't walk away with a large check—usually a nice pen and pencil set. Sometimes a speaker might ask that a donation be made to a favorite charity; this is problematic for a non-profit organization, but can be circumvented by giving the individual a check that can be endorsed over to the charity.

Police and Fire

These two public service arms of government are always of interest to the public, both young and old, because they are so directly involved in the protection of our persons and property. Most police departments have officers who regularly speak to youth in the schools and to adults at meetings and banquets. Some of the topics of interest to adults are crime, traffic safety, drugs, gangs, and domestic violence. Some speak about personal experiences while on the force, what motivated them to enter law enforcement, or perhaps the inner workings of a police department. They can give the audience tips to keep them safe and secure at home and on the streets and sidewalks—something that everyone can use.

There are two types of local fire departments: full-time professional and volunteer. This distinction is a matter of funding, not experience and training, because members of both types of departments are well trained and knowledgeable in their work. A firefighter might talk about such things as smoke detectors in the home, what to do in case you are trapped in your home or another building during a fire, fire extinguishers and their proper use, and outdoor burning regulations, among many other topics. Although it was a children's program, the Peabody had the local volunteer department bring one of their fire trucks to the library for an up-close and hands-on experience. This sort of thing would obviously appeal to the inner child in many adults as well.

City Hall

Don't forget the mayor and the town council. Even when they are not actively campaigning for office, they will be happy to keep your patrons informed about what is going on in town. You will probably get a better turnout than the average town council meeting because the parliamentary structure of a formal meeting would be absent. Heads of other city and county departments, such as parks and recreation, roads and highways, and water and sewage treatment are also good candidates for speakers because people rarely directly contact such officials and might not understand all of the things they are responsible for. If you are having a special event at your library—a festival, a conference, an anniversary, or a really important author or other luminary, consider having the mayor or council president on hand to give a keynote address, dedication, or introduction; this will give an official air to your affair and make people realize that the library is also an essential part of their local government.

Speakers from the Courts
Down at the county courthouse, a lot of folks like to talk; talking is what they do for a living, so why not have them do it at your library? These people are, of course, the lawyers and judges. Judges have always been known for their speaking abilities (although some seem to make the news by talking when they should keep quiet). Judges, prosecutors, and public defenders should all be approachable for a possible speaking engagement at the library. They are able to talk about a number of legal topics, such as the problems of doing your own legal work, how to act in court, and what to do if you are being sued, among others. While at the courthouse, don't forget all those ancillary offices, such as clerk, recorder, and treasurer.

Local Utilities
In the past dozen or so years, utility companies have been going out of their way to tell us just how wonderful they are. Could this be because of the spiraling costs of energy during that time? Ignoring economics and politics, we will give them the benefit of the doubt and take advantage of their good natures. Besides telling people about themselves, they can give tips on saving energy and even alternate forms of heating and cooling (the local electric cooperative in our area offers a geothermal heating program).

Private Sector Speakers

Businesses have speakers as well, and although they might relate to their particular area of profit making, they will still have information important to your patrons who are, after all, their customers. Try contacting the local chamber of commerce to see if it knows what businesses and industries might have speakers—it will save you some time trying to make individual inquiries. However, several types of establishments will most certainly have speakers available for public functions. Like hospitals and caregivers, they exist in the public's mind as noble and necessary institutions.

Banks and Financial Institutions
Banks seem to go through regular image changes in our society. During the Great Depression, they were seen as soulless money grabbers who would not hesitate to toss someone off a homestead the family had lived on for generations. After restructuring during the New Deal, and the Federal Deposit Insurance act, they seem to have grown in stature as they helped people to achieve the post-war American dream of suburban home ownership. Local banks would go out of their way to approve loans and encourage people to deposit their money rather than keep it under the floorboards. Those of us from an older generation can remember such services as free checking, free overdraft protection, and free stock transfer. At the dawn of the Twenty-first Century, the juxtaposition of "free" and "bank" in the same sentence is pretty well a thing of the past. Gone are the neighborhood lending institutions where the tellers all knew you and your parents, and probably your grandparents, as well. The 1980s' cartoon-like feeding frenzy saw bigger banks swallow small ones, and even bigger ones swallow the big ones, in turn. This has gone on until, it seems, there are only about three bank corporations left in the entire country.

Although these goliaths enjoy such things as charging us for access to our own money, they still want to be our friends, at least the local branches do. Doing outreach is one way to maintain or build a good name in the era of nameless and faceless banking. If a bank does not have a speakers' bureau per se, they will have people who can speak on all aspects of modern finance, as part of their overall commitment to the community.

Among the many topics a banker might speak on, and which will be of interest to the general public are:

- How to identify and protect yourself against fraud
- What to do in case of identity theft
- How to maximize your chances of getting a loan or building equity
- Avoiding bankruptcy
- Saving for retirement or college

Other financial institutions in your area are investment brokers, savings and loans, and tax accountants. Check with any of these offices to see if they have someone to speak on topics with which they are concerned. Even the most casual of investors and the most basic of taxpayers will want to hear what they have to say.

Insurance Companies

Like banks, insurance agents feel the need to talk to the public about what they do because the stereotype of these institutions is the adjustor who will find every possible way to avoid paying even the smallest claim. Unlike banks, most insurance agents are perceived as local, hometown types—even if they work for a large company. They have a small storefront office, and often represent several companies at the same time, giving you the chance to find the lowest premium available.

Insurance is, to say the least, confusing, and an agent can talk to your patrons about various types of policies, what they mean, and what they do for you. S/he can explain premiums, what factors are involved in lowering them, and that old but confusing favorite, the actuarial table. The agent can also discuss the various uses for insurance: investments, college funding, lawsuit protection, and more. To most of us, insurance is one of those necessary evils in which, as the old joke goes, you bet against the company and your bet is that you are going to lose. A few scheduled programs could help to clear up such misconceptions.

Business and Industry

Although the small shopkeeper in town might not have much to speak about or, if he does, might not feel inclined or equipped to do so, large businesses and industries in your community certainly will. Even small communities have businesses and manufacturers that employ a goodly number of area people yet remain enigmas to the general populace. Having a speaker explain the business's operations to a library audience will help to take the mystery out of their presence in the community.

Another type of industry that needs to be heard by your patrons is the one steeped in controversy. A company like this will undoubtedly have a public relations department and it will be a busy, prepared one. Several years ago, a steel company decided to build a plant in the Columbia City area. This created an outcry among many people—especially those in the rural townships near the proposed foundry. The basically "not in my backyard" response included incendiary billboards along the highway, inflammatory letters to the editor, and the formation of a coalition, known as Citizens' Organized Watch (do the acronym). Despite the people who had a cow, the plant was built, the hullabaloo died down somewhat, and the steel plant has a solid community presence, with charity work, speakers, management people in community groups, and more. Public relations are a wonderful thing.

Professional Speakers' Bureaus

You should be aware of one other breed of speakers' bureau. You might have run across one or more while searching the web, or you may even have ended up on a mailing list. The professional speakers' bureau acts as agent for a number of celebrity speakers, such as sports figures, authors and journalists, actors and comedians, well-known business executives, motivational speakers, and "icons du jour." The one thing that these bureaus have in common is that their speakers are expensive. You—or someone with real money— could pay anywhere from $5000 to $25000 dollars. Some have "bargain" speakers for less than 5K; some bargain. Of course, the top dollar getters are usually very well known and could fill several auditoriums, but you would have to charge admission to recoup the fee, and that is not what we are about in this book. It is rather fun to speculate on the impact one of these people would have on the library and its image.

Academic Speakers

We all remember our professors from college; some were very good speakers and motivated us to great heights. Others were passable. The worst of the lot could rent themselves out as sleep aids. All of them however, knew their topic and loved to talk about it, if not enthusiastically, at least knowledgeably. If the professor was stimulating enough, she might have swayed our career intentions in some direction or another. These people could entertain and educate your audience.

Talking for Tenure

Many colleges and universities—especially public ones—have public offices that offer academic speakers to the community. These people are most often lecturers and adjuncts, still working for a full-time position or tenure. A fully tenured professor does not have to do much of anything he doesn't want to do, so if you find one on a speaker list, it reflects the true love that this person has for the subject and, moreover, for imparting knowledge to others. You will find these bureaus—often masquerading under another title—in the individual schools and colleges of a university, or even at the department level.

Among the most interesting academic speakers are those in the sciences, history, the arts, and politics. Science is a large field, but most large universities have specialists in most areas; the same is true of history. The public offices that make these people available to the public go out of their way to ensure that the academic is able to address a group of nonspecialists (which should not be a problem for those who deal with undergraduates on a daily basis). For the state of Indiana, Indiana University has a science speaker's bureau that will find a specialist on just the topic you want. The Peabody Public Library, in conjunction with its on-premise wetland, was looking for an entomologist to talk about aquatic insects. It took some time, but they found one in the School of Public and Environmental Affairs. We have had a few of these academic speakers, and the experience has been uniformly good. These people are able to both talk to a lay audience and not condescend to them. This combination might be the most important factor for success when dealing with a group of patrons of mixed educational levels.

Scheduling Academic Speakers

Not quite as much red tape is involved in the booking of academics, as opposed to those of the federal government, but as anyone who has tried to get a transcript or drop or add a class can tell you, bureaucracy is alive and well in higher education. Usually, if there are any problems, they lie in the use of proper channels. You must do all you can to ascertain just what the proper channels might be. Obviously, if they have some form of speakers' bureau, you needn't worry about protocol; if nothing is self-evident, it is best—odd though it might sound—to start at the bottom. Those at the lower levels of an office will know what is going on above them; that is usually not the case from the other direction. If the lower-level staff (and this term is used solely in the structural sense) does not know, they will cheerfully send you on to the next highest level; you will either reach someone with a definite answer or you will come right out the top unsatisfied. At this point, it is permissible to throw your hands up in frustration before moving on to more promising prospects.

Once you have found the person or office in charge of booking speakers, you will need to provide a detailed description of what you want and why—and then leave it up to them to find the proper speaker for you. Because a number of factors are involved, some of which are the sheer number of requests, office time that can actually be spent looking for the speaker, and the literal tracking down of the person, you could end up waiting for some time. Be patient, factor in plenty of lead-time, and don't bug them too much—clerical university staffs are experts at dealing with people who are capable of being much more annoying than you.

Once a speaker has been found, she will most likely be given your contact information; on occasion, you might be required to initiate the proceedings.

Once contact is established, it will be up to the two of you to work out the details. Academics—especially the ones not yet tenured—can make themselves extremely busy, so it is imperative that you work with their schedules, rather than vice versa. Give the person the widest range of dates and times possible so that they might find something that fits their schedule. These folks are very agreeable, but you have to work with them. A while ago, we had scheduled one speaker from the university who had to cancel out at the last minute because of a family illness. He voluntarily called back some months later to schedule another program.

Finally, unless they are retired, listed on some outside speakers' bureau site, or a personal acquaintance of yours, it is probably not a good idea to contact the academic directly. As mentioned, there are proper channels, and stepping on toes is bad business—especially if you want to deal with those same toes at a later date.

Most communities have a number of colleges and/or universities located close by. Start with these for all the obvious reasons. Small colleges are good contacts because they are often easier to deal with; they do not have as large a faculty to hunt through, nor is their red tape quite as deep. The larger the institution, the bigger the bureaucracy. Don't ignore the two-year colleges and technical schools; their offerings are often of a more pragmatic nature and their speakers might lend themselves well to a general library program. As an example, Indiana has a statewide system of technical colleges, and the one nearest to the Peabody Public Library has such diverse courses of study as culinary arts and auto mechanics. These could prove more interesting than something like late medieval architecture or nineteenth-century Polish poetry.

Author Visits: Are They Worth It?

Very recently, the Peabody Public Library had an author visit the library. He writes historical mysteries set in Roman times; his books are in our library and get checked out on a regular basis. We had exactly three people show up, two of whom were library staff. When you have an author visit you, the point is to have someone visit him at the same time. While apologizing profusely for the poor turnout, I mentioned this book and the above section heading. The author, gracious in a somewhat awkward circumstance, assured me that he had attended readings and signings where no one at all had shown up. Speaking with fellow writers, he has come to the conclusion that they could very well say the same thing: are they worth it? Monetarily, perhaps they are, but there is much more than money at work here; people want to be recognized and lauded for their talents, and that can be especially true of authors who have yet to obtain celebrity status. Sometimes, contact with readers is the only feedback they have.

As libraries, we are more or less expected to have authors visit us and talk about the process of writing. As libraries, we mostly cannot afford to bring in the best-selling authors who would undoubtedly fill our facilities with eager fans. The Peabody usually books three or four authors a year (they tend to draw more than three people), but those writers are the sorts who have a topic on which they can speak with some authority, rather than writers of genre fiction. Most people who attend their signings are there to learn more about that subject, rather than to bask in the presence of authorhood.

Two essentials for holding successful author visits are a budget (while some are free, you still need to pay expenses) and a good knowledge of your patrons and their reading habits. We have relatively few Stephen King fans at our library and I have the feeling that he would not draw very well—even if we could afford him and he would actually leave Maine. Several years ago, fiction was circulating at a much higher rate than nonfiction, and we were able to draw respectable audiences for these authors; now nonfiction has overtaken its story-based counterpart, and we can begin to shy away from the novelist as speaker. This is something you will have to determine for yourself, through a systematic search of your circulation patterns.

Contacting Authors or Their Representatives

Finding authors is not difficult; finding ones close enough to come to your library is even easier. Unlike actors, authors are not particularly bicoastal, and tend to live in the area where they grew up. This tendency could be in order to research their topics easier (if their topics tend to center in that area), or it might be the reclusive nature of the craft of writing. Writers do not need to be near the giant publicity machine like other celebrities; their books are their publicity, and publishers are their marketing experts. Stephen King has always lived in Maine, which has not hurt his stature in any way; Kurt Vonnegaut lives near Indianapolis. Proximity to such authors does not ensure their presence at your library, but if such luminaries as King and Vonnegaut can live on Mainstreet, U.S.A., so too will the more approachable ones.

Author Groups and Associations
Writers might not be union activists, but they do have associations and guilds to which they belong, usually specific to the type of writing they do. Very few authors are total loners, and most feel they can benefit from peer input, which they can get through conferences sponsored by these organizations.

These groups also establish criteria for excellence in the field, issue awards, and give advice on legal and artistic matters. For our purposes, the best thing a writer's association does is make available contact with their members. As a clearinghouse of sorts, they will list URLs, agents, or direct mail contacts (e-mail or regular). Some important writer's associations you may want to visit online:

- Mystery Writers of America—The biggest and best known of the genre associations, the MWA awards the prestigious Edgar (after Mr. Poe) for best work in the field. www.mwa.org
- Romance Writers of America—The premier site for romance authors big and small, hardcover and Harlequin, their site includes a librarian's page as well as links to member web sites. The major award of the RWA is the Rita. www.rwanational.org
- Horror Writers Association—Bestowers of the Bram Stoker awards, the HWA web site has an e-mail contact to get information about their members. www.horror.org/librarians.htm
- The Authors Guild—The largest advocacy group for all published authors, they have a web site directory for their many members. www.authorsguild.org
- Novelists Inc.—For long-form fiction writers, they too have a directory of the member web sites. www.ninc.com
- Poets and Writers—A large organization that publishes a print version of its directory, and has a smaller online directory that can be searched by name, place of residence, or type of writing. www.pw.org
- Western Writers of America—there are still a lot of western writers out there, and still a lot of fans reading their work. The WWA is the home of the Spur Awards, and their web site offers either the URL or e-mail of its members. www.westernwriters.org
- Sisters in Crime—A large organization of female mystery and crime writers, their directory lists members and their place of residence (city and state), web sites (if they have them), and a list of their major works. www.sistersincrime.org
- Science Fiction and Fantasy Writers of America—Home of the Nebula Awards, you can find a directory of member web sites as well as a listing of future author appearances. www.sffwa.org

Author Web Sites

If you know the author you are looking for, it might be more expeditious to go directly to their web site, if they have one. Not all authors have entered the cyber age; in fact some of them are still stuck in the Underwood age. Author fan pages abound, but these will not do you any good. Some authors will, however, have an "official" web site created and kept by someone else, perhaps even a fan. Some of the writers' organizations mentioned previously will offer their members small informational pages on their web site. Authors who are academics might also have some pages of their own on their institution's web site. Sometimes though, an author will just have to be contacted the old-fashioned way. Electronic mail has really spoiled us.

Book Festivals and Writers' Conferences

Just like librarians, writers spend a lot of time going to conferences. These are places to meet fans, talk to other writers, sell their latest book, and attend some serious writing workshops. Some conferences are strictly for writers, centering on their craft and advancement of their chosen field. These conferences feature writing classes, panel discussions on issues of concern, and educational seminars on such topics as copyright or working with agents. Although you might not be strictly barred from such conferences, you will be very out of place there, trying to buttonhole an author for a personal appearance. These are not the kind of gatherings where they expect such a thing. You probably wouldn't care to have patrons come up to you at a state conference and ask you why you don't buy more romance novels with Fabio on the cover.

A far better place to approach an author is at a book fair or festival. Although the main focus at these events is the books, many authors are invited to share their expertise—and their autographs—with attendees, most of whom are fans, booksellers, or librarians. Some of these festivals or conferences are put on by publishers, some by writers' associations, and some by colleges and universities. If you have ever attended one of these get-togethers, you will find yourself redefining the meaning of fan. The nonindustry people who are there will eat, breathe, and live these authors and their books. Their knowledge of authors and grasp of detail of their books can astound even the writers themselves; a writer has no idea of who said what to whom on page 359, but one of these fans certainly does. Most of the authors who attend these events are expecting to be approached by people, and a librarian asking for a visit is probably the best conversation they have had all day.

Many of these events recognize their appeal to library personnel, and will often have a special rate for us. Individually, we might not seem to be much in the publishing world, but if you take into account the nearly ten thousand public libraries in the country, you are approaching bestseller territory if each of us buys a single copy of a given title. Scores of these festivals, fairs, or conferences are scheduled all over the country; some are very large, some are of more modest proportions. You should consider attending one of these instead of, or in addition to, the usual library-based event.

The biggest book fair in the country is *Book Expo America*, sponsored by the American Booksellers Association. The event is held in a different city each year. There is a writer's conference combined with the expo, and autographing sessions have scores of midlist authors in attendance (the kind you can afford). Grabbing authors at signings, especially if you have a newly purchased book in hand, is a good way to catch them in an effusive mood. Ask if they do library visits, and get some contact information. Follow up on it soon thereafter, while you are both in post-conference euphoria. *Book Expo America*, despite being run by booksellers, welcomes librarians and even gives them a special rate (shows how scared they are of us). Librarians do, however, have to brand themselves with a special "librarian" name badge—so that the big publishers can see them coming, no doubt.

Many other such festivals exist across the country. Some of these are of a general nature; some focus on a specific genre; some will celebrate the gender or ethnicity of writers and their art. Mystery conferences seem to be the most numerous, with evocative names like *Malice Domestic*, *Mayhem in the Midlands*, and *Magna cum Murder*. Usually, these events will have a big-name guest of honor and a few dozen new and midlist authors. Romance and science fiction and fantasy also have similar events (be sure to go to a literary-based sci-fi convention, not the dress-up-as-your-favorite-Klingon type).

Getting Authors to Contact You

Believe it or not, there are ways to get authors to ask you if they can come to your library. That doesn't mean that you get to charge them, but it certainly makes a nice windfall.

Of course, you might not want a particular enterprising author at your library even though he goes out of his way to contact you; in that case, a simple "thank you, perhaps another time" message will do. After all, we have all been turned down by them with some gracious excuse or another. There are, however, many authors you will want to book, and advertising themselves to you does not mean they are desperate, cranks, or self-published. The Peabody recently booked an Agatha Award winning author who had contacted us directly via e-mail. More and more, the connectedness of society makes such things possible, and word will get around about you and about them. If an author, or any other program-giver, has had a good experience at your library, that information will be spread amongst her peers in short order.

Writers Associations Registry

At the time of this writing, the Mystery Writers of America had a database of libraries that are interested in having authors at their facilities. Authors also sign up for a speakers' database, detailing information about themselves and their criteria for an appearance. Librarians can access that list by contacting the MWA at service@mysterywriters.org. If an author finds your address on the library database, she can contact you to set up a visit. The Romance Writers of America offers librarians contacts to authors in their area who do book signings. These services go beyond the mere listing of author information and web sites; you are being offered writers who are actually willing to speak at libraries.

Authors @ Your Library

The American Library Association began a registry of its own a few years ago entitled *Authors @ Your Library*. Like the MWA service, it is a two-way street although you don't really get to contact authors directly. Instead, you contact only publishers, who may or may not list their individual authors. On the other hand, authors and publishers (and presumably serial killers, as well) have full access to the information you give to the registry. The best way for you to actively use this service is to find the publishers in your area (assuming you can't afford long-distance travel expenses) and read their profiles to find out what and whom they offer. You will find information on the types of books they publish, author names in some cases, upcoming book tours, and whether or not their authors require honorariums (the usual answer is, "in some cases"). One problem I have run into when contacting so-called regional publishers is that not all of their authors are actually in the region, so what seemed close and cheap suddenly becomes distant and pricey.

The passive method of using *Authors @ Your Library* is to simply input your library's profile and wait. You will be asked for your library's name, a contact person (you, presumably), what sort of programs you are looking for, information about your facility (room size, audio and video equipment, etc.), publicity methods and typical audience size, and your ability to pay fees. Unlike the publishers, you will need to be a bit more specific about the amount you can afford, entering a general price range. Your library's name and location will then be placed on one large list that is arranged alphabetically by state, but by no particular order within the state list (the Peabody, for some reason, is listed first among Indiana libraries). This makes it very easy for authors to find libraries close to them. The publishers list is simply alphabetical by name, so you will have to search the entire thing for those near you. Yes, this site is provided by the American *Library* Association.

Once you have submitted your information, all you have to do is sit back and wait. Don't forsake your other duties in order to wait for responses, however; we get three or four a year. Probably if we were in a more populated area, or offered larger honorariums, we might do better. Still, it is a rather fruitful source of programming for having to do nothing.

Local Authors

The ALA service will not result in John Grisham knocking down your door to get a speaking date, but rather bring you the ubiquitous new and midlist authors. You are probably taking a chance with these people, no matter how excellent their work or how often it gets checked out. You might live in a community that embraces all things literary and will fill your program room to see any published writer, but, in reality, you will run into uneven attendance. You might have better luck with local authors—either from your immediate community or your state. Even if they are someone few have heard of, that magical connection to home will have a positive effect. Bookstores in your area might have a local author section that you can check, or there may be writers' groups that you can contact. Because a library is such a logically literary place, the authors might come around to see you. A local author will be sure to draw someone, if only his friends and family.

Selling and Signing

When an author makes an appearance at a bookstore, what she mostly does is sign copies of her latest book purchased at that establishment. Meeting and hearing the author will often prompt sales, so the author can count royalties with each signature. With a rather fine line between success and failure, each copy sold becomes important, and time spent on a visit is time that should result in increased sales. An author will, of course, realize that your small library is not a mega bookstore, but even ten or twenty more copies per venue will add up over several libraries. Although you might think that payment of an honorarium is sufficient, the author is thinking about that next book deal, which might be dependent upon the success of the present one. Long-term financial security is something we should all be able to relate to.

Library policies concerning for-profit enterprises vary greatly, with some being quite adamant about the free nature of public institutions and the library's place in society as a haven from crass commercialism. Others, like the Peabody Public Library, look at the way things are and realize that our survival might well rest upon our getting into step with the rest of the world, rather than waiting for the world to come around to the logic of our way.

Who of us have not heard patrons utter those immortal words in our sacred institutions, "Can I rent this video?" We might still cringe when they say it, but we will never counter commercial advertising's hold on the American mind. If patrons are constantly thinking in terms of profit and loss, will they notice if we bend a bit before the winds of reality?

Even if your library staunchly refuses to allow the sale of books at an appearance, most authors will still agree to talk to your patrons. All publicity is good and might result in sales at some point. Remember, however, that word does get around. You should at least attempt to fill in gaps in the author's work on your shelves before having him in for a program.

If you do allow selling and signing, several options are open to you. The author might have copies available for sale. In all likelihood, he has purchased these at discount from the publisher for this very purpose. If the author does not have any copies, you may be able to work with a local bookstore, which will provide the copies and collect the profits. Another option is to work with your friends of the library, who can use the occasion as a fundraiser.

Epilogue

The last several pages may or may not have answered the question of whether author visits are worth having. In fact the question might well be moot; we are libraries, and books are still our business, and books mean authors. We have given so much ground to bookstores as it is—that whole sit-in-a-nice-chair-and-read-without-bring-disturbed idea was originally ours, if you will recall—so let us not give them proprietary rights to every literary endeavor in the book world. We are expected to have authors, so let us have them, no matter who shows or doesn't. In the business world, this is called a *loss leader*.

CHAPTER FOUR

~

Educational Programs

The Educational Imperative

That the library is an institution of learning is an empirical given. What else does one do with thousands of books, dozens or hundreds of computers, and the knowledge of trained librarians, except learn from them? The problem with our world is that it is neither empirical nor logical. Just as everyone's favorite vegetable, the tomato, is not a vegetable but a fruit, a public library is not an educational institution in many eyes. We do not employ members of the NEA, nor do we create curricula, and not one person has ever been pinched by the truant officer for playing hooky from the public library.

Like army sutlers, we are viewed more as support than frontline troops. The public library is where you go when the school library is short on your subject, or everyone else in the class has beaten you to the books. It is now also the only remaining option when your Internet search comes up empty. We are now the arena of last resort, somewhere down the line from Joe's-Game-Cheats-and-Encyclopedia-of-the-World.com. Teachers might view us askance, as usurpers to their thrones or at best, another bit of multimedia or a field trip to relieve the tedium of lectures. We do not fit in to the world of formal education very well; an ill-defined yet crucial piece of the puzzle, our indeterminate role may be one of the things that plague the librarian's self-image. We feel the need to collect "Library Stories" about what the library means to individuals, in order to justify ourselves to—mostly—ourselves.

Yet the library as a place of learning need not be tied to any course of formal education; it only needs to exist on its own, as it has for millennia, as an important and necessary adjunct to the growth of human intellect. We have always had our own missions and goals, which may or may not be tied to the educational system. These missions and goals should drive us and help us to perform the task of education in programming, whether its end product is a formal degree or a simple feeling of accomplishment.

Missions and Goals

We are many things at a public library: teacher, merchant, program director, impresario, instant bet resolver, and supplier of popular and other culture. Not every library has to be all things, but the things they decide upon had best be written down as precisely as possible, or everyone on staff will invent their own.

While a mission statement is deliberately vague, and the more inventive among us could possibly fit anything from a herd of library camels to world domination into it, our goals are usually much more specific, and it is here that we will find those supports for educational programs.

Support of Secondary Education

Because we are dealing with adult programming here, this book does not discuss primary education. Many adult services librarians, myself included, have the responsibility of services for high school-aged young adults. If that is so, they probably feel the frustration of trying to get that particular constituency into the library at all, let alone attend something that might be for their coursework. Yet, getting them into the library on a formal basis is precisely the thing to do. Perhaps if they attend a program, or come as a class on a field trip, they will experience the 21st-century public library for themselves, rather than relying on the tired old stereotype that Hollywood and most of the world continues to perpetuate.

If you are to work with the schools to provide programs (and more) for students, it is best to have someone in those schools who is receptive to the idea that libraries are an important part of their students' education. There could be many such teachers or only a few. Even if every member of the faculty is in favor of hauling their kids to the library every day of the week, that does not mean they are going to act upon it. You need to find those who will.

Teachers are incredibly busy people, and to expect them to find time to help you do your job, as well as theirs, is asking a lot, even if you promise great and wonderful things in return. They also do not run on the same timetable as you do. One of the main stumbling blocks to school–public library cooperation is the fact that teachers schedule much of their year far in advance, and there just isn't an easy way to fit our sudden brainstorms into their class work.

This is where the school–library liaison comes in. You need to find that person (one is probably the preferred number with which to work) who can get you curricula, schedules, and more. One of the truer, if sorrier, statements of our society is, "It isn't what you know, but . . .," well, you know. Rather than beating your head against a brick wall, let your liaison walk in through the front door.

What do you have to offer secondary teachers in the line of programming? Well, unless you have a laboratory on premises, science experiments are out, but most anything else is fair game. History and literature are sure to tie in some way with curricula, as can lectures and presentations by scientists, such as those from NASA. If you have videoconferencing capabilities, and the schools do not, the potential is limitless. If you are not aware of videoconferencing and its possibilities, check with your systems administrator. She might have a list of companies and organizations through which you can work.

Higher Education

What can a small public library offer a college, or its students? That depends on the school, your capabilities, and your location, among other things. Your collection librarian is probably not stocking up on college texts and technical journals, but it is a safe bet that if an institution of higher learning is within driving distance of your facility, students are using your services.

No college or university is in Columbia City, but there are probably a dozen or more within thirty miles of the Peabody Public Library. That translates into commuters, lots of them. Returning students are now a larger part of the college campus than anytime in history. Between 1980 and 2000, there has been an increase of over 63% in the number of college students over the age of thirty.[1] This figures out to 25.8% of all undergraduate enrollments in the year 2000.[2] It is more likely that these students would have a home and family and would commute than younger students. Perhaps even more telling is the fact that 26.9% of undergraduates were parents[3], also a limiting factor when it comes to spending a lot of time on-campus.

What we see in these statistics, which will be higher or lower depending upon local conditions, is that a substantial and increasing number of people are fitting college into an already busy life, rather than making it their life for four or five years. These students do not hang out on campus before or after class, and can be hard-pressed to use the library for research and/or study.

But what of programming for these people; what can we do for them besides order journal articles and provide Internet access? They probably don't need entertainment (they might want it, however); they might only need a quiet space. If that is something usually hard to come by in your library, then make a regular "study hall" date for them to use a room for uninterrupted research and reading. Perhaps you can assist literature students by bringing them together in a discussion group that centers on their course readings. It only takes one request for help at the reference desk to bring to light the needs of your (yes, they can become yours) students. It only takes a bit of creativity to heed them and craft solutions.

Another kind of student is the distance learner. In the 2000 school year, 8.7% of all undergraduates took distance education courses, and a full 19.4% of part-timers participated in off-campus courses.[4] These courses can be live, interactive videoconferencing, Internet-based, or prerecorded. We, as a learning institution, should be able to deliver this sort of material to the student; even if it only seems to be saving them a few miles and minutes, these savings could be immense to them. We also could become integral in all of their school-related activities, from study to relaxation, if their only campus is our facility.

One other area of programming we might consider is that of basic skills. The returning college student has probably forgotten, or never known, the basics of writing and researching a paper, using the library, or searching periodical indexes. College instructors take these skills for granted, and even if they did not, there would be no time to teach those skills. A simple class on proper citation and footnoting could be a boon to the returning student.

Lifelong Learning

Now here's the stuff! Lifelong learning is what we do best, isn't it? People walk in off the street, search our catalog and use our services, and go away smarter than they were before. What more could there be to lifelong learning?

A lot, as it turns out. Lifelong learning is not the higgledy-piggledy sort of thing described above, but a more guided, yet still informal, way of imparting knowledge to those no longer in a formal educational setting. Much planning, development, and outside help is necessary to make lifelong learning successful in your library. The two (probably more, but we'll stick with two) definitions of lifelong learning are: continuing education or professional development and informal, self-enrichment classes. The former are usually used to update and keep current the skills of professionals and business people, such as lawyers, real estate brokers, etc. These classes might be held in the library and even in partnership with the library; they will not, for the most part, require much more than you booking a room and putting up a sign. They certainly cannot count as adult programming on your year-end statistics sheet.

Enrichment classes, however, are something with which we can do a great deal. Beyond literacy and GED programs, we can involve ourselves in the community's efforts to provide casual learning to citizens, either in the arts, the humanities, simple crafts and home economics, or more traditional subjects, such as math, science, and language refresher courses. If the community already offers such classes, we can offer our help, either in the form of our own expertise (teach a class on the Dewey Decimal System!), our ability to coordinate and locate, or even our facilities. If the machinery is not already in place for community enrichment, the library can begin to build it. Locating qualified instructors is not difficult; many people in the community have a skill they wish to share, and many retired educators will be happy to remain involved with the learning process. Once you have determined what is needed or wanted in the line of personal enrichment, it is simply a matter of finding a willing teacher and booking a spare room. Enrichment classes can go on and on, and really add to your regular calendar of events.

Library Education

Back about ten or fifteen years ago, when online catalogs and informational databases were new and strange, we all spent a lot of time giving one-on-one instruction to our patrons, with decidedly mixed results. We then hit upon the bright idea (once we had enough computers to do it) of giving classes on the subjects, again with mixed results. Lo and behold! A dozen years later, we still spend most of our reference desk time telling people whether or not we own an item that could simply be looked up on the catalog. A lot of people are still in the dark about using the library of the 21st century. There will probably continue to be a lot of these people for the foreseeable future. We have more ready-made programming waiting for us.

Because library staff (hopefully) is well-versed in the use of the library's own databases, we have a built-in faculty for these classes. It need not be the same person, forced to stay past quitting time, or to come in early, who teaches the course week after week or month after month; rather, change off and keep the role of instructor fresh and interesting.

Computer instruction is not the only area of library education that can be taught to your patrons. A short course on the Dewey Decimal System, the shelf arrangement of your building, the way to research a subject, or any other area of bibliographic instruction is always in order.

As Samuel Johnson said, "Knowledge is of two kinds. We know a subject ourselves, or we know where we can find information upon it." The educational imperative of the public library gives us the opportunity to deliver both kinds to our patrons.

Supporting Educational Programs

We all know that adult services librarians have the toughest job in the world (controversial? How could this statement be controversial?); they are given the proverbial pile of mud and told to make bricks out of it without straw. All the strategic goals and board decrees will not help to get the job done, even if Moses appeared with his staff (yes, it's a pun). When we are told to develop educational programs from any or all of the above directives, we must look beyond what we may view as our stupendous talents and simply cry "Mommy!" Or at least, "Money! People! Friends!"

Money is always the first thing we need and usually the last thing we get. Budgets have been discussed extensively in an earlier chapter, and we need not bring up the obvious differences between the lucky haves and the rest of the library world. Even a good budget, however, can disappear quickly in support of education. (Look at your school taxes and compare them to library taxes.) Luckily, the very word education often opens up the hearts—and hopefully the checkbooks—of the grant givers out there. It is true that working on a grant request is akin to playing the green numbers on the roulette wheel, but there is money out there and you need to try for it.

Another source of funding might come from your friends-of-the-library group. They are always raising money selling books, or popcorn, or something. Put in your request for a few of those dollars. As mentioned earlier, the word education usually softens the most solid of resolves. While you are touching the friends for their capital, how about asking for some time and ideas as well? There is probably at least someone in the group willing and ready to teach, and everyone will probably want to help think up and put into motion some great ideas.

It takes a village, as someone once said, and you are part of that village; planning, reaching out, working together with the community, to continue to raise that child well into adulthood.

Programs in the Creative Arts

In any community, there are two sure bets: very talented amateur artists are out there, and any number of people wish they were very talented artists. If a librarian plays his cards right, he can be the instrument through which these two elements come together—at the library. Although it is pretty much a maxim that the talented are born that way, the somewhat competent and blissfully unaware are usually able to be instructed to the point of a passing fairness at what at least resembles art. Our attempt at Gainsborough-style portraiture might end up looking like a Picasso that has survived (barely) a landslide, but our minds are such that we can easily persuade ourselves that that is what we meant to render in the first place. Thus, the semi- and untalented plow ahead, drawing, cutting, singing, and generally making a muddle of the word *art*, but, nevertheless, are pleased with their attempts. Let us happily aid these people in those attempts.

Graphic Arts

The graphic arts generally lend themselves well to library-based instruction. Beyond a room and some tables, we only need a teacher and whatever supplies that particular form of artistic expression requires. They don't smell bad, take up a lot of room (unless you are Diego Rivera), or, leave much of a mess (given a few precautions). The best part is, most of them are practiced by someone right in your community.

Drawing and Sketching in Pencils, Chalks, Charcoal

The easiest to supply, and the best place to start, at least for the rank beginner is the simple (for some!) sketch. In most artistic and craft classes, the library has two choices: charge (or have the teacher charge) a fee for supplies used during class, or donate the supplies, if you have the budget. Like many areas of programming, this is a two-edged sword. You promote a great deal of good will for the library in general and your programming in particular when you do this. You also run the risk of creating the monster that knows no satiation. Patrons come to expect something for nothing, and will demand it even when the cost is unreasonable for you to bear. Of course, the cost for some pads, pencils, pastel chalks, and the like are rather minimal, and you probably won't find a cheaper place to make up that goodwill, but you have been warned.

Another facet of the charge/don't charge argument is that people in our overwhelmingly consumer-oriented society might view a freebie somewhat askance. You get what you pay for is their motto, and what do you get for nothing? Sometimes, it is best just to put a fee on it and be done.

Even if a fee is charged, it might be best for the library to actually purchase the supplies with their discount at an educational art supply company. Few amateur artists spend enough to earn any sort of deal from their art supply store.

Painting in Oils and Watercolors
Moving up the talent meter, as well as the mess-o-meter, we come to everyone's favorite, painting on canvas. Oh, did we forget to mention the cost-o-meter? Yes, it is a fair jump from a crayon and a piece of paper to oils, canvas, easels, and palettes. No wonder Van Gogh cut off his ear. Nevertheless, there will come a time, if your drawing class is a success, when you will hear the call of would-be Rembrandts asking for painting classes.

If you have a talented watercolorist in your community (Columbia City has several), you might convince your patrons that is the way to go. Of course, watercolor takes no less talent than oils, but it does appear to this untalented eye to be a bit less messy and a lot less smelly (or vice versa). The transparent beauty of watercolor, lacking in sharp definition, might best appeal to those who have worked in chalk and charcoal.

Whichever way you go, invest in some good tarps and keep everybody in the center of the room, unless you want Jackson Pollack walls.

Calligraphy, Block Printing and Silk Screen Printing
The use of inks in artwork is an old and honorable tradition. Chinese calligraphy is one of the more popular of amateur arts. Just take a look in the local Michaels or Hobby Lobby crafts stores and you will see an entire section devoted to this ancient art. Art it is, much more than a way of fancy writing. Oriental masters spend years before they consider themselves more than scribblers. That, of course, will not deter your patrons when you offer such a class.

The pluses for calligraphy are many: it's quite inexpensive; a passable product is easily produced after a few lessons; and it is seen as a practical art by many, being used for invitations, certificates, and the like. The only drawback is in forgetting the one thing that can make all of your patrons happy: be sure that you have some left-handed pens. No, this is not a joke like the left-handed screwdriver. Because left-handed people (yes, that includes yours truly) push, rather than pull, the nib across the paper, the traditional curve of the nib must be reversed to avoid tearing and puddling.

Block printing is similar to the craft of stamping, except that you are creating the designs on the block as well as transferring them to the medium, which could be paper or fabric. Originally, the blocks were of wood, but today's material is softer and easier for design cutting. Linoleum and hard foam are among the more common. Although not nearly as popular as stamping, block printing does allow for more originality in the creation of the final product.

Silk-screen printing, or serigraphy, is also an ancient art, which has become very popular in today's world, thanks in large part to the popularity of the printed t-shirt. Screen printing is a sophisticated form of stenciling, in which the stencils are held in a wooden frame and placed over a mesh, through which the ink is pressed. Again, as an art form, silk screening has many possibilities for creative expression and, as a craft, it can decorate a lot of t-shirts cheaply.

Textile and Paper

Textiles are a very broad area of the arts. They can range all the way from spinning thread and weaving cloth to such finished items as clothing, hangings, and other adornments. Some of the more familiar textile arts are embroidery, tatting (lace making), knitting, weaving, and crocheting. Most of these abilities are easily learned, if mastered with greater difficulty, and are prime candidates for library instruction. Although such pursuits as sewing, weaving, and spinning can involve large and expensive machines (although they need not), many of these other activities involve no more than a cheaply had item that can be held in the hand. The threads and yarns are also widely available at craft and variety stores, and ample victims for finished wearables can be had amongst family members. As a child, I remember a lavender knitted tam-o-shanter gift from an aunt that my parents thought was so adorable. The disposition of such articles is, of course, not the province of the library, so there is no need to feel guilty.

Paper arts include the obvious, such as origami, and the not-so-obvious, such as *scherenschnitte*. Most people are familiar with origami, the oriental art of paper folding, and this art certainly has a wide range of possibility, from the most simple of designs to involved masterpieces. Less known, but just as visually stunning is the art of paper cutting (*scherenschnitte*).

Papier mâché and paper making are two rather messy, but often fun activities, which also have some practical applications. Perhaps paper making and calligraphy could be combined for those who want to do something really special for notes and invitations.

Many other paper arts, as well as crafts, are being created in your area. A visit to the local craft store and a quick perusal of its shelves will determine which ones. If someone is doing them, they might also be willing to teach them. Ask at the store, and you might find some willing instructors. Take a chance on some of the more esoteric arts; if they garner interest, you have turned people on to a whole new world of art. If not, then simply go back to the drawing board.

Ceramics and Pottery

Ceramics classes are not as difficult to host as you might think. Many confirmed ceramicists take their work to a shop with a kiln and pay to have their items fired. Your instructor, depending upon her immersion in the art, might have a kiln that can be used by the class (usually for a fee because firing is not cheap). Any number of small ceramics, from cups and mugs to bowls and ash trays, can be made in a library setting. A room with a sink, to facilitate cleanup, is needed for this, as well as many other, artistic activities.

Some beginning ceramics pieces, it is true, might resemble your kindergartner's Mother's Day offering, but that first cup of Joe out of your very own mug can hook you for life. That, hopefully, will mean a regular series of ongoing classes for all skill levels. Like some other arts-and-crafts classes, it is necessary to have some sort of storage available for partially finished work, or work that has been glazed and needs to dry.

Throwing pottery on a wheel is a different sort of ballgame. We probably all can picture Demi and Patrick in that famous scene from the film *Ghost*. Even minus the sexual hanky-panky, a rank amateur on a runaway potter's wheel brings nightmare visions of permanently spackled walls, doors, windows, and more. Actually, such scenes are more the stuff of Looney Tunes rather than reality. Wheels are much more controllable than that, and no instructor would leave a novice alone at something of which she has little (or no) knowledge. Your main problem might be in having enough wheels. Even though many are portable and easily brought to the library, they are not inexpensive, and you cannot expect your instructor to have enough (or more than one) for all the students. It would not make for much of a class, or for many repeat sign-ups, if the students are forced to spend most of their time waiting for a turn on the wheel. You might find a way around this problem, but with beginner's wheels running several hundred dollars, it might be best to stick to nonpottery ceramics.

Jewelry Making and Lapidary
By now, it is probably obvious that many things artistic can also be considered crafts. This has been a bit of a concern in the arrangement of this book. Art probably involves more originality than the craft level of the same pursuit. However, just where does that dividing line run? Using someone else's pattern to knit a scarf is not really artistic, but what of painting? Short of painting by numbers, when is it a craft rather than an art, just because the skill of one painter is less than that of another? If the expression is sincere, then it must be art (or not?). Perhaps the best bellwether for our purpose is the popularity of the activity, as well as the ease with which it is mastered. Perhaps also, we can take into account costs—at least startup cost—as a determining factor. Thus, the very creative endeavor of quilting is also the terribly popular endeavor of quilting, so it appears in a subsequent chapter.

Having been involved in the lapidary arts heavily, I really wanted to make a case for them as a hobby craft. But they are not, at least by the criteria stated previously, even though many approach those arts that way. Jewelry making can be as mundane as setting a stone into a purchased finding or as stunningly inventive as any of Faberge's work; either way, the tools, time, and investment needed take it out of the realm of casual crafting.

The usual starting point for lapidary work is the *cabochon*, the oval or round unfaceted polished stone found in rings and pendants. Even this item requires a lot of machinery, from grinders and sanders to polishers. It also requires a steady flow of water because dry rock tends to overheat and crack. Rock dust tends to get everywhere, and wet rock dust resembles concrete in its persistence.

Actual jewelry making can be more easily accommodated at the library. Silversmithing of small items can be done at a table, with simple tools and small butane torches. The silver will cost more than the equipment. Another popular type of jewelry making is wire twisting, using pliers and flexible wire of silver, gold, copper, bronze, and other metals. Believe it or not, silver casting (we do not recommend gold because of the cost) small pieces is not that difficult to accomplish at tabletop. Just be sure to have plenty of fire extinguishers about.

One final lapidary art that needs mentioning, mainly because it can be done on a table, is faceting. Resembling an engineering project more than art, the precise geometrical cuts of translucent precious stones that dazzle us in diamond rings, ruby bracelets, and emerald necklaces, can be done by the determined amateur. A faceting machine is used to cut the precise angles, and the beginner can practice on a less-precious material, such as tanzanite, garnet, or peridot. The master amateur usually uses manufactured, rather than natural, stones.

Lapidary and jewelry classes, if undertaken by the library, have the advantage of easily displaying their work at the library, thus alerting others to the potential of taking a class. Even if you don't have any lapidary classes, find some enthusiasts to display their works at your library. Such work always garners a lot of attention. While you are at it, ask those enthusiasts if they would consider teaching some aspect of the art.

Sculpting and Carving
Sculpting at the library—at least the traditional idea of sculpting in stone—is probably not a good plan. Hauling even small pieces of stone into the building, and perhaps up or down stairs, is a lot of work—work that no one is going to appreciate. Quality stone—marble, limestone, alabaster, and the

like—is also very expensive (when it is even available). Cost consciousness and budgeting can go right out the window. Even the best sculptors can shatter a piece of stone, so imagine what would happen to people who are not familiar with the particular fault and fracture patterns of marble? Sculpting is slow work, and it would take several sessions to finish a piece. What do you do with the partially finished masterpiece from session to session—especially if your facility is short of storage space?

Beyond the obvious problems of stone sculpting, there are also distinct health concerns. Working in stone creates a lot of dust, and some of that dust is toxic to the human body and other living things. Alabaster, for example, can contain asbestos, and all rock dust breathed in will settle into the lungs and stay there; after all, most rock stays where it is put. The tools of the sculptors also are not conducive to the continued ownership of digits, eyes, and assorted body parts. Neither you nor your library's insurance company need these potential troubles.

Sculpting in metal is also going to pose all of these problems, as well as a few others no less serious. Making art from structural steel, scrap iron or other bits, and pieces of metal involves welding, an art form of sorts itself. Welding makes sparks, and we all know what sparks make. As for casting in metal, if you have never seen a sculptor's casting studio, you should know that it resembles a foundry more than the creative space of an artist.

The carving of soft materials, such as wood, clay, or soapstone, is a much more realistic class for the casual setting of the library's program room. You won't even need access to water, for most instances. In carving and its backwoods cousin, whittling, the tools are usually of a type that are held in one hand, while the potential piece of art is held in the other. Tools include knives, scoops, chisels, gouges, and other wood-handled implements. Power carving is also done, using Dremel tools and their kin. Like stone sculpting, carving is a negative art, meaning that the finished product is the result of removing, rather than adding, material. As the master decoy carver said when asked how he managed such lifelike work, "I just take off everything that don't look like a duck."

Carving, especially woodcarving is a fairly popular pursuit, and a local woodworker's store, in addition to selling tools and materials, can probably put you in touch with some local carvers. Woodcarving is also relatively inexpensive for beginners, and most of the tools can be used for general woodwork around the house if the patron decides not to pursue the art. One piece of equipment you might want to insist upon for your beginners is a metal mesh glove, of the type that fish filleters and butchers wear. Best of all, a very nice piece of work can be made the first time out.

The Peabody Public Library has sponsored woodcarving classes, which ran for a course of several weekly sessions. The students seemed to be well pleased, and produced several excellent items by the end of the class. Unfortunately, the library's janitor was much less enamored of the whole experience. Even with tarps down, chips and splinters got caught in the carpet and were not removable by any option but hand. In all fairness to our instructor, he did forewarn us of the problem, and suggested that it might be better if the class were held in a room with a hard floor (which we did not have). You might want to keep this in mind.

The Written Arts

Creative Writing

Everyone wants to be an author. We all have at least one tale to tell—our own—and most of us feel we can pen the great American novel, or perhaps the national epic poem. As voracious readers, library patrons are naturals for the would-be writers' brigade. They have probably experienced the best and suffered through the worst that the publishing world has to offer, and feel they can emulate that best and improve upon the worst. Spend some time at your library's reader's advisory or reference desk, and you will see that the area is full of Steinbeck want-to-bes.

Your community more than likely has someone capable of teaching creative writing to adults: retired (or active, for that matter) teachers or college instructors, actual authors, and journalists. Most writers are happy to pass along their expertise, and can be retained for small or no fee. Many publishing houses specialize in books that teach writing, and if you have the budget, their authors could give a workshop at your facility (and sell their books at the same time).

An adjunct to actual writing classes are seminars on how to get your work published. Magazine and newspaper editors, book publishers, and literary agents, as well as the previously mentioned actual authors, can be recruited for such programming. One word of caution, however: beware of vanity publishers who promise authorship for a price. No one needs to be told that she is good enough, but it will cost her. Either you are good enough to be published in the traditional manner, or you are good enough to continue writing for yourself and your friends. You need not be scammed into parting with a large sum of cash just to soothe your ego; you can always author a web page, if that is your desire.

Business and Resume Writing

Sometimes we write because we have to, not because we love it. Even those fond of writing know it is a hard task, and will not hold kindly to the type of writing they are often forced to do: business writing. Reports, grants, plans, and policies are to most of us dull, boring, and difficult to read; to write them is downright gruesome. If writing is hard work, then writing without the slightest clue is impossible work. Like its creative counterpart, business writing has rules to follow; unlike creative writing, it has a lot of specific rules that come across more as a set of blueprints than as a guide to self-expression.

Another important business-related document is the resume. Gone are the days of taking the sign out of the window and immediately putting on the apron; almost every open position now requires some sort of documentation of background, experience, and personal merit. Even those of us who are in the professions and have a resume may not have used it in many years. To be thrown back into the job market would leave us as helpless as the millions to whom a resume is a totally unknown quantity. Any help in fine-tuning their chances of landing a new job will be greatly appreciated. A resume class can be a formal workshop on the actual writing of the document, from placing of the name through experience and awards, or it might simply be an informal meeting with an expert who can suggest changes and updates.

Business writing experts can be found at the same source as your creative writing instructors, except in the business, rather than the English, department. Contact your chamber of commerce to see if they know of someone; they might also be able to put out the word that you are in need. Finally, college career counselors are usually very knowledgeable about what constitutes a good resume.

Rare and Old Book Seminars

One of the most common questions the reference librarian deals with is that of the worth of old books and magazines (and sometimes, photographs). Someone is always cleaning out an attic, disposing of an estate, or inheriting great uncle Ludwig's library. They are usually convinced that they have stumbled onto a fortune, simply on the vague memory of a price they once heard placed on a Gutenberg Bible.

As librarians, we are at once identified as the neighborhood experts on the subject, at least until we try to dissuade them of the notion of quitting their day jobs over that worm-eaten copy of *Alice of Old Vincennes*. What is needed is a real expert to tell them of their misfortune or, in the rarer case, their great windfall. There are many serious used and rare bookstores (as opposed to the local paperback exchange), even in the small community. Booksellers will often oblige you and give a talk and price your patrons' old books; after all, these tomes could become their old books if the patron is in the mood to unload. Teaching patrons to recognize valuable books from just plain old books can hopefully presort some of those boxes they are going to inevitably give to the library for the book sale. If only we could educate them about those fifty years' worth of *National Geographic* they have decided to get out of the garage.

For those who have decided to keep their old volumes, or for the dedicated collector, a class on archival methods might prove to be popular. Cleaning, storage, handling and repair, all aimed at prolonging the life and retaining the value of rare books can be taught. Begin in your own tech services department in your quest for an instructor; there might be someone with the training, or at least someone who remembers someone from library school. You might also have a local archivist working at a college library, a historical society, or a church. They, too, can be recruited for the role of teacher.

Antiques and Collectibles

Small-town America seems to have turned its downtowns into antique malls, as "real" businesses flee to the outlands for that mega-store acreage and the all-in-one, grab-your-money, experience. As a result, many of our towns are overrun by the curious animal known as the antique shopper. These people live anywhere, but most know that the rural surrounds are the place to find the good stuff. The recent popularity of shows such as *Antiques Roadshow* and *The Incurable Collector* point to the increase of interest in this area. Check your own circulation or ILL records to see how often price guides are checked out. You can continue to buy these guides to satisfy the collectors in your community, but it will be like trying to empty the ocean with a bucket: everything is a collectible to someone, and the guides just keep on getting published.

Like old book seminars, you can locate an antiques expert (even more plentiful than their bookish counterparts) who will come and do a class or two for your patrons. Also, like the old book dealers, they might go home with more than they arrived. Few experts can come to these affairs armed only with the knowledge in their heads; most must be somehow forewarned of what to expect, either specifically or at least in general subject area. Those that need very specific information, such as provenance, photos, and the like, beforehand usually detract from the spontaneity of the program, and many prospective attendees will shy away from having to do so much work rather than just showing up at the library with the item in question. There might be a speaker's fee for the appearance, or the expert might charge a flat rate for each item evaluated. If you can find one to do it for free, more power to you.

Just as with old books, antiques and collectibles need to be cared for to retain their value; once they have been discovered, most people want to keep them in good condition. Likewise, they also need to know what to do with those items in need of restoration. Of course, some antique restoration, such as furniture refinishing, can be a bit smelly and messy; you might opt for a lecture rather than a hands-on workshop. The main thing in preservation and restoration is a thorough knowledge of what not to do, so as to not ruin the item as an antique. Grinding that annoying rust off of your old Zorro lunch box may not only unmask the cunning fox, but cut the value to nothing. An expert can save your patrons from that heartbreak.

The previously mentioned television program, *The Incurable Collector*, is not really a pricing show, but rather a sort of travelogue through the vast and tangled world of antiques and collectibles. With more and more people collecting more and more things, the budding pack rat might be terminally confused as to what he should start collecting. Availability, prices, future values, and the variety and form of the collectible are questions the neophyte collector often has when starting out. Finding library patrons who are inveterate collectors can give you a source for programs on the subject. A collector of old fishing lures might be happy to do a "show-and-tell" presentation about his collection, how he got started, the direction he took, conventions and shows, and many more details that might inspire others along the same path. Of course, not all collectors want to be so sharing; the more people in the field, the harder it will be to find new items, especially at a reasonable price. This has happened countless times, with such items as depression glassware and metal lunch boxes. Nevertheless, collectors usually feel some sort of camaraderie with others who share their addiction, and often will encourage others to join them.

Courses and Lectures

When most of us hear the word "lecture," we probably want to run and hide under a blanket, much as we used to do in our college dorm rooms when that 8:00 A.M. chemistry lecture loomed. For those who, many years out of school, still dream of not having studied for a test or standing in front of the class in our underwear, the prospect of attending anything remotely resembling a structured unit of learning is enough to make us head on down to the fishing hole for a great day of playing hooky.

True, many adults will not want to hear what some expert or another has to say, no matter how interesting or pertinent the subject might be, but many others will, and lectures and more formal courses will reflect your library's mission very well, if that mission includes education and lifelong learning. Moreover, they don't have to be boring, as many lecturers have taken up the mantle of entertainer well as teacher. Visual and other aids break up boredom, and lend immediacy to the subject that people have come to expect in the age of leisure.

History and Travel
The popularity of cable's History Channel belies the old notion that people find history dull, incomprehensible, and useless. We have moved beyond the memorization of dates and names in our teaching of the subject, and everywhere in today's shrinking world we are reminded of why we need to understand what has happened to humanity and where it is headed. There is no doubt that history is more popular than ever; when David McCullough can put two super heavyweight books like *Truman* and *John Adams* on the best-seller list for weeks, we know people are paying more attention to the past.

Local History
While people are discovering that history on the whole is a worthwhile subject, local history is probably going to stimulate them even more. If the patron has long-reaching family roots in the community, or if she is new and wants to be immersed in the local heritage, you can bring a good number of people into the library with a local history program. You may or may not be competing with the local historical society. If they have a series of lectures, and a home for them, you might need to back away for the sake of community harmony; however, the historical society might be looking for your help, and you should stand ready to give it.

Local is a relative word, and may refer to the town, the county, a contiguous geographic area, or the entire state or region. Whatever way you view it, you are looking at history beyond the textbooks, and can market your programs as something much more immediate than the impact of the machine gun in World War I (or some such thing). Several areas of local history are common to every place in the United States, and knowing these will make it easier to plan.

Native American history. Wherever you are in the U.S. of A., there is or once was a tribe of American Indians. There will also exist in that area some people claiming heritage to the native traditions and life ways. People of Native American descent, even those with less than the "official" amount of blood to be considered a tribal member, are very proud and also very knowledgeable about their culture. You should not have any trouble finding these people because they are often involved in local heritage groups, powwows, school presentations, and other community endeavors. They might simply be wearing an inconspicuous piece of jewelry or clothing that identifies them; if so (after learning to identify such items), engage them in conversation and see if they would be willing to talk to a group of library patrons.

Famous sons and daughters. Sometimes fame stretches beyond borders; sometimes it is purely local; nevertheless, most people in the immediate area have heard the names of these people and will want to learn more. Whitley County, Indiana, the home of the Peabody Public Library, is one of the state's smallest counties, and rather rural—even by Indiana standards. Nevertheless, the area (28,000 souls as of the 2000 Census), has produced an inordinate number of stars, including two governors, a vice president of the United States, an Academy Award-winning actor, and a best-selling author. Twenty or so miles to the north is a town that claims famous naturalist and author Gene Stratton Porter; twenty miles to the south is Huntington, home of another United States vice president of much more recent vintage. Even if you don't possess such a plethora of riches, your historical personages will be just as important to your patrons as Thomas R. Marshall and his "good five-cent cigar" is to Columbia City.

Famous landmarks. You don't need to have the Statue of Liberty in your town to qualify for this one; anything that existed in your community before the people who are alive today will qualify. People will want to know about those grand old homes, or the ruins of the mill on the river; you are in a unique position to provide that information. Local historians, the owners of such properties, or someone in records at the local courthouse or newspaper might have an interest in such places and can put together a program. Sometimes, the famous is also the most commonplace. Whitley county is host to a section of the famous Lincoln Highway, the first coast-to-coast auto road constructed in this country. Many towns, villages, counties, and waypoints can make this claim, and you might also be sitting close to an historical byway such as Route 66, the Natchez Trace, the National Road, or the Dixie Highway. Check to discover if you have such a piece of history and if there are people (such as the Lincoln Highway Association) who can help you create a program around it. Other possibilities include well-known industries or organizations, railroads, or unique local landforms that might have a history.

Military veterans. Your local heroes might be from the Revolutionary War, or as recent as the headlines of your newspaper, but you can bet people will want to hear their stories, either from their own mouth or the mouth of a descendant or local historian. Contact veterans groups to see who is willing to give a talk.

Living History and Reenactors
History can come alive for people when they see for themselves how the populace lived, worked, and dressed at a particular time. If you can bring Harry

Truman to your library, rather than someone lecturing on his presidency, wouldn't you find it more exciting? If you could enter an Ojibwa wigwam, rather than see a picture of it, wouldn't you have a better understanding of those people? That is what living history is all about, and you don't need to be Colonial Williamsburg to do it. Many people in your area will be either collectors of historical items, or one of a large social group known as *reenactors*. Not only do they have artifacts (or reproductions of artifacts), but they will become the people whose history they are sharing. You can find these people by going to fairs, reenactments, powwows, and rendezvous in your area. This is wonderful stuff and fun for all ages.

Tie-Ins to Historical Events

It seems that some important historical anniversary is happening all the time in this country. Ever since the bicentennial in 1976, we have become enamored of historical celebrations. Of course, since the nation hit 200, many of its subsequent events are now also hitting 200. The bicentennial of the Lewis and Clark expedition is a recent example. This one is perfect because it goes on for three years and involves a very large area of the country. Not only can you tie in a program to the time of the event, but you can also boast of it as local history. The entire nation doesn't even have to celebrate the event; you can name your own. Check history timelines, *Chase's Calendar of Events*, or your local history society to determine what can be turned into a timely event. It needn't even be some major round-number of an anniversary; what's wrong with celebrating the 196th Birthday of Abe Lincoln with a series of programs, rather than waiting another four years?

Geography and Travel

If we as a society are in need of historical knowledge to understand our place in the world, then we most certainly need to understand other places and peoples. Despite, or perhaps as a result of, the abysmal performance of American students in geographical identification, travel literature is very popular in most libraries, and people are very interested in hearing about foreign lands and people (as well as our own). Presenting such programs can both inform and involve the community.

Many people travel, and the days of out-of-focus slides of the family standing in front of the Leaning Tower of Pisa are thankfully fading into distant memory. The digital revolution has brought us out of the grainy 8-mm silence of fading Kodachrome into a new video age, in which it doesn't take much to produce professional-looking results. You or someone on the staff knows who is going where, so it is an easy business to round them up for a series of travel lectures. They can bring their videos, their souvenirs, and their impressions to the library and your patrons. They might not be competent lecturers, but their presentation can be jazzed up by you and your staff into a multimedia affair, and you can always turn it into an interview or Q&A show. If you can't get an hour out of a person who has just completed a baad-farten tour in Denmark, then you need to hang up your programmer's hat.

Literature & the Arts

Literature lectures and programs can range from the incredibly dull to the wonderfully inventive; it is up to you to get the right ones. You can make literature come alive in your library by booking storytellers, authors to read their works, literary impersonators, and more.

Professional storytellers are all over, and many form guilds of varying cohesiveness that you might contact for bookings and information. Many storytellers also have their own web pages. Because they make their living telling stories, they are usually very specific on their advertising as to what sort of things they do and the audience for whom they work. Some storytellers deal only in children's stories, but many are of a dual nature and can do programs for both children and adults. This is a chance to share some costs with your colleagues in the children's department. Often, storytellers have a discount if they are asked to do shows for both children and adults. They will usually do the children's program in the morning or afternoon, and the adult stories in the evening.

Literary impersonators are really actors who take on the persona and act out the words of a famous author. Hal Holbrook as Mark Twain is perhaps the most famous example. The Peabody Public Library has hosted both Henry David Thoreau and Laura Ingalls Wilder in the recent past. The presenters of these pieces are professional actors, dedicated amateurs, or even college professors, as in the case of our Thoreau. Usually the audience participates in some form, with the patrons suspending their disbelief and getting into the time and spirit of the presentation. Needless to say, professional productions such as these can range into the several hundreds of dollars, but some amateurs do it for little more than expenses. A search of the web using the desired author's name and the modifiers "impersonator," "tribute," "portrayal," or "re-enactor" can often find people; also searching the web for people on the Chautauqua circuit can prove quite fruitful.

Appreciation Classes

You probably don't want to get too heavily into the more formal class structure with your educational programs, but appreciation classes can be an exception. Art and music are two things that everyone appreciates, even if not understanding it. You can remedy that by having courses for the interested but uninitiated. If you or anyone on your staff has a background (e.g., took an art history class at college), you might be able to stage a series on your own. If no one has a proper grounding in the arts, or the ability to talk for forty minutes without driving the audience to thoughts of suicide, you may want to go the professional route and start asking around. Again, the retired or just interested teachers and practitioners can be a good source of instructors. This sort of thing has the potential to get rather dry, so make certain that whoever is doing the class has plenty of multimedia to keep things interesting and rolling along.

Social Issues
Depending upon the situation in your community, you might want to delve a bit into the controversial world of social issues and current events. At the time of this writing, no issue is hotter than gay marriage. Imagine this as a theme for a library lecture, or a debate. Then imagine, if you would, the likelihood of such an event staying above the level of a Jerry Springer show. If you can imagine both, and can be certain that enraged citizenry won't be calling for an end to all library budgets, then you can probably press that hot button with some degree of certainty. You can, of course, steer clear of the really divisive areas and concentrate on the social issues we all more or less agree upon: the danger of drugs, juvenile crime, and unemployment. What? You say those topics can be controversial as well? Yes, you might be correct, but they are probably less fractious than some. What you need to do is carefully assess your community and decide what it can handle or, more to the point, what your institution can handle without a general uprising.

The structured debate or roundtable might be the safest way to deal with controversy. Presenting all sides in a controlled environment is a way to give your patrons exposure to differing opinions so that they can form their own beliefs in an informed manner. However, the middle has always been condemned by the extremes, and you can bet that Geraldo Rivera did not expect that one of his guests would end up breaking his nose.

The Peabody Public Library has toyed with the idea of presenting local political debates for offices, such as mayor. In the absence of any civic group that would normally take on this job, it could be a viable community service. One must be careful, however, to make certain that all candidates are invited to debate, even those of the Pansexual Peace Party. You might want to rethink the whole thing.

Local social service organizations can supply people and topics for programs. They are always looking for ways to get their message to the people who may need their help. Aid to dependent children and mothers, prescription drug help for seniors, elder law, estate planning, and home health care are some of the topics that might be of inherent interest for your patrons. There are many more, some of which might be of particular need in your community. Take the time to familiarize yourself with them and determine if a program is possible. We know that people come to the library looking for this kind of information and contact with these agencies; why not bring the two together at your facility?

Technology

Very few of us do not have some Luddite leanings in our souls. On the surface, we seem to work well with our technology: we drive our automobiles, press our remotes, e-mail our business associates and friends, and write our books on word processors. Nevertheless, who among us has not shuddered when the dashboard gauges go wild, or uttered a not-so-silent oath at the VCR, or secretly wished for a sledgehammer when the computer (the one at work, not the one at home we are still paying for) freezes up? We have mixed emotions, at best, about the tools that lighten our everyday load; when they work, they are our friends, but when they become recalcitrant, we anthropomorphize them into enemies and long for the simplicity of the age of our parents, who, of course, had longed for the same.

As librarians, we see ourselves somewhat as experts on the use, if not the witchcraft of building and caring for, computers. We have used them long before they became household products, perhaps as far back as college, and certainly as part of our jobs. We can use them so dismissively that we are unable to see how others can fear and loathe them. We wonder why they keep asking us about the availability of materials when the catalog station is right there; we snicker when they ask for the Reader's Guide and find a perverse pleasure in their reaction upon finding out that periodical indexes are all online. Really, though, has it been so long since we were in that very same situation, wondering what all those bits and bytes had to do with books, and how an ALT key will help us assign a Dewey number? Don't we still shudder when we see people turning away from expertly written books and instead putting their faith blindly into the hands of the great god Dot Com? What our entire schizophrenic attitude toward computers boils down to is knowledge: we have it and our confidence rises; we lack it and fear takes control. Lack of knowledge is a lack of power, and the 21st-century American does not like to feel powerless.

Computer Classes

Because the library is often the first place a computer neophyte comes into contact with the dreaded nemesis, it should be the first place they turn to in an effort to overcome their foe. When they are ready to learn, we must be ready to teach. We have all been asked for help by patrons and we all know the frustration of trying to deal with someone whose computer literacy quotient is unknown to us. Do we just assume they can use a mouse; that they will understand when we say, "Just click on the link," and then walk away? Can we even use words like "link," "enter," and "backspace" without causing even more confusion? Do we just give up and do it for them? One-on-one computer instruction from the reference desk is a no-win arrangement. We are not in a position to judge a person's skill level "on the run," and we are never in possession of enough time to devote solely to one person's entry into the world of the viable computer user. Nor are we fulfilling our mission to that patron by just taking over and doing it ourselves, just to be done with it. A structured class setting is what is really needed.

Basic Computer Skills

Teaching the basics of computers to adults will continue to be a viable pursuit for many years to come. Not only among today's seniors, but also tomorrow's— the Baby Boomers. Many seriously lack any computer training—or at least not PC training. True, many people have jobs that entail the use of specialized computer machinery, such as foundry workers and cashiers, but these people have been trained to do a particular job on a particular machine in one and only one fashion, and it rarely translates into the wider world of CPUs and keyboards.

A first course in computers should begin with the most elemental feature— turning it on—and progress to the point where the student is comfortable with exploring the possibilities of the machine and its programs. In short, we need to eradicate fear and replace it with confidence. Finding the right teacher is the first and most important step. Providing follow-up opportunities and help is the next.

A good computer instructor must have empathy for her charges and realize the fear and inferiority caused by this prepossessing piece of wire and plastic. Too many people who are "into" technology and the binary world come off sounding the way computer manuals are written. Jargon has its place, in helping to define the previously indefinable, but its place is rarely at the beginner's level. It should be used only for clarification, and all too often it leads only to obfuscation. Patience is also imperative; what we need to remember is that just because we "get it" does not mean it is clear to everybody.

It is probably true that just about everyone on your staff is capable, skill-wise, of teaching an introductory computer class; but who, if any, has these special talents to really make it worthwhile?

Computers, like musical instruments and sports, are best learned through repetition. To simply hold a class or two or three is not enough. Beginners at computers often do not own their own machines; in fact, that is usually why they come to the library: they want to know if it is worth it to have one of their own. To avoid this sort of Catch 22, frequent computer labs should be held—open sessions in which the student can drop in and do some pre-assigned exercises with an instructor or lab monitor present to answer questions, should they arise.

At the Peabody Pubic Library, a basic hands-on, step-by-step text is required for purchase, and is the only fee charged for the class. A clear, illustration-intensive manual should be used; some of those books marketed as being "for dunderheads" are far from the beginner's texts touted in their titles. Remember, this is the kindergarten of computer schools, and written—or drawn—material should match the grade level.

Specific Computer Applications

After the student has mastered the basics—using the mouse and keyboard, understanding files, and the nuts and bolts of an operating system—she is probably ready to move on to the good stuff. Most people have specific uses in mind for the computer, and would happily continue learning about them at the library.

Of course, one of the most important "destinations" for the new computer enthusiast is the Internet, with all that entails. Maneuvering on a page should not be a problem, but they will need to understand the use of browsers, search engines, and directories. They must become familiar with links and URLs. They particularly need to know that the cyber world is not all Dot Coms. Library staff can easily handle a class like this.

Another popular online feature is e-mail. A class based around two or three of the most popular free mail services will give a patron a background in composing, sending, receiving, and attachments. All of the things learned on these e-mail servers can be easily translated to any other programs they could end up using. E-mail is becoming one of the favorite sports of older Americans, who find it a dandy way to keep in touch with far-flung family, and for rediscovering old friends. Many casual Internet users, who don't want e-mail, but are forced into having an address in order to use online ordering, will also find such a class helpful.

Staying in the cyber sphere for a moment, one of the most successful series of computer classes offered by the Peabody Public Library has been e-Bay instruction. As a result of brainstorming sessions among the adult services staff, it was suggested that teaching these people to use the service, rather than having a reference librarian, who has never bought or sold via the 'Net, pulling her hair out, would be a good idea. We ran the class monthly for almost a year, and after a brief hiatus are ready to offer it again. That is definitely a good idea. The classes cover the processes of buying and selling, tips and cautions, examples of good deals, deals gone horribly wrong, and general protocol and courtesy in the online auction world.

We must not forget the old standards, the ones that made people want to use a computer back before there was a World Wide Web, or even an operating system called Windows. These are the office tools, the word processors, spreadsheets, and databases. What particular brand you teach is, of course, dependent upon what brand you have loaded on your computers. Because networking licenses can lead to real serious money, you probably are not going to get the boss to spring for some program like Quicken, which is a popular home product, but has little value in a library setting (would you want to balance your checkbook on a public computer?). To those of us who use these programs every day, we see the similarities between Word and Word-Perfect, between Lotus and Excel. We might not know the finer points of the unfamiliar program, but a spreadsheet is a spreadsheet and switching from one to the other, we do manage to get by. This situation, however, is not likely to exist with your patrons; the intricacies of one program will be enough for them, without expecting crossover.

Thanks to the software company that ate the world, we don't have to worry too much about this problem. Most people buy PCs and most all PCs come loaded with Microsoft products. Unless your director has been living on Rigel Seven, your library is also loaded with them. So, you will probably be scheduling classes in Word, Excel, Access, and perhaps Power Point and Publisher. The first two will probably be your most popular.

A beginner's class in any of these does not require that the instructor be a complete master of the program, but he must be ready to answer a number of questions that might fall outside the syllabus of the course. Then, if you are successful with these tyro classes, the logical progression will occur and you will begin to get requests for intermediate and, perhaps, advanced classes. You can continue, or you might decide that this is not in your means and beg off, pointing to some nearby community learning organization.

Library-Based Applications
Once you have your patrons all squared away on using the computer, the Internet, e-mail, office programs, and the like, you still have one chore left: teach them how to use the library's special programs. They might be able to

type in a book title on your catalog's search page, but what else can they do? Can they formulate a subject search? Can they even read the record? Most library catalogs have many added features, including reserving material, self-renewal, e-mail notification, and more. Your have paid a great deal of money for a system that can do all this, so it will behoove you to maximize its use by teaching your patrons.

What about a periodical index? Do you have a proprietary online product, or are you part of a consortium that makes these databases available to libraries in a given area? They are all rather different, and even if your patron knows how to use the one at the local college, she might need help with yours.

Depending upon your budget and your patrons' needs, you might have any number of specialized online databases available and enough people interested in them to hold one or more classes. Don't ignore the opportunity.

New Technology

Beyond PCs, there is a plethora of digital equipment that is just waiting to befuddle the unsuspecting. It is rather wonderful to listen to people reticently speak of buying some of these things, of both their amazement and fear of the new products. This has probably been the way things have worked since the first time Oog the caveman took his new invention, the wheel, for a spin.

"What that!?"

"Don't know, but me bet it going to take longer to get to work."

"Don't care. Me got have one."

My grandparents came to this country from Lithuania in 1907, and I can remember them never wanting to use that newfangled invention called *the camera*. Now we have people wondering about digital cameras. The opportunities for programs never end.

New Product Showcases

Here is a chance to partner with the businesses in your community, if you are allowed to do so. Call the local electronics outlet—preferably one that deals more or less exclusively in the new tech, rather than the neighborhood mega store that sells goldfish and tires along with computers. You will want real experts and, as far as that everything-under-one-roof place, their experts are probably at company headquarters. Simply check with the store manager to see when the new products generally arrive, and arrange to have someone come to the library to do a presentation.

This might sound dangerously close to crass commercialism on the part of the library, but there are many good reasons to work with the private sector.

First, they would not strictly be selling anything at the program; they would simply be presenting new items and answering questions about them. Your patrons might indeed run right down to your presenter's store and fill his cash drawer to overflowing in consumerist zeal, but they might also go to said megastore, or not buy anything at all. They certainly will not be buying anything at the library. What you are doing is aiding them in making an informed choice—similar to giving them the auto blue book to find used car prices. Area businesses also pay a great deal of tax money to the community, and just like your average wage earner, probably expect some services beyond snow removal.

Strange New World—PDAs and Other Little Gadgets

Just when you figured out how to make the most of your Franklin Planner, along comes this media blitz for this thing that is a bit larger than a credit card, with a little stick the size of a toothpick, and a keyboard so small that any self-respecting leprechaun would refuse to use it. Nevertheless, it is going to change your world, and you just have to have it, how did you ever get along without it, and, while you are at it, why not buy one for all the kids? The personal digital assistant has descended upon us like a spring blizzard, and we still haven't managed to shovel out.

These little gadgets are not quite as in-your-face as cell phones, or nearly as annoying, but they are still there. Either they are quietly and efficiently being used in the halls of power and for the family shopping list, or they have taken their place in the back of the dresser drawer, next to that fancy chronometer no one has ever been able to figure out. If the latter is the case, then you have the makings of a program. This goes for just about any new and popular piece of personal electronics on the market.

Digital Cameras

Speaking of popular personal electronics, nowhere has the digital revolution had as great an impact as on photography. It has been a rather quiet revolution, but nonetheless a persistent one. Digital cameras are changing the way we record our lives, and have afforded greater control and creativity to more people than ever before. A steady stream of shutterbugs are falling under the spell of the new cameras, even a dyed-in-the-wool 35-mm SLR man, like me.

We have had a workshop—or rather an informational session—on digital still cameras at the Peabody Public Library, and patrons are continually asking when the next one will be scheduled. An informational session should embrace the basics of digital photospeak, such as pixels, memory cards, optical vs. digital zoom, special in-camera compositional features, such as red-eye reduction, grayscale, and monotones. It should also include a demonstration of a good photoediting software program. You can let the prospective Cartier-Bressons snap a few frames, download them, and do some manipulation in the editor. Send them home with a few prints, and you have a successful program. Oh, and don't forget to have some handouts that compare different makes and models.

Another possibility is the digital photography club, which could be organized through the library and use its facilities and equipment (projectors, etc.).

Other Tech Program Ideas
When it comes to the new technology, you are only limited by your own imagination and other peoples' befuddlement. How many of us really know how to program a VCR or record DVDs? How will we do it after the kids move out? It might sound silly, but you can never know what will attract a crowd when it comes to this stuff. If you bring people in, and they learn, you have done well. If you don't, then try something else; a "program cancelled" sign doesn't take much effort.

MP3s, fax machines, GPS, electronic book readers, and anything that confounds the mind while charming the pocketbook is fair game for a program.

Health, Welfare, and Nutrition

Next to do-it-yourself legal counsel, do-it-yourself doctoring seems to be one of our patrons' favorite pastimes. We check out medical books to them, guide them to the latest edition of the PDR, and if it weren't for the public library, Medline Plus would have to shut down. We might be worrying about such developments, and being a part of this mass-migration to self-medication, but if they don't get it from us, they might end up getting it from some guy on the street with a bag full of bones and a few dead chickens. At least our information comes from respected professional sources.

Why all this interest in health, when we keep hearing what an unhealthy society we are? Do we enjoy abusing our bodies, and then obsessing with guilt about it? Is this a recent trend, or has it been going on for a long time? What part should we as program librarians have, if any? Of course, self-administration of health problems is nothing new. The medical profession has only relatively recently gained credence as an effective alternative to home care. It has only been a half century since medical science proved it could help us by taming the polio pandemic and barely a century since it even turned from the purely defensive after centuries of doing little more than providing comfort, or worse, adding to the harm. It was often better to treat your family at home, and the tradition seems to have effectively passed from generation to generation.

We need only look at the over-the-counter drug business in this country. A multi-billion dollar industry, a recent study found that 90% of all Americans have taken OTC medications, 59% take them regularly, and 36% take three or more different ones every month.[5] Do we think that such activity will cease if we refuse to be a part of it?

Whether carrying on the family tradition, avoiding the high out-of-pocket cost of an office visit, or reacting to the stifling effects of the insurance industry on the health care they are allowed, people will continue to turn to the library as one of the more sound sources available toward living a better, healthier life.

Partners in Health

Whether we like it or not, we as information experts are part of a large, pervasive web of health-care providers that keeps the community healthy and fit. Just as traditional roles of the library have changed, the health industry has managed to stretch itself beyond the halls of hospitals and the waiting rooms of clinics. The local supermarket is a part of this new network, as is the gas station/convenience store that sells aspirin and antacids to truckers. Newsstands display health and nutrition magazines, the morning network television assures you that you can extend your life and improve your looks, and bookstores—small and mega—tout the latest by Dr. Phil. Some stores have nothing on their shelves but vitamins and nutritional supplements, while others stock organic food products exclusively. Even your child's school cafeteria is worrying about the fat and carbs in that mac and cheese they keep shoving across the counter.

It must be obvious by now that this book does not err on the conservative side when it comes to suggesting the types and numbers of adult programs public libraries should offer; this certainly holds true for health-related programs as well. We certainly need to be careful where our patrons' health is concerned, but they could just as easily lop off a few fingers thanks to that book on deck building you found for them last week. Thus, lectures, round tables, information sessions, and classes on health and nutrition, diet and disease, exercise and pain relief—anything short of diagnosis and on-the-spot surgery—is to be pursued. If we do it right, and do it with the right people, we end up creating yet another important service.

Working with Local Care Givers

Some sort of care-giving organization or individual will be on just about every block in your town. Nursing homes, assisted-living centers, and senior citizen organizations abound to help older Americans, and older Americans are among the library's best patrons. Gyms, health centers, and aerobic and martial arts instructors are helping the young and fit to stay that way. Groups and governmental agencies dedicated to the health and well-being of our children assist parents in making the right choices. Pain centers, massage therapists, and chiropractors are there to relieve our aches and stress. Grief counselors and hospices facilitate in the face of the inevitable. What a choice we have when shopping for library programs in the health field.

Nursing homes and assisted-living centers are often looking to get together with some organization that can provide a public forum for their outreach. A good nursing home (this information is easy enough to obtain from the state agency accountable for their licensing) will want to be a part of its community and give people an idea of what they do, how their services can be used, and even the best way to never have to use those services, if possible. The person to contact will be either the public relations director, or head of outreach or community awareness. While you are at it, do not only think in terms of what these establishments can do for you; imagine the community good will if you were to offer to take one or more of your programs to them.

Exercise classes are another natural for the library. Not all aerobics and workout instructors are affiliated with a particular business or institution, and they might be available to teach a class. Local governmental health units might also have trainers or physical therapists on staff, and making your facility available to them could be mutually beneficial.

The Red Cross

The American Red Cross has regional offices in most fair-sized cities in your state. They might not have a physical facility in your town, but will still be operating in some capacity. Blood drives, CPR and other classes, collections of food and clothing for disaster victims are all services they render on a regular basis. Contacting the regional office (check the Red Cross website, http://www.redcross.org/, to find the closest one) will let you know exactly what they do in your area. Offer to hold CPR classes, or even a blood drive. Many businesses and organizations require their employees to be certified in CPR or biohazards cleanup, such as blood, vomit, and excrement (sorry). If these groups need instruction from the Red Cross, and also need a place for the training, perhaps you can perform that function. Invite speakers from the

Red Cross to tell their story and to recruit volunteers; never forget that programming and outreach are two-way streets.

Doctors and Health Practitioners

Doctors don't make house calls anymore (except on the PAX network), so why would they make a library call? Don't be too hasty to discount the willingness of the individual physician to engage in community service. Ask your own doctor, or identify library patron physicians and approach them; they might have a favorite topic that they would be happy to expound upon given the chance. Nurses—home health-care nurses and others—are also prime candidates for the health-related program.

The local hospital often has classes and support groups for specific health concerns, such as diabetes and hypertension. However, they also practice community outreach and most have speakers' bureaus. Topics range from diseases and conditions to job-related injuries, affordable care, and the future of medicine. Using these speakers wisely will give you a large variety of programs for a long time to come.

Nutritionists and Dieticians

Nutritionists and dieticians often work for hospitals and clinics, but can also be associated with universities, school systems, the government, or the private sector. Their work deals either with groups, such as a school lunch program, or with individuals. They can lecture on diet, food groups, nutritional needs, food toxicities, and similar topics. A consulting nutritionist will develop a diet plan or nutritional regimen for a variety of individuals, from heart patients to athletes. Any of these areas would make a fine program, either as a lecture, or as an informational session.

Another Way of Seeing—Alternative Medicine

Almost as common as treatment with OTC drugs is the use of alternative forms of health care. It is not correct to say that these methods fly in the face of traditional health care, because in many cases, such as herbs and acupuncture, they are the tradition rather than the intrusive new kid on the block. As more mainstream health-care providers admit to the efficacy of such treatments, the "natural" noninvasive and nonpharmaceutical approach has gained greatly in popularity. As an adjunct to modern medicine, the "chicken soup" approach has much to recommend it; as a wholesale replacement to societal norms, however, it may become problematic both for the practitioner and the patient. Depending upon the comprehensiveness of their claims, and their denial of mainstream medical practice, some alternative solutions can bring lawsuits, government involvement, or even jail time. You and your library most probably do not want to go there. Still, with careful study and choice, there are a number of topics in the wide spectrum of alternative health care that are welcome by most and can make for interesting programs.

Herbalism is one of the very popular areas of medical alternatives and supplements. It cannot be denied that plants have medicinal powers; we need look no farther than foxglove or the poppy. Lectures on any one of a number of herbal topics could be popular at your library. The health-and-beauty uses of specific herbs, the best way to prepare them, their history (herbs in the Bible is always popular), or even their cultivation are just a few of the subjects on which a knowledgeable herbalist can speak. Contact local herb shops or growers for speakers, or your local herb society. A visit to the Herb Society of America's web site (http://www.herbsociety.org/) will get you a list of speakers by region on a large number of topics. Please note that the society does not dispense actual advice on the medicinal use of herbs.

No matter what area of alternative medicine you decide to explore, be aware of the aforementioned problems. Research your speaker, and do not hesitate to make it clear that, as a public institution funded by tax dollars, you are agreeing to present her view as one of several possible positions on the subject; nor will you allow any bad mouthing of mainstream or other systems of health. For the latest information on the medical establishment's points of view on alternative medicine, check out the web site of NCCAM—the National Center for Complementary and Alternative medicine—at http://nccam.nih.gov/.

Notes

1. United States Census Bureau. *Statistical Abstract of the United States 2002.* Washington, DC: Government Printing Office, 2003, 136.

2. U.S. Department of Education. National Center for Education Statistics. *Profile of Undergraduates in U.S. Postsecondary Institutions, 1999–2000,* NCES 2002-168 by Laura Horn, Katharin Peter, and Kathyrn Rooney. Project Officer Andrew G. Malizio. Washington, DC: 2002, 14.

3. Ibid., 16.

4. Ibid., 58.

5. Harris Interactive, *Attitudes and Beliefs About the Use of Over-the-Counter Medicines: a Dose of Reality.* Prepared for: National Council on Patient Information and Education (NCPIE), 2002.

~

CHAPTER FIVE

Cultural Programs

On the scale of popularity, cultural programs will probably rate at or near the top in your library. Film, music, drama, and literature seem to go hand in hand with the public's view of the library's place in our society. Reading is entertainment for many, and the ascendancy of what is viewed purely in entertainment terms—videos, music CDs, and computer software—has helped to cement the idea that we function as part of society's galaxy of amusement, rather than for educational betterment. Thus, if that is what they expect of our collections, then why wouldn't they also look forward to it when it comes to library programming?

Another obvious reason for the popularity of cultural programs over educational and other types is that they are just a lot more fun than listening to a lecture. Didn't we all prefer to go play in the park rather than listen to mom tell us yet again to watch out for traffic, don't climb on the fence, stay out of the flowers, and on and on? Lectures can seem more like formal schooling, and for many, those may not be the best of memories. It might take some real soul searching and perhaps rationalization on the part of many of us to face up to the idea that we are purveyors of popular entertainment rather than essential knowledge. You might not be able to overcome your anathema to such a situation, but you will be doing your library, its continued viability, and the majority of your patrons a real service if you can accept the challenge.

A decade or more ago, when the Peabody Public Library began to seriously build a video collection, a study was made concerning its placement within the building. Some thought it ought to be at the front, near the circulation desk, to facilitate easy access to this popular item. However, it was decided to place the video shelving near the back of the library and, when a new building was planned, that decision remained in effect. Like a supermarket that places its staples—bread, milk, and meats—in the rear, we decided that if people were going to use us as their video store, they were going to have to see what else we had to offer. The main point was to get people into the library who would never set foot in it before, and then take it from there. Why then should we worry about scheduling programs viewed as popular diversion, when they might very well bring into the building people who have never been there and would probably never see the inside of our facility under any other circumstances? True, you might not be dragging them on a guided tour past your book collections and reference department, but you impress them with your talents, creativity, and organization. If you can "put on a show" that entertains them, then what else might you be able to offer them?

As a final point to bring you over, cultural programs are not only great for attendance and a good way to connect with library nonusers, they can also be rather inexpensive (if not totally free) and easy to book and set up.

As described in this chapter, many talented and generous amateurs are willing to put on a cultural program for you, and some professionals are surprisingly affordable. Also, the ease of finding and booking this talent is a joy for the oft brow-beaten program librarian. Musicians and actors have unions and guilds, and many have their own web sites through which they can be booked (and through which you can often sample some of their product). Publicity photos and press releases are usually supplied by the artist, making advertising and publicity a snap.

Remember, no matter how entertaining or fun a program is, most people are still going to derive something valuable from it. They might also discover the hidden gem that is their local public library. So don't be shy; start booking those people today!

Film

Why would anyone want to go see a movie that can be watched at home on VHS or DVD, in the comfort of your own La-Z-Boy, one that might not even be in color or in English? Well, people do this all the time; there are old film festivals, theaters dedicated to revivals, showings at colleges, community events, schools, churches, and other nontheatrical venues. Many times, a person needs to be with others in order to experience the full power that a particular piece of cinema can bring. Knowing that someone else shares your interest in and love of a particular film or genre can make the experience more meaningful, and you might find yourself sharing thoughts, and ideas, and perhaps forming new friendships. Film is a social occasion, and your library can keep it that way.

This is a passion of many and we should be there to tap into it. Film, for better or worse, has become the main medium of expression in the United States and probably a good portion of the rest of the world. The film industry, for a number of reasons, is more profitable than ever in its century-plus lifespan, its stars are worshipped and scrutinized under a barrage of publicity, and so much of what was once considered the news media has now been devoted to this pastime. Offering films for public viewing at the library only makes sense because we are simply continuing to do what we have always done: make an author's creative statement and vision available to our patrons.

Procuring Film Rights

Before you begin to plan a film series, a festival, or even a single showing at your library, you need to thoroughly investigate the wonderful world of public performance rights. Like books, films are protected by copyright; unlike books, which are basically a one-on-one affair, movies are actually meant to reach a massed, gathered audience, and the simple purchase of a single legal copy of the item does not assure us of the right to project it to the world— at least not all at once. The vast majority of videos sold in this country are labeled "for home use only." These are the ones we commonly see at the local mega store, or the neighborhood video rental, generally retailing for under thirty dollars. *At-home use* means a private, unadvertised showing among friends and family—even if your family is several hundred close-knit cousins.

To be able to advertise and have the public attend a showing of a film, even in a public, nonprofit venue like your library, you must have public performance rights to that particular work. Public performance is not just some vague term that no one is quite sure of, but a very specific definition in the copyright law.

To perform or display a work publicly means:

1. to perform or display it at a place open to the public or at any place where a substantial number of persons outside of a normal circle of a family and its social acquaintances is gathered; or
2. to transmit or otherwise communicate a performance or display of the work to a place specified by clause (1) or to the public, by means of any device or process, whether the members of the public capable of receiving the performance or display receive it in the same place or in separate places at the same time or at different times.[1]

You will notice two things about this particular definition: the place or places mentioned are in no way limited to the traditional designation of a movie theater and there is absolutely no mention of whether or not admission is charged.

The wide-ranging laws covering intellectual property convey many rights to the author or creator of a particular work. Outside of fair use of parts of a work (a limited number of quotes), copying by libraries or archives, or face-to-face teaching (all of which have myriad and often nebulous rules attached), there are no exceptions to the procuring of rights. A work need not even to have been published and distributed to be covered by copyright. Because of the nature of film, and the ease with which it can be disseminated to a mass audience, restrictions can appear to be even tighter for them than for other creative products.

There are several ways by which you may obtain performance rights for the films you wish to show. You may actually purchase a copy with the rights attached to it. Some distributors sell these in both video and celluloid versions, and you might have some in your collection right now. You need to check with the vendor from whom they were purchased because they will not usually state that performance rights are included. These films tend (obviously) to cost more than those only with home rights; although the film has the rights until it falls apart, it can always be shown, and it need not particularly be shown at your library. Of course, if you only intend to show the film one time, this is money better spent elsewhere. Some documentaries come with performance rights if purchased directly from the producer rather than a vendor. As stated, you might not find performance rights stated on the packaging; you might not even see a copyright statement, but it does exist. You must assume nothing when dealing with intellectual property. If in doubt, obtain the rights, if not in doubt, doublecheck to be certain. You must have all your permissions in some hardcopy form.

Another method of obtaining rights is to go through the distributor, who may or may not have the authority from the copyright holder to grant or sell permission rights for a public performance. Well-known companies like Kino or Criterion are such distributors. The problem is, of course, that a particular distributor might not have the film you are looking for, and might lead you to a lot of additional work on your part, as you attempt to track down the distributor who does have the film and the authority. In the case of many esoteric works, independent films, and foreign films, this might be necessary labor, but if you intend to show mostly mainstream cinema from major Hollywood studios, a lot of your work has been done for you by a few companies that understand the needs of libraries and similar institutions.

Licensing agents have taken most of the work out of tracking down copyright holders and seeking permissions. For one fee—usually paid yearly—you are granted the nontheatrical performance rights for a variety of commercial entertainment films. What, who, and how many will depend upon the agency that will have agreements with a number of distributors and studios. It happens that one of these agencies is actually owned by one of the largest distributors of Hollywood films.

Why would the studios and other copyright holders agree to do such a thing, especially at the affordable rates that are charged? First, tracking down violators is a lot of time and money spent, and so is prosecuting them. Second, how does it look for your publicity and goodwill if you start harassing libraries and churches over dimes and nickels? Better to collect some money that normally would not be available, than to have all these hassles.

At present, two major licensing agencies deal with libraries and know our wants and needs: Motion Picture Licensing Corporation (http://www .mplc.com) and Movie Licensing USA (http://www.movlic.com). Other agents deal with different groups, such as churches. Signing an agreement with one of these firms is the quickest and easiest way to ensure your library's copyright compliance on the largest number of feature films from mainstream studios and distributors. Covering studios like Disney, Universal, and Warner, and distributors such as Tri-Star and Orion, a yearly site license will cover practically all of your needs. You may then use your existing collection of "home-use only" VHS and DVD, as long as you do not alter them in any way for the showings.

The cost of a license will vary, being dependent upon such factors as population served or average attendance at showings (according to which agent you choose). You might pay less than $100 or more than $1000, as your circumstances vary. If this seems a bit pricey for your adult programming, there are several justifications beyond your department for having a license. First, we are not looking at copying a few pages out of an old book; this is the movie industry, the big leagues of the copyright game. After what has happened with Napster and the music industry, it is just not a good idea to play fast and free with the rules. If you think you are too small to be bothered, think again. In a former life, I happened to be a bartender at an out-of-the-way country roadhouse that featured live music every weekend. The owners, bless their hearts, did not know about royalties, and never bothered sending any money to ASCAP or BMI. These two giants in the music world pay people to go honky-tonking and ensure that all the rules are being followed. After several years, they finally showed up, and the owners learned all about the seriousness of copyright protection and the fact that ignorance of the law is no excuse.

Second, we have already determined that showing films at the library is a programming gold mine, so don't turn your back on it. This license will allow you to run wild in the film program area, as you strive to get your money's worth.

Finally, you will probably not have to foot the bill for the license at all; the children's department and young adults will be able to use this just as well as you. It will also cover the library in general. If an outside group is booked for one of the rooms, and that group shows a film, you will be liable if you have not purchased a license.

You should be aware of several restrictions. The license agreement is for your site—your building—not your movie collection. You do not pass on the rights to a third party when you loan out a video. Nor can you loan the video to another library or organization for public performance unless they, too, have an agreement (the exception is the face-to-face teaching clause for schools). There is also a rather odd provision concerning the advertising of movies you show. You may not mention the title of the film outside the library itself. You may send out flyers and press releases, you may advertise on radio and television, you may fill your newsletter to the margins with information about your series or your festival, but you may not mention even one specific title. You can call it a "classic horror film," but you may not call it "Frankenstein." You might, presumably, advertise that your patrons will find the names of these films at the library on prominently posted flyers. Having read of this caveat, I took a good look around and realized that this rule is not being obeyed on a regular basis; libraries, churches, social clubs and others regularly advertise the titles of their offerings. Nevertheless, the rule does exist, and you should be aware of it and the limitations it might impart.

No matter what licensing agency is used, you will need to determine exactly what is and is not covered by the agreement. Beyond determining which studios are covered, it should be resolved if there are any exceptions to their offerings. There are also limitations and exceptions when it comes to the broadcast of the films. If your library has several branches connected by closed circuit or other electronic media, you might not be able to send the movie from one location to another in this manner.

As stated earlier, "umbrella" agreements from licensing agents are fine for mainstream, major studio presentations, but what do you do if you want to expand your patrons' horizons beyond the usual Hollywood fare? Independent, foreign, and experimental films may not be distributed by one of the companies covered in your agreement—the less mainstream or familiar, the more likely this will be the case—and so must be procured by other means. A fair number of companies distribute this type of cinema, and they will be the ones who will often have authority to supply the rights. Some will have an offer of an umbrella agreement for the films they distribute, and some will grant license for a single showing of a single film, while other still will sell films with the attached rights. For most of these companies, their inventory of VHS tapes, let alone DVDs, is small compared to their stock of 16-mm and 35-mm reels of film. If you have the equipment, you might want to look into this possibility.

Several of these distributors have already been mentioned: Kino (http://www.kino.com) and Criterion (http://www.criterionco.com) are probably well known to librarians who have purchased their fine products. Some other distributors of art house and foreign film include Facets (http://www.facets.org), Cowboy Films (http://www.cowboyfilms.co.uk)—not what you think it is—and New Yorker Films (http://www.newyorkerfilms.com).

Hopefully, you will still want to show films at your library after having read this section. If nothing else, a simple umbrella agreement from a licensing agent will give you a wide range of titles from which to choose, with little work and at a small price, and a great deal of peace of mind. From there, you are ready to take your next step as a film impresario.

Film Festivals

An occasional showing of the desultory film might be a good schedule filler, but it won't attract much attention, except perhaps for the occasional comment of "why?" A much better approach to the scheduling of films would be the festival—a block of films shown over a fixed number of days—or the series, which is a regular offering at a fixed time (weekly, monthly, etc.) usually set around a theme or a particular genre. Such offerings will concentrate interest and expectations, will facilitate publicity and advertising, and focus your staff's efforts upon creating a successful event.

A festival can operate over a very short period, such as a week or less, or over a more protracted period of time, typically a month. Timing is important in planning your event and how much of the community's time you can take. If a lot is going on locally—sports, festivals, school events, etc.—it could necessitate finding the slow nights and fitting your festival into them, even if it takes a longer time. Knowing the habits of your patrons is also essential. Will they come to a showing every night during a week-long event? Will they become bored and lose interest if it is stretched out too long? Even the best choices of theme and film titles are not enough to overcome patron miasma.

Festivals can be more than just the screening of several movies—they can become interactive events. Depending on your festival theme and setup, you can integrate judging, discussion sessions, quizzes, and more. The patrons of the Peabody Public Library seem to be inordinately fond of contests and quizzes. We have devised several such contests around the Academy Awards and the AFI announcement of the 100 Greatest Films. A small movie-related prize enlivens the competition, as everyone tries to show off their knowledge of the movie world. Film discussion groups can get together following the showing of the film (immediately after or at a later date). Held like a book discussion group, they can sometimes turn into a permanent phenomenon. Offering your patrons the chance to judge the festival will involve them beyond the surface level, and perhaps force them to show up for all the events. Besides the fun involved, looking at films a bit deeper and more critically than they normally do could well be a learning experience. After the judging, make certificates and send them to the winning filmmakers (depending upon whether they are still alive, of course), or to the studio that produced it; you might receive an acknowledgment that will thrill your budding band of critics.

Building your film festival into a successful event requires the development of a theme; you should not just say, "Let's have a festival" for no particular reason. Look closely at your own community for a theme, or let your mind travel the world and the events of the day for an idea. Local historical events, a successful high school basketball team, or an award given to a local institution or individual can be the inspiration for a festival. The Peabody Public Library has several local luminaries that are just crying for a festival: the local Academy Award-winning actor (Dean Jagger, if you are dying to know), and the best-selling author, several of whose books have been made into films. You may not be in the hometown of John Wayne, but you probably can find some local hero around which to build a festival.

If you are absolutely convinced that nothing local is festival material, or perhaps there is, but someone might take exception to what they might view as a trivialization of an important event or person, then you can look a bit farther afield. As of this writing, one of the hottest topics of conversation both in the news and the entertainment world is the release of the Mel Gibson film, *The Passion of the Christ*. Around such a theme could be built a festival that analyzes Hollywood's portrayal of Jesus over the years, or even a survey of Biblical movies. We're currently smack in the middle of the bicentennial of the Lewis and Clark Expedition. A lot of films could be worked into this theme, and a lot of tangential themes spun off from it (America's treatment of the Indians, for example). Luckily, as we move through the first part of the 21st century, we will be seeing a lot of these bicentennials with which to work.

Of course, the theme could be as simple as the emulation of well-known festivals and events in the film world. The most obvious event is the annual Academy Awards and its attendant hullabaloo. Outside of late year, last-minute releases, nominees will be available on video for showing at your library. In fact, some distributors make available, for nontheatrical purposes, recent films that have not yet been released to video. They are available for a one-time showing and doing this might attract a large audience. An Oscar festival will also allow your patrons to pick the winners. Film fans can invest a lot of personal emotion into their favorite films and actors.

Several major film festivals garner a great deal of media attention; these might be enough of an excuse to have your own parallel festival. While most every major city on the globe (and a goodly number of little-known localities) has a film festival of some sort, only about half a dozen will be familiar to the general public. This is changing, however, as the practice of the festival gains in popularity and events in such places as Seattle and San Francisco attract growing media coverage.

Here are some of the largest and best-known festivals, with some interesting and usable facts:

- AFI Filmfest—Held in early November in Los Angeles, the American Film Institute's festival began in 1971 and was organized to spotlight the best of American film.
- Berlinale—The Berlin Film Festival is held in February of each year. It was started in 1951 as an affirmation of the freedom of expression possible through film—a response to the Berlin blockade of 1948–1949. The Berlin festival awards a statue called the *Golden Bear* for best picture.
- Cannes Film Festival—Arguably the most famous of all the festivals, it is held each May in the French Riviera town of Cannes. Founded in 1939, but, for obvious reasons, first held in 1946, Cannes has hosted films and filmmakers from more than sixty countries. The major award given is called the *Golden Palm* (the tree, not the extremity).
- New York Film Festival—Anything happening in New York City is going to be important, and its film festival is no exception. Now in its 42nd year, this festival—held in October—features all manner of film, including a good number of experimental and avant-garde titles.
- Sundance Film Festival—Founded in 1981 by actor/director Robert Redford as a showcase for the best in American independent filmmaking, this trendy event is held in snowy (yet stylish) Park City, Utah, each January. Despite an emphasis on American film, there are foreign

categories as well. If any festival is able to overtake Cannes in importance, it is this one.

- Venice Film Festival—Older even than Cannes, this festival has been
around for sixty years. It is a non-specialized competition for feature
and short films. Held in late August and early September, its number-
one award is the *Golden Lion*.

Film Series

Film series are a lot less work than festivals, and probably better for both library and patron in terms of overall attendance. A series shows films that are
somehow related, however tenuously, over a period of time that may be either
definite or ongoing. Showing films at regular intervals—once or twice a
month—will allow you to advertise them thoroughly and will allow your patrons to adjust their own schedules in order to attend. Setting a regular time
and date will ensure you a regular attendance, as well. We see the same faces
at many showings of the Peabody Public Library's two ongoing series.

The two series at the Peabody appeal to vastly different interests. One, put
on by the friends of the library, consists of Hollywood "classics" from the
golden era—roughly the mid-1930s to 1970—and draws people who are
older or appreciate the refinement of well-crafted mainstream film. The
other series was devised by the adult department staff and reflects their collective personality rather closely. Entitled Cult*Ural Movie Night, the
monthly offerings include such "masterpieces" as *Robot Monster in 3-D*, *Plan
9 from Outer Space*, and *Reefer Madness*. If nothing else, we do know our patrons and the series is now in its second year (there are a lot of cult films out
there). The series has become something of a community (okay—the weird
cross-section of the community) icon, with patrons offering suggestions for
future titles. It will certainly play itself out one day, and we will be ready for
that day with another just as successful (and probably just as strange) series
to replace it. We have been thinking strongly on this, and herewith offer the
following (partial) list of ideas.

- Alternative Shakespeare—Most people are aware that *West Side Story*
was simply *Romeo and Juliet* moved to the barrio, but how many know
that the 1956 sci-fi classic *Forbidden Planet* (Walter Pidgeon, Leslie
Nielson, Robby the Robot) was an off-world version of *The Tempest*?
Don't forget to check out Japanese director Akira Kurosawa's transla-
tion of several Shakespeare tragedies into the world of the Samurai.
- Book vs. Film—This one can be a combination of reading and viewing,
with discussion groups formed around each offering. Many people are

probably not aware of the liberties taken by Hollywood in their adaptations of classic literature and contemporary best sellers.

- Famous Characters—Bring out the big guns, like James Bond, Dirty Harry, Tarzan, and more; you can follow the evolution and/or the transmutation of ongoing characters and the actors who portrayed them.
- Films of a Decade—Pick a decade—any decade—and its films will parallel the historical events and social concerns of that era. You can also track the improvement in film technology and artistry, as well as the rise or fall of a particular star.
- Major Director—Follow the career of a famous director, such as Hitchcock or Scorsese. Don't start at the beginning, however; some of their early works might drive people away. Instead, begin with their best and then, in best Hollywood form, flashback to where it all started.
- Major Star—The same premise as the director series.
- Guy Movies—Sure, you might think you will be limiting your audience with this premise, but you will be drawing people to the library who don't generally come for any other reason. If you care enough to show something like *Patton*, *Field of Dreams*, or *Die Hard*, they might think the library is a pretty cool place, after all. All you need are car chases, action, explosions, and male bonding when you look for selections. Oh, and bodily function jokes don't hurt, either. Ask a guy for suggestions, just in case you don't happen to be one.
- Sequels—This series, by its very nature will start out with the best and go downhill. Given the film industry's aversion to originality, you will never run out of material.
- Women's Films—Romantic comedies, period pieces, general dramas, and perhaps all the things that guys like as well. If you need help with choices, ask a woman, in case you aren't one.

Special Audience Films

Like fiction, film nicely fits itself into types or genres, some of which have rather limited appeal. You might wish to show some of these features in either festival or series format. The last thing the Peabody Public Library would probably plan is a foreign film festival, but for your library, it might be foremost on your list of ideas. No matter what form or genre you plan to show, you will need to know something about your patrons' preferences, as well as a bit about these films themselves. You probably know your patrons well; you might not know that much about the film types. Luckily, yours truly is a bit of a film buff, so the following may be of some assistance.

Foreign Film

Rule number one when planning to show films to fans of foreign cinema: never, ever, use a dubbed version. Even the best dubbing studio, paying close attention to the match of lips with words, voice timbre with actor, and inflection with emotion, is often not enough to keep a good film from descending into slapstick. This is especially true of non-European films, where language is very different, and human emotions are not visibly expressed in the same manner as ours. Much of the Godzilla movies' kitsch derives from atrocious dubbing as from the subject matter itself.

Contrary to popular belief, not all foreign cinemas consist of two people sitting around for an hour talking to each other or the telephone—that's French cinema (just kidding). You don't need to be a fan of drying paint to enjoy much of what the world has to offer. Japanese and Russian films, for instance, can be quite lavish and filled with action, scenery, costume, and lively plotting. Italian films can be playful, surreal, action-filled, and sexy. Third World cinema is gaining a following, and can help to open many new and little understood cultures and ideas to our sometimes-closed Western minds.

It is not this book's intention to present a course on world cinema; there are many fine guides for the beginner, both in book form (check the bibliography for titles), and on the web. One such online site is Movieline (http://movieline.com/reviews/archive.shtml#foreign), which offers its list of 100 Greatest Foreign Films, ala the AFI list. You can also check the aforementioned film festival sites for current and past winners. Luckily, much foreign cinema—at least the major award and publicity winners—is readily available through major distribution channels and carried by regular library vendors. This means that a title like Kurosawa's *Ran*, released through Fox Lorber, should be covered by an umbrella license with an agency that has contracted with that particular distributor. Many of the distribution companies mentioned previously have lesser-known titles (and rights) available, as well.

Ethnic Film

Ethnic films are generally (but not always) small, independent productions by producers and directors who attempt to bring a vision of their particular ethnicity to the screen. Afro-American films, from such directors as Spike Lee, Gordon Parks, and John Singleton, are an example of this type of cinema. Hispanic films are also becoming a very large segment of this market since the 1992 release of Robert Rodriguez's *El Mariachi*. Native American film is a growing phenomenon, and some festivals (and parts of festivals—see the Sundance website) are dedicated to this form. For an excellent example, see Chris Eyre's *Skins*.

Unlike foreign film, which is first and foremost a nationalist artistic expression, ethnic films center around and reflect the lives and concerns of a particular group, which can be a part of a nation (as in Afro-American film), or can reach beyond political boundaries and borders (Kurdish, Gypsy, and others). Thus, Australian film is foreign, while Aboriginal film is ethnic. And yes, Kurds, Aboriginals, and others do make many fine films.

Ethnic films allow you to tap into your ethnic population and bring them into the library on a regular basis, not just for Black History Month or Diversity Week. Even more importantly, like foreign film, this type of cinema will help open other cultures to the homogeneous community. Unlike the cultures displayed in foreign film, these are liable to be a lot closer to home.

Film Noir
Despite the French name, noir is an American, Hollywood-made product. It was named by the French, who were flooded with these Hollywood "B" pictures in the post-war period, and were intrigued by the "dark" themes of alienation, greed, pessimism over the human condition, and moral bankruptcy. Not the original intent of the moniker, but just as telling for the overall mood of the genre, is the stark use of light and shadow, resulting in oddly lit interiors and foreboding, alien exteriors. These stories are often told in flashback, with one of the main characters narrating his or her tale of woe; in one famous film, the narrator was already dead, and told how he got that way.

The reign of film noir stretches from the early 1940s to the end of the 1950s. They appear to have evolved directly from the gangster film of the 1930s, but with a very different bent; while the latter were a rather preachy extension of J. Edgar Hoover's crusade against crime and usually resulted in the demise of the gangster and the salvation of society (*Little Caesar, Public Enemy*), noir took a more cynical view of a world in the gutter. Often the criminal was just a regular guy, never dreaming of anything illegal, but turned to crime by a corrupt, unfair world. This poor sap may get his in the end, just like the gangster, but there is little satisfaction and much ambiguity in the typical noir denouement.

Film noir had its regular players, if not a regular audience (popularity ranged widely throughout the genre): Richard Widmark, Robert Ryan, Barbara Stanwyck, Claire Trevor, and Gloria Grahame made appearances in many classic noirs. Directors were often European refugees from Nazi-controlled areas: Edward Dmytryk, Billy Wilder, and Otto Preminger, among others.

If you are wondering what sort of patron might be drawn to film noir, you will need to know what the typical noir movie contains in way of plot, action, and dialogue. The plots usually contain a twist or two, with double-crosses and a fair amount of violence; often, the main character gets beat and pushed around a lot. The language and the cops are all hard-boiled, everyone boozes and smokes and the "dames all have legs up to there." As mentioned, the main character (it is hard to call him a protagonist) is usually a decent person overwhelmed by the evil that is inherent in society, but he (and it usually is a he) can also be a small-time thug who simply spirals into the whirlpool of murder and mayhem. Women are of two types: the good girlfriend/wife who tries to keep her man honest and make ends meet, and the femme fatale, who leads him down the inevitable road of doom.

Selecting noir films is a simple matter of obtaining a few of the many fine books written on the subject. Eddie Muller has written a pair of fine volumes, *Dark City: The Lost World of Film Noir* and *Dark City Dames: The Wicked Women of Film Noir*. Using these books will not only give you a critical analysis of some of the most important films in the genre, it will immerse you in the dark and twisted back streets of this wicked world. Michael Keaney's *Film Noir Guide: 745 Films of the Classic Era, 1940–1959*, is a compendium of over 700 titles and plot lines in the genre, as well as some that might not be strictly noir. He also provides a rating for each film, so you won't get any turkeys.

If you want to view a few films yourself (although you probably already have, but just aren't aware of it) to help you decide if this art form has a place in your library, two highly regarded and typical films will give you a good idea of what noir is all about (as well as entertain you for a few hours). *Double Indemnity* (1946), starring Fred MacMurray and Barbara Stanwyck, is the story of an insurance agent embroiled in a murder/fraud plot against his own company. *Murder, My Sweet* (a.k.a. *Farewell, My Lovely*, 1944), stars former song and dance man Dick Powell as Raymond Chandler's famous P.I. Philip Marlowe. The twisted plot, back-story narration, and just plain meanness and untrustworthiness of the world make this one a classic. Together, these two films will give you insight into the workings of 80% of all film noir.

Cult Films

Cult film has been mentioned before, but it will help if you are aware of the exact definition of the phrase. Actually, it won't be very helpful at all because no one has ever been very "exact" about its definition. As a rule, cult films have a rather narrow, but extremely devoted, following. Unlike genre films, however, there is little homogeneity within this following, save for a certain bent outlook on the world. Cult films may be very old (even silent), quite recent, mainstream Hollywood, or independent, big budget, or grainy backroom schlock, but something in them appeals to certain people in a way that is totally out of proportion to the film's intrinsic worth. The best overall description of a cult film is that you will know one when you see it.

Many, if not most films that achieve cult status (they do not start out as cult, despite at least one studio's attempt to manufacture them) did poorly during their initial theatrical releases, but caught on at some later point because of the single-minded fanaticism of a few loyal followers. It is much easier for a movie to reach cult status in the age of video release than in the past. One that did so, and is probably the archetype of the "genre" is *The Rocky Horror Picture Show* (1975), which, by almost any standard of taste, should have slipped (or time warped) into oblivion soon after being put onto celluloid. It almost did, but a few midnight showings in a New York theater attracted just the right sort of crowd to forever change cinematic history.

Other films have managed to raise themselves from a perdition not always deserved because of changes in the moral, social, and political attitudes of society. Two such films did this in the 1960s, but for totally opposite reasons. The anarchy of the Marx Brothers' *Duck Soup* (1933), so contrary to the somber mood of the Great Depression, struck a note with the counter culture generation. Its anti-war and anti-authoritarian tone (of course, all Marx Brothers films were anti-authority) seemed to be a message from the past that what they were doing in the present had precedence. *Reefer Madness* (1936), an over-the-top propaganda piece decrying the evils of marijuana, set hippies and stoners to giggling, with or without the aid of a joint.

One thing you need to be aware of is the habits of a typical cult film fanatic, just in case you really want to invite them into your library. First, they will often dress up for a showing, plying a character part from the film in question (if you show *Monty Python and the Holy Grail*, be sure not to let anyone come as the Black Knight—you'll be finding body parts for a month); they often bring props related to the film (during our showing of *Holy Grail*, we had several people clacking hollow coconut shells for most of the film); they throw things at the screen and each other; and, they know every line of the movie and feel compelled to shout them out ("She turned me into a newt." "A newt?" "Well, I got better."). Other than that, they are a fairly harmless bunch.

A simple Internet search using the terms "cult films," "cult film guide" or similar wording, will bring up a plethora of listings for sites that espouse a particular person's ideas on great cult films and what makes them that way. A few of the more linguistically intelligible sites might even be of use to you. Perhaps a bit more authoritative, *The Psychotronic Video Guide*, by Michael Weldon, will give you a lot of detailed information about the low-budget, sci-fi/horror end of cult film. Filmsite's web site has a large section devoted to cult film, plus its own list of "greatest" (http://www.filmsite.org/cultfilms3 .html); and the magazine *Entertainment Weekly* has also weighed in with its opinion on the matter, although their list has some real head scratchers.

Genre Film

Common genre film parallels fiction genre, for the most part: Westerns, science fiction, horror, mystery, comedy, and romance. Westerns and sci-fi attract a large male following, while mystery and comedy appeal to a wider audience. Horror—at least today's slash-and-bleed variety—tends to draw a young crowd of both genders. Romance, of course, makes men run in the opposite direction, even if that direction is a burning building. Some genres are not quite as well-defined as these; like their book-world counterparts such as "ice-age" or "caper" novels, they tend to actually be part of a larger genre. At the Peabody Public Library, the term "action/adventure" is applied to any film whose cover art includes a speeding vehicle or an explosion (or an explosion of a speeding vehicle); nevertheless, these films might simply be fast-paced science fiction or mystery. Likewise, the cop movie, the historical drama, and others, tend to be attempts to put some new spin on an old ball.

One relatively new and unique genre (or perhaps just a sub-genre of comedy), is the mockumentary, a comedic social satire masquerading as a serious, stuffy documentary. This particular form has garnered a lot of attention from both fans and filmmakers alike in the last few years, and is worthy of a closer look. The granddaddy of such films is *This is Spinal Tap* (1984), and the grand master of the mockumentary form is Christopher Guest. Actually bordering on cult status, these films are quite popular across a wide section of the populace, touching funny bones at many levels of awareness. Because there are not yet that many of them out there, you could conceivably create a festival or series and show every one of them, thus avoiding upset patrons who have had their favorite example of the genre left out. For example, in addition to the boys of Spinal Tap, Guest has given us *Waiting for Guffman* (1996), about a small-town theater troupe; *Best in Show* (2000), focusing on the strange world of dog shows; and *A Mighty Wind* (2003), which follows the reunion of 1960s folk musicians. Others have also delved into the field, with titles such as *And God Spoke* (1993), wherein two filmmakers attempt to shoot a Biblical epic on a short budget (Soupy Sales as Moses?), and *Fear of a Black Hat* (1994), the gangsta rap version of Spinal Tap. Finally, one of the oldest mockumentaries is Eric Idle's spoof of the Beatles, *The Rutles* (1978).

Documentaries

We have mentioned the problems with fact-based programming, whether it be lectures or, as in this case, film. People do not generally enjoy a school-like situation when it is not necessary, and certainly not when they expect to be entertained. Documentaries might give them that suspicious feeling that they are being taught, and might actually be expected to learn something. Also, a documentary brings up visions of PBS or the History Channel, and why would you want to go to a film series to see a television program?

Luckily, both of these statements are only partially true. Many people enjoy lifelong learning experiences, and will come to see a documentary, especially one they can't see at home, which brings us to the second statement. Although nothing is wrong with televised documentaries, many theatrical documentaries are released each year, and are not usually seen outside of a theatrical setting. The Academy of Motion Picture Arts and Sciences has awarded an Oscar each year since 1943 for best documentary (*Scared Straight* and *Woodstock* are among the winners), and many of the festivals mentioned earlier also award prizes for this form of the cinematic arts. This will give you a start on your selections.

Needless to say, the audiences for documentaries will be more erudite and serious, the non-fiction purists among your reading public, although the vast amount of subject matter in the documentary field can really make such predictions worthless. How cultured would an audience for *Woodstock* be? You will probably end up with a bunch of ex-stoners, like me.

Equipment

Now that you have all of your festivals scheduled, your film series lined up and in reserve, and the popcorn machine buttered and ready, what are you going to do next? Roll out the 23" TV on the cart and pop a cassette in the ol' VCR so that your patrons can squint at a glaring screen for the next two hours? You might have little choice, but if you have any discretion at all in the matter, please take the following sections seriously. If the Peabody Public Library did not have a 10-foot flat projection screen, we would either have no film series, or have a town full of people with serious vision problems. The alternatives to the small television screen will make viewing easier, turn your festival into an experience not to be duplicated at home and, above all, make your audience return again and again, rather than thinking solely about getting rid of their headache.

Projection

While all film and television is projection, even the back to front of the cathode-ray tube in that twenty-three incher, projection in this case means the external casting of an image because of light traveling across an interval of space—that is, the room or theater.

Theaters—real theaters—show their movies on mechanical projectors us-ing a high-output light source capable of casting a film image for several dozen of hundreds of feet. These projectors handle 35-mm color or black-and-white positive image film, the standard of the industry. The image is su-perior, obviously, because it can be projected to many times its original size. The multiplex theaters of today use screens that are half the size of what can be sharply presented; those of us old enough to remember the 1960s and ear-lier know the size to which theater screens could go. The images projected back then were, except for a few experiments in 70 mm, all standard 35-mm film, the same size that is probably in your still camera at home.

As you might imagine, there are quite a few drawbacks to owning a 35-mm film projector, even a so-called "portable" one, as opposed to the sta-tionary type found in movie theater projection booths. Cost is the number one factor. These units can run into thousands of dollars, and even a cheap one will not be below the four-figure range. Even if, for some reason, you have that sort of money to spare, there are the problems of storage, hauling it out for a showing, the heat it generates, and the noise it makes. 35-mm projectors are best left in the projection booth.

If you pre-date the video revolution, you might remember your school showing feature films, either at assembly or in the classroom. There was usu-ally an out-of-favor teacher or an in-favor student running the projector at the back of the room or hall; they would inevitably mess it up about ten minutes into the first reel, resulting in general pandemonium while repairs were attempted. Odds are that you were watching film projected in 16 mm. At roughly half the size, the image quality remains good for projecting onto the typical pull-down or portable screen. These units are certainly within the affordable range for the library committed to the showing of films. Moreover, 16-mm film versions of many theatrical releases are readily avail-able for rental.

Perhaps the most sensible and versatile solution to the showing of movies without a television is the LCD projection unit. These are available in both portable and mounted (usually on the ceiling) models. They usually connect to VHS, DVD, and computers for a variety of display and projection uses. With a ceiling-mounted version, you can maximize your seating and avoid "shadow heads" problems. The portable unit can, of course, be taken to any available room for your event.

Battle of the Formats
You want to make your screenings the sharpest, brightest, and least prone to skips, glitches, and problems in order to maximize your patrons' viewing ex-

perience. You will have to balance that against the realities of location and budget, not to mention what you can actually find available for purchase or rental. It will be worth it for you to look into the pluses and minuses of the different formats, in order to make informed choices.

Film, as mentioned earlier, is going to give you the brightest, sharpest picture, especially in 35 mm, but also in 16 mm. We have all been subjected to uncle Willie's home movies, so you know what kind of quality you will find in 8 mm. Because you are projecting light from a very hot, very close bulb through a sprocketed piece of plastic, you are going to have occasional problems with skipping, breaking, melting, and even the ubiquitous piece of persistent lint. Film is usually rented rather than purchased, and film is often the only option when wanting to show rare, out-of-the-mainstream movies.

VHS tape has been around for a long time, at least since the early 1980s, when it triumphed over its competitor, Betamax. VHS is convenient, inexpensive, and will become part of your lending collection. It has acceptable quality, but loses some crispness of detail when projected. It also slowly deteriorates, as the magnetic particles are sloughed off and the tape stretches over the course of repeated showings.

DVD is a purely digital representation of an image, and as a result, it has very good quality in sharpness and brightness, as well as color and shadow renderings. Because it is read by a light, it can theoretically retain this quality forever. The problem with DVDs at present is that they are stored on very fragile discs, which are easily scratched or soiled. Because they have multiple layers of information encoded on them, rather than just one, as in CDs, the protective coating is much thinner. Projection of DVD images will be better than VHS, but still not as lively as film.

Screens

Size matters with screens, as does quality. You can, of course, project an image onto a blank white wall or even a sheet, but you are going to end up with a picture that is dull and, in the case of the sheet, one that waves in the slightest breeze. Movie screen are designed to reflect light, as walls and sheets are not, and that is the difference between them. The amount of light they reflect is also a measure of their quality and their cost. Thus, like your choice of projection, a good movie screen can contribute greatly to the experience of watching a film. Size is a matter of comfort for your patrons; you have already concluded that a big television is not acceptable, so make certain that your screen is large enough so that even patrons in the back of your room are afforded a good view. A 10- or 12-foot screen should do nicely in a room that seats 75–100 people.

For convenience, a screen that pulls or automatically descends from the ceiling is preferable, but not portable. You might want to consider having both. Make certain that you have the ability to completely darken your screening room, either by choosing one without windows, or by equipping it with blackout shades. This is especially important when projecting VHS or DVD.

Concessions

Perhaps food does not seem to belong in a discussion of equipment necessary for showing movies in the library, but can you imagine an actual movie theater without a popcorn counter or a Multiplex without Raisinettes? You will want to make available, either for a small price or for free, at least popcorn and soda. Make your popcorn fresh because the smell permeates the entire building and is irresistible. If you are showing the film during regular hours, it could draw in people who might not have otherwise attended. Cheap pop, in two- or three-liter bottles, can generally be had for less than one dollar, and is worth much more in good will.

Certain films lend themselves to a theme snack, and knowledge of the movie you are showing can help you to plan your food menu for the event, making your "theater" a unique and fun experience. The Peabody Public Library has served beans and cornbread for a showing of *Blazing Saddles*, and gummy lizards (advertised as "newts") for *Monty Python and the Holy Grail*. Whether you serve fish sticks for *Jaws* or Reese's Pieces for *E.T.*, it doesn't take a lot of work, just a bit of imagination, and a slightly warped way of looking at nearly everything.

Musical Performances

What could be more wonderful for the body, the soul, and the basic emotions that make us human, than a live music performance? When we want to relax, meditate, dance, or socialize, we turn to music. It is in our automobiles when we drive, our supermarkets when we shop, our elevators when we rise and descend, and in our dentist's office while we are drilled. It is the number one mood manipulator, used on ourselves, our customers, our friends, and strangers. It sells, it cajoles, it massages, and it inspires.

Libraries have always been a source of music. Growing up in Detroit, I remember checking out LPs and musical scores, from the Beatles to Wagner. Like the music industry itself, libraries have changed with the times and the technology, moving from vinyl to tape to CDs, all the while gaining shelf space and struggling with new security issues. More often than not, the library is a source of music that is not readily available at the typical retail out-let. With few stores allowing people to sample before they buy, the library can provide a service for the patron trying to expand her musical tastes. Of-ten, patrons are in need of music for weddings, school projects, presentations, special events, celebrations, and parties. If they stage a Hawaiian luau, they will want to have some authentic (or somewhat authentic) Polynesian mu-sic for the occasion; they probably will not, however, want to buy it for their own collection. Likewise for kodo drumming, Zamfir's pan flute, or an hour's worth of Swiss yodeling. Of course, a patron might become enamored of Zamfir and end up buying the box set, but that will be because you have pro-vided the opportunity for him to hear it first. We end up teaching through a medium others view as pure entertainment.

When we start offering music as programming, we need to keep in mind that we are being given the chance to expand some cultural horizons for our patrons, while showing them that the library's role in their lives is not nec-essarily limited to the written word. There are a variety of program options involving music, from the passive experience of a formal concert to the hands-on education of a workshop. Some styles of music will fit your library better than others, and not all musical events need be confined to your build-ing, or even to your premises.

Concerts
The most common form of live musical entertainment is the concert. The musician or ensemble perform on a stage (or at least at the front of the room), separated from the audience, which watches the artists from regu-larly arranged seating. For the vast majority of people, this is what they ex-pect from a musical experience and what they most likely will prefer. Find-ing musicians for a concert is not difficult, even in the most rural of areas, and drawing a crowd is almost a given: people like music. If you want to get people coming to all of your programs, make certain that you include a good number of concerts on the calendar. At the Peabody Public Library, concerts generally draw three to four times the average of all our programs. Outside of school bands and choirs, and the occasional church concert, there is very little musical activity in the area, so a concert is quite an event. Even if your community is a hotbed of music and musicians, you should still draw well for concerts.

Music That Works, Music That Doesn't
Our library collections are likely to have all manner of musical style, from many cultures and many ages, to every instrument or group of instruments,

imaginable. Sounds, groups of every size, amplifiers, grand pianos, symphony orchestras, and opera companies all take up an equal amount of space on our shelves, all at the same sound volume—namely, zero. We may or may not fret over the parental advisories concerning lyrics or the album artwork, but, for the most part, all music on our CDs is equal, and equally able to do what is expected of it: check out to our patrons for their personal use. Although it might sound rather callous, what our patrons do with the music—volume, time of day or night, or number of half-intoxicated friends invited over to listen to it—is no longer our concern. If they bring it back on time and in good condition, we have played our role, and they could have used the music to hypnotize people into thinking they were chickens, for all we care.

When our library's music originates from live programs in the building, however, we suddenly have a whole new set of concerns and obligations. Despite the changing nature of our library, from a place of quiet (almost morbid) contemplation to a lively community center, we still have the responsibility to keep our particular public place open and attractive to the entire community. We might shudder now at the past practices of librarians who existed only to quiet people, but we certainly are not going to start handing out bullhorns at the front door. We need to follow the same sort of societal standards we expect our patrons to heed when they check out our collection of heavy metal CDs.

You need to follow a few commonsense rules to have a successful musical program in your library:

1. Don't fill the room with musicians—It would be a real coup for your library were it to engage the local symphony orchestra for a benefit concert in the community room; it would be a real disaster if the ninety members of the orchestra had to squeeze into a room the only holds 100 to begin with. Although this is an extreme example, you really need to think about the possibilities of overwhelming the audience. Your facility might indeed be able to hold the symphony orchestra—and a full chorus besides—but for most of us, a smaller group is more realistic.

2. Mind those amplifiers—You have probably been sitting at home when your windows started rattling and the walls began vibrating to what seemed certain to be a Richter scale–bending earthquake; yes, that rock concert on wheels owned by the teen down the block is out for an evening cruise. That same brain-shaking scenario is just waiting to happen at your library, if you don't pay attention when you book a musical act. Not all amplifiers are bad for your patrons' hearing, and may

even be essential in some instances (a solid-bodied guitar is fairly use-less without one); however, some musicians like to crank their Peaveys so high that your facility's windows might be in real danger. This might be why there are no windows in concert halls. Although you might hate the thought of denying your patrons the chance to experience death metal, you might just have to consider the other people in and around your building and advise those headbangers among your pa-trons to try another venue. Besides, acoustic music sounds much better in the library.

3. Don't freak them out too much—Because of music's undeniable effect upon the emotions, it is understandable that music itself would be the target of some very negative emotions. This is not a new phenomenon; it has been at the foundation of generational misunderstanding for many decades. Much of today's problems arise from "questionable" lyrics and the video images that today accompany nearly all popular music. Adhering to community standards strikes many as censorship and it could be, in a sense. It is not this book's purpose to open a de-bate on the topic of censorship and all its philosophical implications; rather it is to promote the use of the library by the majority of our pa-trons through the use of programs. You might want to keep two things in mind when dealing with the problem of being both an open forum and an adherer to local standards. First, we censor every day by what we refuse to deal with. It is a sure thing that your library does not carry x-rated videos, despite the facts that the local video store probably does, and that there are undoubtedly people who would check them out. The video store doesn't care as long as they make money; we need to care because we don't. Which leads us to point number two: we are publicly funded and, however tired you might be of hearing it, patrons do pay our salaries. We tend to remember that when we buy and do the things they want; why do we forget it when it comes to what they do not want? Is a song about killing cops or raping women really as de-serving of our protection as a *Catcher in the Rye* or *Daddy's Roommate*? If you feel that it is, and you believe your community standards can handle gangsta rap and black metal, by all means book such programs if they fit your facility and your mission. Just think before you start adding programs to the schedule.

Finding and Booking Musicians
You will be booking two basic types of musicians for your programs: amateur and professional. These terms can become a bit murky because many amateurs

accept payment and many professionals will only play part-time, opting for a regular weekday job. Some full-time players are reasonable in their rates and some are not (at least by library budget standards). No matter who you book for your program and no matter what they cost, you need to know how they sound. Don't be afraid to ask them for a demo tape or, lacking that, an actual audition. You might get someone for free, but if they sound like Roseanne singing the national anthem, you have overpaid. Even a hefty fee does not ensure dulcet tones or adherence to your wishes.

When looking for good amateur talent, remember that the days of everyone taking piano lessons are long gone, and sometimes the ability to play at all will strike the general public as an acceptable reason for someone to give a concert. You need not be that lax in your quest, but somewhere between the virtuoso and the person who cannot even operate a CD player there is a happy medium. Many talented people simply play for their own or their family's enjoyment. Locating such people will result in a good, reasonably priced program for you and the chance to play to a wider audience for them. How better to breed community goodwill and acceptance?

Contact your local high school (or perhaps even the middle school), talk to local music teachers, go to the parks and the clubs (have a mineral water), and check out street corners, bus depots, or wherever street musicians can be found. Churches are a good place to find amateur musicians of a very high caliber. Many of these people will be happy to perform as individuals and, if you talk to their pastor, you might be able to get the chorus or bell choir as a whole. They will be happy to have the public at large hear what normally is heard only by their own congregation.

Attending local or regional festivals can often unearth some fabulous folk, jazz, or other ensembles that might either be playing at the event or, like you, merely enjoying the music. Once, while attending the annual banquet of the local chamber of commerce, I happened to notice a very accomplished string trio playing before and during the meal (much better than the speeches which followed). They were at the library the following Valentine's Day. We should always be on the lookout for such talent, from the jazz guitarist at the local restaurant to the harpist at the art gallery exhibition.

Once you have held a few well-attended concerts, you might be amazed at the number of musicians that appear out of nowhere, seeking to play at the library. Even if they do not actually seek you out, they might make casual mention of their semi-hidden gift. This is when you want your front-line staff to be aware of such pronouncements and relay the information to you. For every nine who will not do it, the one who ends up performing will make it worth the time and effort.

Professional musicians might not always make their "living" exclusively from performing and/or teaching music. Outside of large population and cultural centers like New York or Los Angeles, most musicians subsist on a regular day job. The club or bar musician of the old days has largely been replaced by disc jockeys and karaoke. There is probably no good definition of "professional" outside of the old Olympic model of one who accepts payment—in any amount or form—for her talent. For our purposes, we can consider a musician a professional if he works on some sort of regular basis—a weekly club gig, regular festival or concert circuit, or two to three nights a week at the local supper club. Thus, a predictable, if not major, portion of his annual income is derived from playing music.

Why is this important in any way, shape, or form? A professional is more likely to be found through a variety of regular channels. First, many will have their own web sites, which might have booking information, schedules, and even some .wav or MP3 samples of their sound. They also advertise in newspapers, magazines, and even the yellow pages. If you are looking for a certain style of music, or just shopping around in general for a band or individual, you can also check professional organizations, such as the American Federation of Musicians (http://www.afm.org). Many professionals belong to this union or other national guilds, which act as a clearinghouse for them. The AFM web site contains links and contact information for all of its local chapters.

Professionals might also belong to loose-knit local or regional organizations that work to further public interest in and awareness of their particular style of music. In Indiana (and elsewhere, certainly), several regional groups are dedicated to the advancement of bluegrass music and its kin. Some of them list contact information for their members.

Working with professionals is usually very easy. They are aware of their schedules, usually quite far in advance. Those who work clubs and festivals will normally be booked on weekends and holidays, so you might want to forego looking for people on those dates. At other times, they will go begging for bookings, and will be more than happy that you called.

One thing you can be certain of with professional musicians is that they will have a contract for you (or your director) to sign when you book them. Most have probably been stiffed more than once, or have had friends and acquaintances treated poorly, so they are being certain that this will not happen. This is also a good idea for both parties involved. With a contract, you will be assured that your performers will not back out, a most unfortunate state of affairs if you have spent a great deal of time and money on publicity. We sometimes think that because libraries are a trusted public institution, no one will do anything to burst those warm, fuzzy bubbles we exude. We are first and foremost a business in a country that thinks and breathes business, so it behooves us to act in a businesslike manner and forego the informal niceties of a past era.

Along this line of reasoning, the library should have contracts ready for musicians to sign if they don't provide one of their own. Besides spelling out performance dates and fees, the contract will state what you are required to do for the musicians (setup, electrical, provide refreshment, etc.). A contract should also delineate how long a performance will be, how many sets will be played, and the length and number of breaks. This way, you will know exactly how much music you will be getting, as well as have a timetable for refreshments or whatever else you plan to do during the breaks (if you want to be sure that your audience doesn't drift away, you must provide some sort of attraction or amusement). Check the appendix of this book for sample contracts or consult your library's attorneys.

Festivals—Very Special Events
Mention was made in a previous section of musicians playing festivals. Many of these are actual music festivals that are normally dedicated to one particular style of music such as jazz, country, or bluegrass. Such festivals are typically two- or three-day weekend events, although some major festivals, such as the Detroit Jazz Festival and the New Orleans Jazz and Heritage Fest will run a week or more.

Another type of festival is the local town or county extravaganza, with names such as "pioneer days, " or "summer happening." These will typically include a street fair, parade, amusement rides and midway, and the ubiquitous beer tent. There will also be a number of musical performances over the life of the festival. Related to these local festivals are the historical festivals or reenactments, of which music and musicians are often an integral part. These are the best places to find folk and old-time music performers.

Beyond just visiting a festival to find musicians for your programs, it is certainly within the bounds of possibility that your library could stage such an event. Although attempting an all-music festival may prove daunting, as well as expensive, a multi-event festival staged only one day, might be more affordable and draw a large crowd of people with mixed interests. Again, this can be a great opportunity to showcase your programming skills to the unaware. Time, cost, and (alas!) credit can be shared with other library departments, or with the community in general. You might supply music while the children's department brings in storytellers and community organizations provide refreshments.

The Peabody Public Library held such a festival, and is considering holding it again. Entitled "End-of-Summer Festival, " it included three bands and was held outside on library grounds, of which we are blessed with ten acres. We were pleased with some of what we did, and are considering changing other aspects of the event. Intended as a sort of back-to-school celebration (or lamentation), there was a fairly narrow window of time with which to work. Too early, and we feared people would still be on vacation, and too late, the kids are back in school, sports have started, and papers are due. We also needed to avoid other local events and the Labor Day holiday.

We attempted to make an event that would appeal to people of all ages throughout the entire course of the day, and to that end we tried to schedule events that could be attended by the family, together or separately. During the jazz band's set, we had face painting and crafts for the children. We had a pair of strolling folk musicians during the time when we held our stone-skipping contest and several other simultaneous events at far-flung corners of the grounds. In the evening, for the older folks, we had a classic rock band performing. Throughout the day, community organizations sold refreshments to the crowd, the way they would at any community event.

What were we aiming at with this festival? Mostly, it was a way to thank our patrons and our community, which had supported the building of a new facility, and increased our usage and circulation figures each year thereafter. It was also a showcase for the back acreage of the library, which usually goes unseen and is underutilized by the general library patron. We also hoped to involve the community in our vision and display the versatility of our facility and staff. Mostly though, we just wanted to have fun.

A great deal of thought went into the timing of this festival. As mentioned in an earlier chapter, fitting your events into the overall community calendar is paramount to both success and overall goodwill. The only thing we could not anticipate, even given our outdoor venue, was the fact that, although we billed it "end-of-summer," it turned out to be the hottest day of the year. The only thing it didn't do was rain.

Will we change anything before we try it again? The biggest expense was the bands, and we probably did not advertise it as primarily a musical event. The real target audience was not reached. Given the outdoor location, complete with wetlands, many people were doubtless concerned with the possibility of West Nile Virus, which had spread into the area the year before. The heat continued for eight hours, mostly under a roasting sun and near-100% humidity. An outdoor event is always at the mercy of the weather, but with rain, you can move the crowd inside or to some sort of shelter; with extreme heat, you will find few people leaving the cool comfort of air-conditioned homes to travel to the event in the first place.

When booking musical acts outdoors, a very important consideration is electricity. Not only will you have to provide for it at the location, if there are no outlets, you have to worry about the danger of shock, both to the musicians and the general public. Even lacking rain, dampness in the lawn and on patios can present the danger of shock. It would not hurt to have an electrician (surely, you have one among your regular patrons) look over the setup and make some suggestions.

A festival need not be held outside, or even on one day, or even just one weekend. It is a festival because you call it that, and if the work is such that you can manage an extended event, and you know that it would maximize patron attendance, by all means try it. Whether one day or a month-long celebration, a music festival can do much to draw public attention and praise for your library.

Background Music

What we have with a concert setting or a music festival is culture up front, in the spotlight, and demanding of our patrons' full attention. We want to serenade them, teach them about different musical forms, have them applaud and cheer, and talk to each other about what they have experienced. Concerts also force people to move their schedules and themselves, to make a special effort to come out when they would not have under other circumstances, to sit for an hour or two or three when they could be relaxing in a Barca Lounger watching television or, surprise, listening to music.

Perhaps we have been missing something in our rush to sit people down and show them something, to make them pay attention and listen, feel, or see. Although many people do go to concerts, how many more listen to music in a more casual, passive manner? We have music on while we are driving, while we study and read, even while we sleep. It is an important part of our lives for a major portion of our day, but it is not usually the major part of our attention. It is in the background, helping us to think and to relax, blocking out unwanted noise, and just being there as a friend and companion in our solitude. It might be working on a different level of awareness in this background to our life, but music's ability to move our emotions remains strong.

Background music usually has a bad name, thanks in large part to the defanged pop and rock pumped into our elevators, supermarkets, and dentists' waiting rooms. This homogenized sound, devoid of its bass lines and lacking its dynamic highs and lows, should not be the sole definition of the music that is ambient to our daily lives.

Music "In" the Library
One of the most detested stereotypes among library professionals is that of the "shushing" librarian, telling young and old alike that the library is a place not to do, rather than the place where you can do. Some patrons and writers decry the loss of solitude in the library as a whole, being forced into "quiet rooms" or study areas, shunned and isolated as second-class citizens. This is exactly how their less-taciturn brethren were made to feel in decades past, when children were discouraged and pins had best not drop, if they knew what was good for them. The result was a public place that was not really public, but the domain of a few elite and rather sour individuals.

Beyond any argument of civil rights, the exponential growth of our technological age has pretty well taken the matter out of our hands. We are not going backward anytime soon, to resurrect our card catalogs from the landfills, tying our hair back into buns, and inking up the due date stamp. As long as we continue to compete for the increasingly scarce public dollar, justifying ourselves as a worthwhile and indispensable community center, we will exist at a higher decibel level than before. We make computers available for the public (a service that is overtaking books in its importance), and that results in more than the annoying clickity-clack of the keyboard; it is several students working on a project, someone reading a humorous e-mail, the clatter and rattle of overworked printers and, of course, our own vociferous invectives when the system crashes. We have people crowding our information desks, asking for everything from Mesopotamian pottery to the location of the potty, and no one is bothering to be very quiet about it. Groups tour our facilities, lock-stepping across the tiles, asking where the video section might be. Pages push book carts with squeaky wheels and groaning welds, dropping the largest volumes on the floor, obviously in order to find their way back to technical services. CD players and VCRs preview our AV collection, not always with headphones attached. We try our best to aid those with hearing loss. In short, the library is a diverse, lively cacophony.

Into this mix of dissonance, why not inject a little music? It might even work to keep the noise down.

If you plan to offer music in your library, you need to have a space in which the performers can sit comfortably, and preferably where their sound will carry throughout the building. You should also make it as out of the main traffic areas as possible. If you have room, set up some chairs to accommodate those who would like to sit and listen—in other words, concertgoers—as not everyone will want to put the music that far to the back of their minds.

Groups and Solo Musicians

Some styles of music are perfect for an in-library presentation, and certain performers and groups fit better than others. Heavy metal is not an example of the former, nor is the New York Philharmonic a good representative of the latter. Having tried this form of programming on numerous occasions, the staff at the Peabody has compiled the following list of preferences that work well in keeping everybody (okay—a majority) happy:

- Classical Music—A lot of people will not listen to classical music when left to their own devices, but few have any real objection to it (except, perhaps, soprano opera arias). As background music to their normal library activities, it is a perfect match. The philharmonic aside, small classical groups, such as string quartets, woodwind trios, and duos (or any permutation) provide the ideal ambience and sonic levels. Soloists, such as pianist, harpists, and guitarists, are also appropriate.
- Folk Music—Another excellent choice for background music in the library, given a few simple rules to be followed. Although most folk music is acoustic, you might want to check and be certain that no stacks of amplifiers are being booked along with the group. Because the banjo is integral to much American folk music, you might find that your performers will be bringing one along. The banjo has a very bright, sometimes piercing, sound, so you might want to ask if the player has an instrument without a resonator—the metal back plate that amplifies the sound and gives it that ringing tone.

    The best background folk music is probably the solo instrumentalist. A dulcimer player or a recorder player, even a fiddler, will entertain those who wish to be entertained, and float into the softer parts of the consciousness of those who have other business to attend to.
- Jazz—Some jazz will work in this setting. Mainstream combo jazz requires careful listening, and the musicians, engaged in improvisational art, demand our total attention just as a matter of respect. What has become known as soft or smooth jazz, which is more traditionally melody driven, may work for background music. Your best bet, if you want to present jazz of any sort in this setting, is the soloist. A pianist in the style of Marianne MacPartland or Oscar Peterson, or a guitarist with the Charlie Byrd or Barney Kessel technique should appeal to most of your patrons.
- Accordion Music—No. Never. Bad librarian. No.

Seasonal Offerings

Like so many programs, background music fits well into seasonal and holiday celebrations. At the Peabody Public Library, we have two main times for this sort of musical offering: the Christmas season and Valentine's Day. The Christmas programs are rather obvious in their content: holiday music, be it sacred, classical, or popular. At times, we might have non-Christmas music as well, as long as it fits into the festive mood of the season. Tired shoppers will appreciate anything that can soothe their nerves. For Valentine's Day, we offer small ensemble classical, such as a string quartet. Baroque and Romantic music, as well as American show tunes and standards, make up the repertoire.

Other occasions that lend themselves to such programs include St. Patrick's Day (perfect for Celtic bands), Mother's Day, the beginning of spring (or summer or fall), or perhaps as a part of a local festival or celebration.

Bringing music into the library is a fine way to raise awareness of your programming in the casual library patron. If the background manages to break into their consciousness, you just might get them hooked for other programming.

Musical Styles in Your Library

With all the music styles out there, what are the best ones to bring to your library? Obviously, that depends on your mission, your target audience, and your community. If yours is a popular culture–oriented, rural library hoping to attract more 40–60 year old patrons, you might opt for country music. If your mission is to bring new and diverse culture to that same audience, you might decide on jazz or perhaps world music. As with film, you are the one who best knows your library and community; you might not, however, know that much about the different voices of the musical universe. Because you need complete knowledge to make informed choices, you will need to study and listen to the variety of styles available to you. It might be true that the only types of music are good music and bad music, but you will want to know a bit more than that.

Jazz

Jazz, the great American contribution to music culture, is many styles and many sounds, all under the umbrella of improvisation over chord structure. From its origins in the South in the early part of the 20th century, it has evolved many times. Its former selves, however, have never completely disappeared, and remain to be played and admired by each new generation.

Dixieland is an early form of jazz performed in combos on a variety of instruments ranging from trumpets and trombones to pianos and banjos.

Melodious and danceable, most people enjoy Dixieland, and prime examples of the art can be found in the early recordings of Louis Armstrong and his Hot Five, and the contemporary combo, the Dukes of Dixieland.

Swing is an urbanized, refined sort of Dixieland played solo, in small groups, or large ensembles. Listen to the recordings of Django Reinhardt, Benny Goodman, or Glenn Miller for an overview of this style.

Big Band jazz is a more improvisational and complex offshoot of swing. Duke Ellington, Woody Herman's Thundering Herd, and the Stan Kenton Orchestra epitomize this style.

Be-bop is the beginning of modern, experimental jazz. Consisting of great virtuosity, complex chord progressions, and highly personal musical statement, be-bop was a conscious breaking away from convention and commercialism and was, in this way, a counterpart to the writings of the beat generation. The high priests of this music include saxophonist Charlie Parker, pianist Thelonius Monk, and trumpeter John "Dizzy" Gillespie.

Modern jazz rose to prominence in the 1950s and was definitely the domain of the small combo. Although economics helped to bring about the downfall of the big band, modern jazz and its emphasis on individual expression nailed the coffin closed. Various descriptive names came to be attached to different "schools" of modern jazz, such as cool, hot, and avant-garde. Original compositions (now considered standards) and older works were typical of the offerings of this era. Some works were of an extended length and featured a statement of melody and theme, followed by long improvisational solos by each member of the group. Dave Brubeck, Miles Davis (pre-*Bitches Brew*), and John Coltrane are among the many famous names from this era.

By the end of the 1960s, rock's influence on and relation to jazz was undeniable. Fusion jazz began to blend elements of both music types, often with amplification of traditional jazz instruments, such as piano and bass. Fusion can be both cutting edge and extremely approachable. Groups like Weather Report, Hiroshima, Chick Corea's Electric Band, and Spyro Gyra are all fusion bands.

Smooth jazz borders on the realm of pop and New Age. It is usually instrumental, with perhaps some background vocals (often of the wordless variety). Devoid of the dissonances and convoluted improvisations of most modern jazz, it can function nicely in the background. Many of its artists are familiar names outside of the jazz world: Kenny G, Earl Klugh, Steve Carleton, and Grover Washington, Jr.

Of these various styles, the ones most likely to appeal to the general, non-jazz going public are Dixieland, Swing, Big Band, and smooth. Big Band is problematic, since by its name, it indicates a group of 15–20 individuals, which will probably violate the "don't fill the room with musicians" law. Any of the small combo styles, however, are worth a try, and may win a few converts.

Classical Music

The original "unplugged" music, this is perfect for most library concerts and background, outside of the large group or orchestra. Classical is really a modern term that encompasses the art music of the 17th through the early 20th centuries. Many distinctive styles and artistic movements developed during this time, usually running parallel or slightly behind the same developments in the art and literature world. These movements featured different philosophies of the musical art, entailing theory, structure, and personal emotional statements, all reflecting the social and political realities of the day.

Baroque style dates from the early 1600s through the first half of the 1700s, its end date usually (and somewhat arbitrarily) is given as Bach's death in 1750. The favorite music of mathematicians, Baroque's precise structures and counterpoints—in which several distinct themes or melodies are played over each other—inspire calm, ordered thoughts and peaceful reflection. The most famous of Baroque composers are Johann Sebastian Bach, George Friedrich Handel, Antonio Vivaldi, and Johann Pachebel.

By the end of the 18th century, the form known as *classical* had replaced counterpoint with chordal harmonies and greater sound dynamics. The development of new instruments, such as the pianoforte and the trombone gave the new music greater range of volume and raw emotion. New forms, such as the sonata and the symphony were developed, and some of the formal dance movements, such as the minuet and the gigue were replaced by freer, folk-based structures, such as the scherzo. Classical form was the palette of some of the greatest composers of the Western world: Hayden, Mozart, and Schubert, reaching its culmination in the large and powerful works of Beethoven.

The Romantic era in music came somewhat later than its counterparts in art and literature, actually having its beginnings in some of the more passionate works of Beethoven. Running from approximately 1830 through the end of the 19th century, Romanticism was marked by freer forms, more experimental pieces, rich harmonic textures and long melody lines, as opposed to short statements of theme. The most notable difference in Romantic style is its unabashed emotionalism. Romantic music is the stuff of movie soundtracks and melodies you hum along to in the car. Some elements of Romanticism lasted well into the 20th century, with such figures as Rachmaninoff and Richard Strauss, but the giants of the movements—Schumann, Brahms, Dvorak, Tchaikovsky, and others—all worked in the 19th century.

Impressionism in music was similar to that in art, where the artist used light and color to create an impression of the subject, rather than distinct lines and shadows. So, too, did the music of Impressionism, which usually conjured up pictures of places and events. Mostly a French school, Impressionism was the brainchild of Claude Debussy. Others who dabbled in the form were Maurice Ravel and Eric Satie.

Twentieth-century music is a varied and, at time, atonal basket of styles. Marked by the anarchic disaster that was the First World War, music after that time experimented with tones, key, combinations, and instrumentation. The boundaries of form and mathematical correctness that had always marked music were gradually being erased. From the folk-based ideas in Stravinsky, Copeland, Bartok, and others, to the questionably musical pieces of John Cage, there is much too much to discuss here in a few feeble paragraphs. The reader is instead directed to the excellent work *Musical Composition in the Twentieth Century*, by Arnold Whitall, a fine way to unravel the confusion that is the music of this century.

Folk and World Music

Folk music wears two hats in this country: the popular definition, referring to music that came to national attention in the early 1960s, and traditional music indigenous to the various regions of the United States. The former is often tied, in both philosophy and perception, to the *Sturm und Drang* that marked the political and social upheavals of the decade. The performers of this decade were either soloists or small groups, who began their careers in coffee houses and Greenwich Village hangouts during the "beatnik" years of the mid-to-late 1950s. These artists mixed traditional American and English (and sometimes other ethnicities') folk songs with original compositions in their acts, which were usually highly polished and marked by clean, expert playing and tight vocal harmonies. Instruments included guitars, banjoes, autoharps, upright basses, and harmonicas.

Early groups, such as the Weavers ("Goodnight, Irene"), set the stage for such commercially successful acts as The Kingston Trio; Peter, Paul, and Mary; and the New Christy Minstrels (the "old" Christy Minstrels being a 19th-century musical company). Solo artists, such as Bob Dylan, Joan Baez, and Phil Ochs, added social activism to the mix. By the latter part of the decade, rock and roll influences had spawned Simon and Garfunkel, The Byrds, and other "folk rock" groups.

Music anthropologists, such as John and Alan Lomax, would probably not recognize the above definition of folk music; these musicologists traveled the back roads of America in the 1930s, documenting "in situ" the authentic music of people of different regions, aware that the homogenization of society at the hands of transportation and communication advances had already destroyed much of our indigenous sound, and that the trends toward standardization in the name of commercialism would soon render it extinct. True American folk music, from Cajun Louisiana to Appalachia, to New England's maritime society, was a raw, unrefined, and highly personal experience, far removed from the polish and shine of the commercial folk revival. Artists like Leadbelly (whom the Lomaxes found serving a life sentence in a Southern prison), Big Bill Broonzey, and Woody Guthrie present an urgent and honest reflection of life and its hardships, as well as its glories. These people lived what they sang. Despite its seeming simplicity, this music transcends intellectual dissection, because it is pure emotionalism and experience. Not all of your patrons will accept such edginess in their folk music, preferring instead to "Kumbaya" along with more genteel crooners; however, when presented in its historical context, which is the method of many of today's adherents to this form, it can be more than just a musical interlude.

World music—the indigenous music of non-Western cultures—has also developed a dual personality. As Third World countries fight what appears to be a losing battle against the encroachment of Western culture and values, many musicians in these nations have taken a stand against foreign artists by blending their ethnic folk music with American pop music style to produce their own commercially viable hybrids. Although these are interesting forms, reflective both of the evolutionary nature of music and the struggle of national and cultural diversity in an increasingly global society, the actual native music and instruments of these nations will produce a far better program. An Indian sitar concert is much more interesting than some Hindi ballad dressed up in Britney clothing. When you hire musicians who play such music, you will also be hiring cultural historians, who can recite the historical significance of the music they play and the instruments they hold.

Sacred Music

Does religious music belong in a government-funded organization, such as a public library? Is the presentation of a well-performed musical program a violation of the separation of church and state? Does singing *The Battle Hymn of the Republic* constitute a religious service or a patriotic statement? Perhaps we need to re-visit the statement about both kinds of music—good or bad— before we judge by intent. Some of the greatest music ever composed was done so for the greater glory of someone's god, including much of the music of Bach. Some of the most stirring music—the French National Anthem, for example—has some of the most mundane or barbaric sentiments behind it.

We can enjoy Wagner without the burden of the Holocaust, and we can enjoy *Lift High the Cross* without wanting to go out and start an inquisition.

At the Peabody Public Library, we have the occasional concert performed by local church groups, mostly during the holidays. Like other libraries, we have a large section in nonfiction devoted to religion (we don't plan on wiping out the 200s, do we?). We also have movies, such as *The Ten Commandments*, and music CDs, like Handel's *Messiah*, plus a growing collection of those patron favorites, inspirational fiction. Why, therefore should we deny sacred music as a programming possibility? Just as those who do not care for religious books can avoid that aisle, so, too, they can avoid that program. As long as a religious service is not being performed, what could we possibly be doing wrong, other than exposing people to alternatives? That is what we do, is it not?

Other Music in the Library

Passing mention has been made of some forms of rock music (heavy metal, for example) and the problems that might arise from performances in the library, specifically the volume at which it is played. Outside performance might resolve that issue, but there are also some specific styles of rock (another varied musical briefcase) that could fit well inside of your building. Doo-wop, often sung a cappella, is harmonious, romantic, and much fun; Motown-style R&B has been around long enough and listened to by so many people that it is almost "easy listening"; and the general term "oldies," applied to the top-40 radio format tunes of the 1950s and 1960s, has a great many adherents and practitioners.

Blues comes in several flavors, but is usually divided into electrified (Chicago style) and acoustic (Delta blues). Sharing a history with folk music—of which it is a variety—and rock—of which it is a precursor—blues has a rich heritage of story telling, a tradition that can serve to raise the level of your program above mere passive concert attendance. Electric blues has a unique sound but that sound is not usually above the threshold of sonic pain, unless it has been unduly influenced by rock. Listen to the work of Muddy Waters, John Lee Hooker, and Buddy Guy, and be impressed.

Country music will work in many locations, and its folk-rooted early versions—The Carter Family, Jimmie Rodgers, and Uncle Dave Macon—is a perfect blend of history and music. New Age, a blend of pop, jazz, classical, synthetic, and whatever else gets thrown into the pot, has many followers, and is generally a quiet, meditative sort of sound, most suitable to background music. Once again, unless Weird Al walks into your library, no accordion music!

One final note: no matter which or how many styles of music you choose, don't neglect the possibility of a talent show. Although many patrons, even the very talented, would balk at performing an entire concert, they might just be willing to get up there for one or two numbers.

Theater

You might not be aware of it, but you have in your library and your community the necessary talent and means to produce and present theatrical performances—even if there is no local auditorium for traditional staging. You might also discover that you have a large number of potential theater goers, looking for live productions and an evening out. If not, many people will enjoy coming to see their friends and family on stage acting totally unlike themselves.

Local Groups

Amateur theatrical groups either already exist in your community, or are just waiting to coagulate from the unset gel of frustrated thespians that never got enough of the stage in high school or college. If a group already exists, it might be homeless; that is, it has no place for regular practice, or to store its props and wardrobe and, most importantly, no place to stage regular performances. A theater troupe—unless it is a road show company—will only suffer by moving around and making its followers find them. If your local group does not yet exist, then you can be the catalyst that makes it gel.

If, after long and unfruitful searching, you do not find your pre-made amateur group, you can offer to form one by holding an organizational meeting at your library. You don't need to become part of the troupe, if not so desired. Some people on your staff might have enough interest in the theater to take charge of the task, or you might know some patron who can organize and lead the group to glory. If not, you still can look for talent without putting out a blind casting call. Check with the drama teacher at the local high school to see if she has any suggestions. Perhaps the drama teacher herself would be interested in helming a group for fun rather than for livelihood. If you really want to find people, try digging through old (but not too old) high school yearbooks to see if you recognize any present-day patrons in the old drama club photographs. You will never know what pent-up acting ambitions they might be hiding unless you approach them. Perhaps they are not aware of those latent desires either.

Working with Local Theater Groups

Whether formed through the library or existing previously in limbo, you will need to bind these people to your library with some offers they can't refuse.

When the Peabody Public Library found its little gaggle of amateurs, they were attempting—without a budget—to put on a play and advertise it to the community via flyers ("Can I put this up on your announcements board?" was how we discovered each other) and with the hoped-for good will of the local newspaper. They barely had the small fee required to rent the high school auditorium for a single performance. The library, of course, was as destitute in its own way, needing programs in the dramatic arts. The director had been making her normal "hints" about this deficiency, especially our inability to produce one of her favorite library programs: the murder mystery play. Immediately, the bells and alarms went off: make some kind of a proposition to this person.

Thus, it came to be that we "sponsored" the group by letting them perform the play (without fee for use of the community room) and allowing a collection plate (actually an old hubcap) to help fund future projects. They were able to use the library for rehearsals, and the library put its somewhat more substantial publicity machine to work advertising the group. It mattered not to us that they were basically a bunch of former high school friends billing themselves as "The Village Idiots"; they were *our* idiots. The library has called upon them several times since (including the production of and most of the roles in our library mysteries), and the symbiosis has proved positive for both organizations.

You can provide several other services to foster your relationship (and make them feel guilty for even thinking about leaving you). Like movie licensing, when putting on a play written by someone other than a member of the troupe, you must pay royalties for the privilege. Luckily, these fees are not particularly taxing for the nonprofit organization and are based on the number of performances and the size of the audience you expect. If you are charging for admission, the royalty will be based on a share of the "box office" receipts; if there is no admission, the royalty will be based on some low dollar amount per head. We have paid as little as $15 for the rights to a single performance based on an audience of sixty. Yes, that "we" refers to the library, for this is one thing you should be doing for a group of people who are donating their time and talent. If you have absolutely no budget for this, and the staff is truly committed to theatrical programming in the library, you can find a way to pay for royalties without involving the library's finances. Grants are available under certain conditions from humanities councils. There might be something in the library's gift fund, or you might be able to locate some local Broadway Angel to back your production. Fortunately, you will not need much money for this at all. If all else fails, take up a collection among the staff. It might cut into the director's Christmas present fund, but we all have to sacrifice for our art.

Another small way to serve your enthused amateurs (and keep them enthused) is to offer, if possible, to store their wardrobe and props. Normally, these would be divided among members with garages, basements, and extra rooms, where they immediately become lost forever. Dress rehearsals can result in various stages of undress when someone fails to bring in their share of the costumes. If you have any room at all, keep this stuff where they will use it—where they will have to come to use it. Who says librarians can't be devious in their methods?

The Best Plays for Your Library
Once you have a "group-in-residence" you will probably need to work with them on play selection. As literary specialists, you will have access to play catalogs for them to peruse. Indeed, you may offer them so many possibilities that they may lock up in ecstasy and not be able to make a choice. You will also need to provide some guidance as to what will work in your library, and also what the library is willing to connect its name to.

Your actors will have to consider the scope and staging of the play before they commit to it. This is dependent upon many things, the foremost of which is the size and layout of the performance space. If you are lucky enough to have an actual theater or auditorium in your library—one with a stage, wings, aisles, and lighting, you pretty much have it made. The odds are, however, that you have no such thing, and don't even have old sheets for curtains. You will have, at most, an empty room in which you must create all of the above, including seating for the audience. This means that you will want your troupe of jolly performers to be looking for plays that do not require elaborate sets, zoos full of animals, and the Rhine River overflowing its banks. (Oh, never mind. That's Wagner.) Constant scene changing and a great deal of swashbuckling action should also be ruled out, unless you have really great insurance. An intimate, dialogue-driven piece will work the best. If there must be physical stunts or objects flying around the stage area (this has occurred in some of our productions), be certain that there is adequate space between the actors and the audience.

Concerning content, you will know better than the actors what the library is willing to have in the building. Both you and the troupe can agree that you want something that will actually draw people in, so you will probably avoid the experimental theater pieces; however, the library should decide whether a play meets community standards. If you have your mission in place, an audience you wish to target, and a good understanding of your patrons, you can write up some guidelines that will allow your performers to choose a good play with a minimum of hassle from you. A standard procedure is to have them select several plays, which they can submit for your input or that of the library staff, if you so wish. Make helpful comments, but don't tell them which one you think they should mount; there comes a time when even safe wardrobe storage is not enough to temper their creative outrage. Rather, involve them as much as possible in the decision. Talk about potential problems and see if there is a way to resolve them. Most of all, treat your actors as the artistic and ingenious people they are. They are creative individuals who have a way of making the most elaborate stage directions work for them, so why not trust them? They also live in the community and want to see everything go smoothly; otherwise, they would have moved to New York City.

You and your group will also need to think about play length. As discussed in the section on film, you are not dealing with professional settings here, and you cannot expect the same level of involvement from your patrons as can the Broadway impresario. These people have not paid an exorbitant price for tickets to your event, so they will not be demanding their "money's worth" by feeling compelled to stay for an overly long production. Neither will they (in all likelihood) be sitting in plush theater seats, reclining on armrests and high, padded backs, poised high above the level of those in the row in front of them. You have perhaps 90 minutes to two hours in which to fulfill their expectations and not send them home grumbling, "Never again!" What you need to aim for is one intermission of approximately twenty minutes, during which time your play goers can tend to rest room needs, talk about what they have seen so far, and have some refreshments which you will, of course, provide.

Luckily, purveyors of scripts seem to know what sort of problems the average theater troupe faces, and have made their catalogs—even the print versions—easy to search by several of the above criteria. You can find plays listed by time (average), relative cost of royalty payment, number of acts, and number and gender of characters. A thorough cross-check of these catalogs will convince you that just about anything you want to see performed will be available for production.

Procuring Performance Rights

Play royalties were mentioned earlier, and it cannot be stressed enough just how important it is to comply with the copyright laws of the country. We can only do ourselves further harm if we cut corners to avoid what are essentially peanuts for fees. Luckily, royalty payment and performance rights acquisition is a very easy process, requiring only a letter, a few quick calculations, and a check.

More companies are involved with play royalties than with film rights, but only a few really big players are in the field. Their catalogs of plays stretch into the thousands, so you will not have to go far to find what you need. The stock will include plays by the famous, such as Tennessee Williams and Eugene O'Neil, from English playwrights as well as from Americans, and by relatively or completely unknown authors. You will find dramas and comedies, farce, surrealism, experimental plays, and musicals, and practically everything old and new that is still under copyright. One of these companies you might be familiar with through their huge catalog: Samuel French. You may request their current catalog by writing to them at 45 West 25th Street—Dept. W, New York, NY 10010 (price is $3.50), or go to their website at www.samuelfrench.com and download a copy in PDF format (it's over 300 pages in length). Dramatist's Play Service is another firm with a catalog of plays in the thousands. Go to their website at www.dramatists.com for their online play search or contact them at 440 Park Avenue South New York, NY 10016. They also have an extensive FAQ about royalties, script changes, and copying of materials. The third-largest firm dealing with play royalties is Broadway Play Publishing Incorporated (www.broadwayplaypubl.com). They specialize in modern American theater, but offer much more than just that. Like the other companies, they offer an extensive index of plays, and list low royalty and free plays.

After you have sent in your request and royalty payment, you will receive in the mail an agreement for the staging of the production and details about charges, number of performances, and other things you had specified in your request. Now you may begin to advertise your intentions to the general public (unlike film rights, you may include the name of the play in your publicity). The licensing firms, however, will require that all mention of the play and its staging be accompanied by a phrase such as "by arrangement with" and their firm's name, as well as inclusion of the playwright's name. It looks a little bulky, but it also looks rather professional, so this small concession to form should be no trouble.

There are two further areas of concern when trying to license a play, and these are major items. First, you are in no way allowed to alter the playwright's words in any way, nor are you to change characters (adding, subtracting, changing gender, etc.) without the author's written consent, which is a lot more hassle than it is worth. The exception to this rule is the staging. Because it is impossible for the author to know what sort of setting her play will be produced in, stage directions that include entrances and exits to wings and backstages that might not exist, or thirty-foot runs on a twenty-foot stage might be unworkable. You may, therefore, modify them to fit your venue. You might also run across a denial of staging on the grounds that a particular play is "restricted"; this is not an affront to your amateur stature, but rather is a further protection of the playwright's chance at profit from her work. Play restrictions might not appear in a printed catalog because of their timely nature, but will more likely (but not always) show up on the website. A play will be restricted if it happens to be on a national tour, or if a professional staging is planned or in progress somewhere in your area. You may thus wait until the restrictions are lifted, or simply choose another play.

Finally, remember that you are simply paying for the right to perform this work; that will probably not include the actual working scripts needed for the cast and director. You will also be expected to purchase these, since photocopying is another licensing no-no.

The Talent in Your Library

What if there are no local theater groups and no one else can be cajoled, bribed, or threatened into starting one? You can perhaps give up your dream of live theater in the library, but what then of that director staring a hole in the back of your head, wondering when the play season begins? If you are desperate enough (or, hopefully, just think it is a smashing idea), you can enlist the aid of your staff, burning the same-sized hole in the backs of their heads. You might well have the makings of at least one production at hand, if not a regular troupe.

Collecting "Volunteers"

Starting in your own department and working out to the rest of the library, gently begin to let people know how great it would be to "put on a show" and how indebted you will be to them for considering "even a small role" in any production chosen. This is how it would have to be done at the Peabody, along with several follow-up threats of total change in employment status; you, hopefully, will have a more positive experience and a more cooperative staff. In fact, it is entirely possible that you will have an enthusiastic staff. Many, many people are closet performers, actors who never get it out of their systems in high school and drifting through a dull and boring reality. Give them a chance at the greasepaint and footlights, and you might well be creating the next Barrymore.

Once having recruited at the library, be certain that your co-workers—even those who cannot be convinced to participate—talk to their families and friends. The farther you cast your net the better your chances at landing your cast. Be as devious as you need to be to gather your troupe by promising them anything. Tell the recalcitrant thespians that they can have that "small" role, or the anxious crooner that he can sing his lungs out in *Show-boat*. Once committed, you can shift them to what is really needed.

A Crew Beyond the Stage

Everyone in your library has talent; you, of course, already know that. Those talents might aid in the staging of your homegrown performance. Behind the stage and beyond the glitter, you will need people to help make it all come together. Does someone on staff know how to sew? They can make your costumes. How about the weekend handyman, the hammer and saw virtuoso? You will have your set built and in place. Your props and furnishings are in your homes; the audiophile on your staff can work out the sound system; the creatively noisy among you can do sound effects; and, muscle will put it all into place and move it when needed. The answer to stage fright in this case is to stay off the stage, and the way to play your part is behind the scenes.

A Way with Words

You don't wish to pay royalties for a copyrighted play? Refuse to put on a medieval mystery play to avoid fees? None of your actors understand Shakespeare? Then perhaps you should consider writing a play yourself. Come on, don't sit there and say you didn't enjoy creative writing class in college, the chance to let your mind run free and tell the world what you really think? No? Then consider finding a scribe to do the job for you. There are instances of librarians writing plays for their libraries—especially interactive mysteries. The concept of a librarian with time to do this might prompt such questions as "Who does the work in your library?" or "Don't you ever sleep?", but a dedicated librarian/author will do whatever it takes under sleep deprivation in order to get the job done. (How do you think this book was written?)

Ideas for plays are all around, and those ideas need not be found any farther than the limits of your community. Local events and history can be researched right in your building, with newspapers and old letters just brimming over with material. It need not be some momentous event in your town's history, but rather any interesting occurrence; it could even be the local reaction to a world event, such as war. If you do find a good story, be certain to check for extant family members and ask for permission to include their ancestors in your production (better yet, work with them, and even offer them parts). A totally fictional story with no historical persons can be built into your community, but you will need to know how the populace would react to such "interlopers."

Your efforts can, with a little attention to detail, be quite creative and professional—there is no need to descend to the *Waiting for Guffman* level just because it is a local production. You might indeed draw large crowds to see their town "come alive" on stage.

Full Time at the Library, Part Time on Stage
Perhaps the best use of library staff—and this is what is done at the Peabody Public Library—is to "lend" them out to the group doing your play. If there is need for a bit role or two, and the troupe does not have enough regular members, offer yourself or a staffer to fill in, cutting out the need for a search. You could also make your group aware of the aforementioned special behind-the-scenes skills available on your staff.

Professional Theater Troupes
If you have a budget, the occasional professional production will be a welcome change—and an interesting contrast—to locally developed offerings. Although not directly mentioned in the previous section, it must be obvious that putting on an amateur production, even in your normal role as program librarian, is a long, exhausting, and stressful process. There is much pressure involved in bringing together every aspect of production and hoping the scenery doesn't fall down on your players, not to mention worry about whether anyone will show up for the performance. It might be well worth it to take a break, let someone else do all the hard work, and maybe learn a few tips from the pros.

You are probably not going to hire the national company of *Cats*, no matter what your budget might be. The size of a touring company—its cast members, props, wardrobe, and staging—is the biggest limiting factor when it comes to getting a troupe to your library. The more people and stuff that needs to be moved, set up, and moved again, the more the company will want to limit its wanderings. Why play one engagement in ten towns—setting up and breaking down again—when you can find a town willing to host ten performances? Instead of extravaganzas, you should be thinking small. Some of the best companies feature only a few performers, and little or no props and sets. Hal Holbrook took Mark Twain across the country with little more than a cigar and a white suit. Recently, one man with a cane and a fedora enabled the Peabody Public Library to give its patrons an afternoon with Harry Truman.

Another factor in your ability to hire a touring company is their tour calendar. If they can make it worthwhile to travel to your library, they will do so. If they have to drive several hours to reach you, then several more to get back onto their tour route, they might not do so—certainly not at a price you can afford. However, if several venues awaited them along the way, or when they arrived, they might jump at the chance to pay you a visit. This will be up to you, though, and your skill and experience at partnering with other libraries and organizations will be crucial. Although you certainly don't want the competition right in town, you can contact appropriate outlying organizations and see if they are at all interested. The more you can find, the lower the price for each venue, and finding enough partner sites might be all that stands between a booking and a cancellation.

There are a goodly number of regional traveling troupes, some of which will travel quite a distance away from their home bases. Like traveling salesmen of old, troupes will often divide and cover a predetermined area or territory. If they get a significant number of bookings in one direction, they will head that way. They might send one of their productions north, another south, and yet another east. They will rotate these each year, giving each area a different play and themselves ample time between mounting new plays. You probably will not have a choice on what play can be booked, even if you found half a dozen or more offerings in their catalog or on their website. Just letting you know that they have these other productions is a way to keep you interested from year to year.

The best way to find out about these traveling groups is to contact other libraries in your area, your state, and your region. Ask your counterparts if they have hosted such performers, or even been approached by them; they will be happy to get another venue possibility in the area, so that they do not suffer future cancellations. Also check with yours or neighboring states' humanities councils for a list of performers and groups available in the area. Once you have had a successful booking of one of these professional groups, you will find yourself on a list for other touring companies as well. You might not be flooded by offers, but you will see an increase in flyers, catalogs, brochures, and e-mails from not only theater troupes, but storytellers and musicians as well.

Theatrical Possibilities

Your library and its theatrical troupe in residence have many dramatic and comedic choices. You can use the strengths of your particular facility, target your markets, and maximize the talent at hand by investigating the options opened to you for staged productions.

Working without a Stage

One common problem when trying to program a play is the lack of a stage. Not just a stage in the sense of an elevated platform, but rather all of the necessary areas and mechanics that make "staging" possible: wings, backstage,

dressing rooms, and curtains. Putting actors at the head of the room and expecting the same result as a properly staged event will simply not work. Actors need to be seen, and to make entrances and exits—sometimes for costume change, and sometimes for dramatic effect. You and your troupe will
need to carefully look over your available space for the following possibilities:

A place to change.   Just having a backstage area is not enough for this
procedure because the actors will want some privacy; they are entertainers,
not exhibitionists. Any sort of room or closet that has enough space for a person to remove and put on clothes without it descending into a Marx Brothers routine should suffice.

A way to make an entrance.   Lacking stage wings, your players will
have to come on stage from behind the stage area, meaning you must have
some sort of backdrop set up to provide a backstage. This backdrop can also
serve to hold your background scenery.

A way to escape.   At times, actors will need to make entrances from or
exits to some place other than the stage area, namely the back of the theater.
If they can leave from a door behind the stage setup and come in behind the
audience, you will have solved this problem. If not, you will either have to
cut some new doors, change your layout, or come up with some sort of staging shift to accommodate this shortcoming.

Curtains.   Curtains are not an absolute necessity, but are a nice touch if
they can be worked into your plans. Curtains will allow actors to begin scenes
in place and make for less disruption during scene changes. A portable, lightweight arrangement can be made from aluminum conduit and unlined fabric.

The staff of the Peabody Public Library and our semi-resident acting
troupe, The Village Idiots, closely scrutinized the library's performance space
and turned it 180 degrees from its usual orientation for use. Figure 5.1 shows
a storage room that is normally considered to be at the back of the space being used as a dressing room. Notice also that two doors behind the stage open
on to a hallway, which leads to an entrance at the back of the audience.

We have thus far worked without curtains, but use lightweight plywood
hinged together as a backdrop. If you have a handy person on the staff or in
the group, and the library has storage space, you might consider building a
portable stage. This need not be a massive affair; getting your actors even 6"
to 8" above the audience can make a lot of difference. If you do decide to
build one, follow the plans carefully, and if you want to alter it to make it
larger, be aware that the bracing must be adjusted to continue supporting the
extra weight. A collapsible stage is good; a collapsed stage is not. Although
the term *portable* is relative, your finished product—which might need to be
in sections—should be handled by no more than four people.

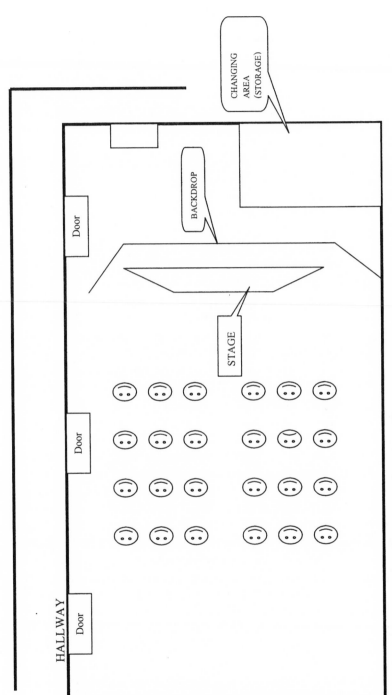

Figure 5.1. Peabody Community Room Set for a Stage Play

Outdoor Productions

Everything mentioned under "Working without a Stage" also applies for outdoor productions. You will need a place for the actors to change, and to make entrances and exits; you will also need to have some sort of sound system, which you might not need in your indoor venue. There are no acoustics outdoors, except for bad acoustics. If the wind is blowing, you will need to be certain that all props, scenery, and backdrops are properly weighted or anchored, and if you are doing Greek tragedy, be certain to wear something under those togas. It goes without saying that you need to have a plan B in the event of rain—either moving to an indoor or covered location, or postponement to a later date.

Although we have not actually staged an outdoor play, the staff at the Peabody has looked at the possibilities and reached some conclusions concerning optimum staging and seating. Several spots on our property gently slope away for thirty or forty yards, ending in a level area at the bottom. Although not actually an amphitheater, this arrangement would allow for seating (on the lawn itself) that would give the entire audience a clear view of the stage area. If you have such a place on your property, you might want to test it first, lest it turns out to be too steep and the audience slides into the performers.

We also have a huge parking lot, and had thought to bring in a large flatbed trailer to act as the stage. Again, the audience would be seated on the lawn in front of the trailer. (We also considered seating in the parking lot, but because we were considering a July play date, decided against the possibility of crisp, fried patrons.) Actors would make entrances and exits via steps at the back or sides of this truly portable stage, and vans or small campers parked behind would serve as dressing rooms.

If you have a series of steps at your library, and if they do not immediately end in a public sidewalk, you might consider using them as amphitheater seating with the stage in front. Although not as scorching as asphalt, concrete can heat up, so you might want to avoid the hottest part of summer.

It takes more planning, more worry, and a lot more courage to attempt an outdoor production, but there is something very attractive about open air theater, probably something left over from the early Greeks. If you go ahead and give it a try, and the weather holds, and the sound system works, and no one gets stung by a bee, it should be a great time for all.

One-Person Performances

The solo theater performance has been mentioned earlier, and is certainly one of the best options for a library—even if it does not involve many of your players. It is also a premier choice when engaging a professional troupe. Usually, the one-person performance features an actor portraying a famous person from history or literature. The person's own words, taken from writings, letters, and speeches, are combined with those of the playwright to give a rounded picture of the character. The person might move through time, aging during the performance, or simply be a representation of an important instance in their life. This is not impersonation, in the style of Frank Gorshin or Rich Little, but rather a fully acted characterization of a role, including mannerisms, accents of speech, and dress. The many impersonators you will find plying their trade on the Internet do not act so much as pose. They might not have any set pieces to perform or offer anything of a literary nature. They often hire themselves out to walk around at fairs, grand openings, and festivals. Be certain that you are booking an actual stage performance, and not an ambulatory statue.

A one-person play, such as *An Evening with Mark Twain* or *The Belle of Amherst* is both historical biography and literature. Entertainment and instruction in one package is a good deal, no matter how you divide it. If you book a professional for such an event, remember that they will be traveling light and you are saving money that would otherwise be charged for moving wardrobes and props from one locale to the next. Although it was mentioned earlier as a local troupe possibility, in reality, these plays are very demanding of the performer, who must be on stage at all times and cue his or her own lines without the aid of dialogue. Rare is an amateur who will take on such a task.

Musicals

Even a small musical play is a large undertaking, with dancing, singing, and instrumentation to worry about, in addition to the acting. The royalty fees can be much more because you are paying for music as well as dialogue, and authors usually come in three and fours, rather than singly. You will also need more scripts and scores for musical and dance personnel. Mainly, you would have a difficult time performing such a feature in the usually limited space of the library. You can consider it as an outside project, but remember that you will have to ensure that the sound is in balance between voices and instruments. The orchestra should be the least of your worries because a fine musical can be staged using just an electronic keyboard.

Comedy Skits and Standup

One option for opening up your stage (or whatever passes for a stage) to your patrons in general is to offer amateur comedy night. Many people fancy themselves comedians, and have probably been told by friends and family

"You should be on the stage." By offering an open mike to individuals or would-be comedy troupes looking to put on some original skits, you can help prove the family right. Or very, very wrong.

You might want to hold some sort of audition, not to sort out the great from the Gong Show rejects, but to make certain that community standards are not exceeded. You can also ask to see a copy of the material before it is presented, but it is always better to actually see it performed because ad-libs and body language are not normally written down.

The Library Murder Mystery

A perennial favorite, the interactive mystery play is not only performed in libraries, but also in corporate training seminars, at reunions, and at dinner theater, both professional and community. Many of these plays are actually written to be performed in a library, or at least have a library-related theme. Those that do not relate directly to the library are still suitable for performance in a library setting.

Because they are normally written for a cast of rank amateurs, these plays are light on actual written dialogue and heavy on stage directions and cues for ad-libs. Because the emphasis is on audience participation, these directions are aimed at getting them into the spirit of the action. Character description and motivation is much of what drives these scripts, and making things up to play to a particular audience is much of the draw. In many interactive mysteries, the identity of the perpetrator is not known to the cast at large in order to keep them from tipping the audience during the questioning period. Thus, the clues themselves are what point the finger of guilt. Reject any play that does not use direct evidence but relies instead on some unknown tidbit of information; it will keep your patrons a lot happier if they don't think they are having their minds messed with.

Some mysteries are presented in formal play structure before a static audience, while others are more loosely constructed, allowing the audience to wander around on their own in search of evidence. A past production at the Peabody Public Library, presented on a Saturday evening after the library had closed, utilized the entire facility as a "mansion, " in which the suspects were scattered in different rooms, giving their side of the story and answering questions. After a predetermined amount of time, cast and "guests" (the audience) assemble at a central point for the classic resolution scene.

Getting the entire staff involved with the production, especially as characters, will add an air of fun and familiarity to the event. Getting local celebrities into key roles would be even better—especially if someone like the mayor or another beloved politician ends up as the killer (or, even more popular, as the victim). We usually make the hunt for the killer rewarding for our amateur detectives, prizes for top guessers in the form of local business gift certificates. We also have the ever-present table of magical disappearing snacks (and a regular staff to keep it stocked).

These mystery plays are easy to find on the Internet, and range in price from a few tens of dollars up past 100 dollars, depending upon the complexity of the writing. These are most often fees for one performance of the play (more than one at the library would rather lessen the mystery, obviously), and may or may not require the separate purchase of scripts. Most of the plays you will encounter are heavy on comedy, with a lot of bad puns and silly names, especially for the characters (Lance Boyle, M.D.; Phil R. Upp, gas station attendant; etc.). The authors also have a propensity to turn any situation or setting into a murder scene, including the starship *Enterprise* (The Next Generation crew, obviously; Captain Kirk would have just shot all the suspects and been done with the whole affair). Here are several good starting points for your search for the perfect murder in your library:

Eldredge Plays—http://www.histage.com/
Samuel French—http://www.samuelfrench.com/
Haley Productions—http://www.haleyproductions.com/
PlayDead.com—http://www.play-dead.com/
Mysteries by Vincent—http://pages.prodigy.net/jeff.ludwig/mystery/game_
    vincent.htm

Most of these people are very easy to deal with, and you will have your scripts, clearances, and whatever questions you might have answered within a short time. The Peabody Public Library has dealt with Haley Productions and Mysteries by Vincent, and they both were very helpful. You might want to drop a line to them after you have successfully mounted your production, just to let them know what a good time was had; they will appreciate the input.

If you would rather try your hand at writing your own, some websites will help you become an instant playwright. No matter what avenue you take, hosting one of these events at your library will result in a grand evening of fun and entertainment. If you have mystery fans among your patrons (and who doesn't?), they will be greatly appreciative; they will also be the most intense, bulldogging, crime-solving detectives you have seen since Colombo retired.

Readers' Theater
This theater style almost ended up being discussed in the following section on literature. It is, after all, similar to poetry or prose readings. However,

several distinct differences landed it in the theater discussion instead. The most obvious distinction is that more than one person is involved, as a rule. There can also be entrances and exits, although the principles generally stand still or sit on stools. The stage area can be empty, have a few props, or even some actual scenic backdrops. Mainly though, people are reading in character, acting out the parts verbally. They may act as far as using body language, but there are no distinct physical movements and character interactions. Rather than speaking to each other or the audience, the actors remain unfocused, acting and reacting to some unspecified stimulus.

The advantages of readers' theater are many. The greatest reward is in monetary savings: no costumes, sets, or props. You will still need to pay royalties, however. Because the script is essentially being read, there is little or no stage direction, rehearsals are kept to a minimum, and a production can be quickly and easily mounted. Finally, this is the perfect opportunity for a fledgling actor to learn the art of characterization without the added burdens of staging, character interactions, and script memorization. Readers' theater is perfect for the smaller program room without any way to create a stage, yet it will still work in an actual auditorium setting, on a real stage. The lack of elaborate staging and traditional acting might discourage some playgoers, but you should still draw interested patrons and, over time, you will be able to mount more of these productions—involving more potential acting talent—and thus maximize patron exposure to the theater arts.

Literature

Programs of a literary nature are in their natural habitat at the library, and we should not only schedule many of them, but excel at doing them as well. A library that cannot offer regular literary fare will not be looked upon kindly by a good portion of its patrons—quite often the portion with money. The book discussion group, dealt with in a later chapter, is the basic literature program of most libraries, but others—more universal in interest and larger in scope—will attract a varied audience.

Poetry and Prose

Reading and writing—two-thirds of the ill-named "Three Rs" are the most basic concepts pictured by a person when thinking in terms of the library and its mission. As librarians who program, we should not simply make material available to patrons; rather, we must give them a stage from which to proclaim their love of literature. If they have found a poet or a poem, a writer or a story, that they have enjoyed and has touched them in some manner, they should have the opportunity to share their love and understanding with others in the community. So, too, with writing. All the frustrated poets, novelists and essayists in the community are just waiting for someone—you— to personally invite them to display their creativity in a public forum, along with others of their kind.

April is National Poetry Month (as well as home to National Library Week) and a perfect time to schedule a poetry reading. It should not be the only time, however. Once you hold your first reading and realize just how many little Lord Byrons are wandering your community, quarterly or even monthly gatherings might be in order because a really "hot" poet can rip off an epic in short order when the spirit moves—and with most poets, the spirit is always moving. Make a few simple rules for your readings: how long each person is allowed at the podium, number of works they can read, and age limits. Content should not be limited, but you should let the poets know that you expect them to conform to community standards. Outside of this, there should be an air of freedom, keeping the event open for all styles of poetry, people reading other authors' work, and perhaps even songs.

You will probably want to keep your prose and poetry readings separate, just for the sake of time equity. A poet will have many short poems to fit into the allotted time, but a writer of stories needs more space to tell the tale, and more time to read it. If you do have separate readings, be sure that there are an even number of each, so that the tender souls of your writers do not feel trampled upon.

Writers' Groups
Something must be in the water around Columbia City, for there seems to be about as many authors as livestock, and there is a lot of livestock around here. Someone is always at a corner table of the library, putting together a manuscript or doing research for a book; there are more and more self-published authors offering their tomes for the library's collection; and it seems that everyone is making comments like, "Oh, you're writing a book? So am I." Perhaps the major publishing houses should consider moving here because there seem to be more stories in rural Indiana than there are in the Big Apple. Of course, Indiana and the Midwest have always had a share of important authors, literary and other.

Most areas of the country can claim their own authors, published and famous or unknown and hopeful. The advent of the World Wide Web and its ability to send a person's written insights (and senseless rants) across the world in an instant will only make the number of authors grow exponentially. Like most endeavors pursued in solitude, writing can only improve by outside advice; a writer craves both justification and helpful criticism. Because his own mind will become obsessed by his particular style, the isolated writer will begin to either glorify or vilify every word put onto the page. The answer to this problem is the writers' group, wherein would-be Faulkners find fellowship and much needed literary direction. As a librarian, you need only organize the group, providing it with a place to meet, access to your collection, and perhaps have something to eat and drink. There is probably no need for a leader because writers are rather anarchic in their lifestyles, and everyone will just shout until they are heard. If you or a fellow staff member are of a literary bent, so much the better; having an "insider" in the group will ensure that they don't slip away and start meeting at the local Starbuck's.

Very few if any ground rules exist for writers' groups, with the concept of simple respect being at the fore. No negative criticism or blanket praise allowed; saying "This story stinks!" or "It's really wonderful" is in no way constructive. The group must provide examples and alternatives. Criticism should never be based on content; if one of the members has written a factual account of her abduction by and subsequent marriage to Bigfoot, the only criticism allowed is that which would further the literary character of the story, thereby enhancing her chances of having it published by *Weekly World News*.

The Library as Publisher

People want to have their words published. Whether or not they are commercially or critically viable is of no concern to them; they need to have someone see and read what they picture themselves to be, to feel that their ideas have merit in this world and can somehow affect others in their thinking. This means that a prospective author might go to any means to get "published," including paying a hefty fee to a vanity publisher in order to obtain several hundred copies of a book they might never have means to market. Under such conditions, why can't the library step in and offer a better solution?

The idea of library as publisher is not new—check your genealogy section and you will probably find some typewritten volumes that have been bound by the library's bindery service; today's product will be much more professional looking, thanks to the variety of home-publishing software available. Whether the library offers access to their bindery service, or pays for the process itself, you can present the budding author with a well put-together product that will win you a friend for life—and perhaps a mention in her first real published book. Besides an offer of binding, classes in the use of publishing software will be helpful to the writer. The one thing that a vanity publisher will do that you will not is to provide an ISBN for the finished book. To receive a barcode as a publisher, you must pay Bowker a fee based on the number of items you plan to publish, and it could run into the thousands of dollars.

By offering a service such as that described, you will be doing the prospective author several good turns:

- They will be getting a high-class copy of their book to send to a real publisher or agent.
- The chance to learn how to get a manuscript into form and the chance to see their words in print could be a good thing or a wake-up call to change their dreams.
- By putting a copy of the book into the collection and giving it a bit of publicity, you will help the author to reach many more people than she could on her own.
- You are saving your patron hundreds of dollars.

Storytelling

Storytelling is not just for children; never has been, really. Go to any fair, festival, reenactment, or Chautauqua and you will encounter storytellers for adults. This oldest form of human record keeping is alive and well across the country, seeing resurgence as more people take an interest in their heritage. Storytellers seem to have a way of touching something deep inside us, as they weave that long thread of humanity across ages and civilizations, binding us to our past and opening a window onto ourselves. Finding storytellers is a lot like finding folk musicians: they are a family that works, travels, and plays together. If you go to a festival to find musicians, you will find storytellers. A more direct method is to find the storyteller societies, guilds, or whatever they care to name the groups, that act as clearing houses for their members' talent. You will find at least one in each state, and usually more, divided by regions of the state. Large urban areas will even have their own guilds. These guilds or societies will list their member storytellers, contact information for them, a brief biography, age appropriateness, and the names and descriptions of programs offered. They will not, however, mention fees; that will be decided after you contact the person in question.

Contacting storytellers is not always as easy as we would like. Many of them are not into modern technology, such as e-mail, and the Peabody Public Library once had to write a letter to one storyteller who had no telephone. Once you do contact them, you will find them quite easy to work with. They are generally not very expensive, and are usually willing to give a financial break to a nonprofit institution, such as a library or school. We might not be the bulk of their working venues, but we do give them broader exposure than they would get at re-enactments and such, and because libraries and stories go hand-in-hand, they usually have a great fondness for us.

Many storytellers cover a wide age range with their work, and most have separate programs to offer to adults and children. At the Peabody, whenever one department contacts a storyteller, the other is informed and given the chance to also book that person. Usually, when they are booked for more than one performance at the same venue, there is a discount price. Thus, both departments get a program, and at a lesser amount than if they were scheduled singly. Generally, the performer will do the children's show in the late morning or early afternoon, and then return for the adult program in the evening. Some storytellers have tapes and CDs, or if they have a web site, there might be some audio samples. This will give you the chance to hear their work first before hiring them, if you care to do so. This is not a necessity because they have probably performed somewhere in your area and will be happy to offer references. Check the library in the next county; your storyteller has probably been there (the pool isn't that deep).

One final bit of advice: if you are not familiar with the program they are doing, find out if they will be including audience participation of some sort. If so, you can advertise this fact to protect the more passive patrons who will attend looking for a nice, quiet evening. Forewarned is forearmed to sit in the back of the room (and hope that the storyteller doesn't pick from that area).

Quiz Games

This orphan of an event had a difficult time finding a place in this book, finally settling into the cultural, and specifically literary, chapter for no better reason than that some questions in a quiz game will be of a literary nature. This does not mean that this is a minor player in the programming game; just the opposite, a quiz game could have the effect of galvanizing the community. Whether you call it Jeopardy!, Quiz Bowl, or Who Wants to be A Genius?, and whether it is a team or individual format, a quiz game can bring out a large number of people who have always wanted to see if they are as good at the real thing as they are in their living rooms. A tournament of this type can be a formidable undertaking and it would be wise to share it (while still claiming proprietary rights) with other community organizations. When the Peabody Public Library first started to put together a tournament, we were not sure what direction it would take; we were just happily engaged in creating categories, questions, and answers. We ended up partnering with the county Kiwanis club. They worked on publicity and prizes, while the library created the tournament itself. The team entry fees went to the Kiwanis and their charitable work with children.

A Power Point template for a Jeopardy board was found on the Internet, and the reference staff created the questions. Lockout buzzers, which allow only one team or contestant to ring in at a time, are also available on the Internet, with prices ranging up to $400. We had many people claim they could build such a device for us, but none succeeded; perhaps your tinkerers will have more luck. We were not able to get a buzzer system in time for the tournament, and did not want to spend the money until we were certain that this would be a recurring event. We ended up going the comedic route and using silly noise makers. It really isn't easy to distinguish which sound comes first, no matter how different those sounds are; do yourself a favor and invest in the lockout system.

The staff spent several months putting together questions and answers, basically using any free moment they had on this fun chore. All answers were verified in reputable reference works, and we actually had very few challenges during the tourney, and those were a result of ambiguity, not wrong information. Included in the categories were a number of "local" ones of historical, cultural, and sports-related nature. This really personalized the event, although the category "Peabody Public Library" did not do too well. You can also purchase questions and answer packets from companies that deal in quiz bowls, but why, as librarians, would you want to do that? This is also a good way to hone those reference skills and brush up on the contents of your reference collection.

We expect to make our tournament an annual event, a way to raise money for charity and connect with the community in a substantial manner. In Bloomington, Indiana, home of Indiana University, the public library has teamed with the local literacy council to produce a yearly quiz game called *Vital Bowl*. Each spring, dozens of teams, usually under sponsorship, compete in what has become a much anticipated community event. Your town might not have the ready-made contestants a university town boasts, but don't underestimate the draw that trivia and game shows such as *Jeopardy!* and *Who Wants to be a Millionaire?* have upon people everywhere.

Note

1. Subject Matter and Scope of Copyright (2000). Title 17 U.S. Code, Ch. 101 Online. GPO Access. Available: http://www.gpoaccess.gov/uscode/index.html

~

CHAPTER SIX

Crafty Programming

I hear and I forget;
I see and I remember;
I do and I understand

—Confucius

We can't be certain if the great Chinese philosopher was into basket weaving, ever kept a scrapbook, or tied a trout fly, but he certainly had the right idea when it comes to hobby crafts: the best way to learn is the hands-on way. And the best way to get that hands-on experience is at a class taught by someone who is an expert in all aspects of the field.

The need to create is a strong urge in humans. After all, the first thing to distinguish us from the apes (well, besides that hair thing) is our ability to make and use tools. The second thing probably was some sort of nonessential craft, like totem carving. *Creating*, in this sense, does not mean writing reports, balancing a ledger, putting together a slide presentation, or any of the other things that Americans do in their post-industrial work cubicles. These things are not solid, physical objects, but rather ephemera that will not last beyond the next strategic plan. This very book, as it is being written, is disappearing into the electronic ether of a word processor, not to be seen as a whole until it is printed out and sent to the publisher. Indeed, one chapter was damaged during disk backup and had to be substantially repaired. What sort of permanence is that? Even as a completed book, it is still only the author's idea, transferred to a medium that can be interpreted by others; there is nothing of substance to it, as far as he is concerned. Someone else ran the press, and repaired it when it broke, someone else made the paper on which it was printed and did the binding. It is more their book, from a physical viewpoint, for they have made a thing.

Until corporate America began sending its manufacturing jobs south, west, and in any direction but here, people could point to something and say, "I made that, and by making it, I have left my mark on someone's life." Okay, so they probably didn't say that, but the unconscious pride was there. Our fathers made automobiles, their fathers built wagons, and their fathers smelted iron into horseshoes. This physical presence, this weight in the hand and the seeming permanence of a constructed object is important to us; it is our mark on this world, the small piece that we leave behind for posterity, for our family and, most of all, for ourselves. The abstraction that is life is given justification in the reality of that which we make.

Maybe this is a bit overblown, but it is nevertheless true that we like to make things. Working with our hands is a stress reliever; why else would someone come home from a week's work to spend the next two days repairing the plumbing or refacing the kitchen cupboards? The home-improvement industry is booming, and not necessarily for the professional contractor. We have also developed a propensity to create things that have no intrinsic value. Ancient humans, of course, carved likenesses of their gods and made baubles to wear, but these were not seen by them as useless; whether to appease an angry deity or to attract a mate, everything they made had a purpose. Not so with today's crafters; take a ride through suburbia some sunny Saturday afternoon and count the number of plywood silhouettes of ladies bending over in the flower beds or men with pipes leaning against trees. What earthly good is a goose decoy dressed in women's clothing? People fold paper into intricate shapes and then watch as it yellows and sags over time; they squeeze puffy paint onto articles of clothing that wear quite well without it; and they sprinkle glitter onto cardboard, thinking this to be a better way to say "I love you", all in the name of creativity. We need to keep our hands occupied in our leisure time, convinced perhaps of the veracity of the proverb about the devil and idleness. This is the modern business of handicrafts, turning what used to be America's way of work into its way of relaxation. Everywhere are craft stores, and the Internet is overflowing with sites that offer supplies, instruction, and chat. At the library, we are flooded with requests for the latest "in" craft books or some obscure permutation of a well-known craft, and suddenly the 700s are crammed to bursting with oddly oversized crafting books.

What does all of this tell us, if not to get the library involved with craft programming? What else are we to do, but follow the community's lead and offer them the one place they can come to have all their needs met?

Scheduling Craft Workshops

Finding Instructors
Unless you are a master at several crafts and have the time to teach them, you will need to find instructors for your library workshops. Being proficient at a task does not automatically translate into the ability to teach it to others; an able crafter who cannot impart his knowledge to another will do more harm than good, and could turn the prospective learner away from the further pursuit of what once seemed interesting. Another thing to consider, when dealing with techniques that require an extreme amount of manual dexterity, is handedness. I learned this personally during a six-week course I taught on tying trout flies, a craft that entails small items being placed on even smaller surfaces, and forces the fingers to work independently at times, rather than in unison. I happen to be left-handed, and the entire class was that other way. Most left-handed people can do more with their other hand than vice versa, but it usually isn't done that well. Although the students all seemed satisfied with the course and several have even continued the hobby, we have not repeated it again and probably won't until one of the non-lefties gets good enough to teach.

This chapter begins with finding instructors rather than the actual classes you want taught for a very good reason: when you locate the instructor, you will have found the craft that you want at the library. With so many handicrafts around, you probably will not know which are "hot" at the moment, as craft fads come and go almost as quickly as rap artists. If someone is bothering to teach a craft, however, you can be assured that there are people interested in it.

Local Amateurs
Calling a craftsperson a professional is somewhat problematic because a craft is a hobby and hobbies are leisure-time activities. A professional in the field will sell supplies at a retail or wholesale outlet, or on the Internet, and derive the majority of her income from that activity; an amateur will do it for love alone, or just enough to feed her addiction. Looking for amateur crafters does not mean looking for amateur skills; these people will be as adept as anyone who dove into the activity for the money.

Finding this craftsperson is much like finding any other community member who is a likely candidate for presenting library programs. Start in the library, with staff and patrons, and begin to work outward. It is likely that some member of the library-going public will be an adept at some popular craft, or know someone who is. The finding should not be a difficult chore; convincing this person to undertake such a project might take a bit more work. Once you have found them, do not let your instructors off the hook with just one workshop; it is your job to keep them committed with a series of classes.

The longest running craft class at the Peabody Public Library has been a monthly (minus a few weeks for summer vacation) basket-weaving class that has met for five years and has gone through several instructors. Some of the weavers from that first class still attend. Crafting is as much a social occasion as it is a learning experience. Craft classes consist of specific projects, rather than ongoing, cumulative instruction; the projects could be of varying difficulty, but most are of interest to novice and expert alike. Some students continue on their own, some will only do the projects in a class, and most will come in to pick up tips for their independent work and renew old friendships. Thus, finding an instructor entails much more than engaging a person for an evening's presentation; it is almost like hiring for a regular position, except that the pay and benefits stink.

How can you possibly get someone to do something like this on a regular basis? Well, the benefits are not quite as bad as first advertised. Doing what you love, passing that love on to others, and perhaps making lifetime bonds with those who share your passion can be very strong incentives to take on this job. We have four such people at the library at the present time. Not only do they give of their knowledge and time, they also bother to take the time to procure the materials needed for each class session and make their own tools available for first-timers, who might not want to purchase their own until they know they will continue on in the work. These instructors' only reimbursement is for materials.

Several special conditions exist in a craft class that are not present in other types of programs. Besides their recurrent nature, class sessions usually last much longer than the average library program, averaging about three hours but possibly up to six or eight. These lengthier sessions are obviously best held on weekends, and even the shorter classes have to start much earlier during the week than your normal programs. Not to worry, because a true craft devotee will gladly take early dinner—or no dinner at all—to get their hands on a new project. Because of the hands-on nature of craft work, and the probability that most students will need some extra attention, instructors limit the attendance at these classes. The maximum will differ according to the type of craft, the amount of instruction needed, and the familiarity with the tools and their functions. Obviously, a craft such as stamping is more familiar to people than basketry, both in the tools involved and the hand dexterity required. Most paper crafts involve tools and materials that are handled by people on a regular basis—scissors, glue, etc.—while a craft like fly tying has many odd things, such as hackle pliers, whip finishers, and bobbins. The minimum attendance will usually be whatever the instructor feels is the number of people for whom it is worth her time to do the class. A minimum is also important if the instructor can get a discount from her supplier for a certain amount of material. Because of these requirements, most instructors ask that the student sign up and pay for the class ahead of time.

Fees vary according to a particular craft, as well as complexity and the material necessary in a given project. You need not be concerned about the fees keeping people away; we have had some rather substantial projects and have had no trouble filling those sessions. It all goes back to the concept of creating a product; people might not pay to improve their minds at a lecture or soothe their soul at a concert (even for free, sometimes), but they will let themselves be put on a waiting list for a chance to pay $25 to make a basket that they will take home, show their friends and family and, in all likelihood, put on a shelf or closet in the spare bedroom. It doesn't matter to them: this thing is theirs; they made it and a part of their life is in it.

Finally, you will need to have two things available in the room that will serve as the craft area: sufficient electrical outlets and water. Many crafts require some sort of electrical tool: grinders, soldering irons, glue guns, hot plates, etc. Sufficient outlets also means that you will not be running cords all over the floor. You will not only need the outlets, but also several separate circuits in the room to prevent overload because many of these tools produce heat and thus draw a great deal of wattage. You do not want to plunge the place into darkness when all the electric frying pans fire up at the same time. Some crafts also require water, although not everyone will need a faucet and sink. It need only be close at hand. Basketry, for example, requires that the reeds for weaving be soaked in order to make them supple enough for manipulating without cracking. They need to be kept this way, or they will dry out quickly. A pan of water at each workstation is therefore a necessity.

Making all of these options available for your instructors will ensure a mutually beneficial relationship, and they will not start looking for another place to teach. Keeping the instructors happy keeps your patrons happy, and classes will continue for the foreseeable future.

Professional Craft Instructors

The proliferation of handicrafts has created a new class of entrepreneurs in most communities, and these people can be very good instructors for you, despite their "for-gain" outlook. Like beauty product or household merchandise firms that use direct sales representatives to distribute their wares to the general public, so, too, do some craft companies, engaging people looking for a little extra income. Some of these people are probably in your area working out of their homes and giving classes in order to sell their products. What better way to create a demand?

How does this impact your library's efforts to get into the craft game? Obviously, if someone is out there teaching the classes you hope to present, that represents direct competition. What we strive for is cooperation with the community, so why not find these people and offer them a sweeter deal, a partnership of sorts? Because using one's home for classes is not the ideal arrangement, and most other venues will charge rental fees, these crafters will be glad to take you up on your offer. If this sounds like we are partnering for profit—someone else's profit—it might very well depend upon your library's policies and strictures on how far you can go in this direction. In fact, it might be impossible for you to do this if your director and/or board have decided that anything that even resembles profiteering is to be banned from the library. As you might have by now figured out, this is not a big problem at the Peabody Public Library; we are more liberal in our interpretation of personal commercial gain because so much of what we offer can be seen in that light. If you really want to argue the point, providing books and information on the startup of a new business can be a form of aiding and abetting capitalism; the author who gives a talk is hoping to sell more books; and the band that plays your festival is looking for more bookings from the exposure. We are not, after all, going into business with General Motors (although we seem to have no qualms about taking computers from Microsoft); we are helping people who are community members, library patrons, and taxpayers.

Lest you think that we have lost all of our scruples and are pocketing payola faster than it can be printed, there are ground rules for engaging a commercial crafter (or any other program presenter) at the Peabody. First, remember that these people are really only selling things to feed their own craft addiction, and these materials and tools would be purchased by our patrons, regardless. When we find someone like this, we simply ask them not to actually sell anything during the class, but simply to mention themselves as a possible source of material. This arrangement has worked well for us, made us friends in the business community, and we do not feel that we are party to any commercial venture.

When you find these instructors, remember that they have a built-in incentive to stay with you for a long time. By giving them a permanent home, you are building your program base and pulling in a steady group of patrons who will spread the word about what a great place the local library is for so many things. You will need to do two more things to ensure optimum return on this prospective goodwill you are building: first, you will need to ensure that your collection has sufficient numbers of up-to-date books for the crafts you are offering and second, do try to get the instructor to commit to at least six months of classes when you sign her up (a year is even better). In this way, you can publicize them well ahead of time (even if the instructor hasn't yet decided on the project) and you will be able to offer the greatest selection of open dates and rooms for flexibility of the instructor's calendar.

A Trip to the Craft Store

If you are not interested in crafts yourself, you still owe it to the library to find out just what goes on in this strange little subculture. A nice leisurely trip to the craft store will soon convince you that these people are having some serious fun. As you walk past piles of foam, pounds of feathers, paint, glitter, more kinds of glue than you ever knew existed, and every material ever imagined, you can only gaze in amazement at the colors, sizes, feels, and smells of all these materials. Someone obviously forgot to tell you that kindergarten was in session for the adults of this country. These are the building blocks of the crafter, just waiting to be assembled. Whether you go to one of the craft super stores or to the few aisles devoted to crafts at the local everything mart, you will be overwhelmed by the feeling that this stuff goes on forever, and that crafting is an endeavor without an end. A careful perusal of the shelves will show you what crafts are "hot" at the moment. Although some items, such as silk flowers, flower pots, and other floral materials just naturally take up a lot of space, this is not necessarily an indication of popularity. Look to see what is up front in the store, what dominates the center aisle, and the variations—color, size, brand—of a particular craft's materials and tools. Go to the book section and determine which crafts dominate.

While you are in the craft super store, drift to the back of the building. This is generally where the classes are held, if they have any. You will be able to check their schedule to see what the store is featuring and, logically, what you should be thinking about for the library. If you are of especially bold material, you may even want to hang around and see if you can collar one of the instructors.

Going to the Fair

Another fun place to go in order to check out the current handicraft crazes is the county fair. They will, of course, have the traditional crafts one associates with a fair, such as quilts and home canning, but look for the "unusual" items and most importantly, the interest they generate. Although many of the events at a 4-H fair are dominated by children and teens, look for the adult entries as well. The people who gather around these displays are not all 4-Hers, but rather the regular citizenry who have an interest in crafts. Strike up some conversations, and get their opinions on these works; see if they would be interested in taking classes in them; most importantly, take the names of the crafters entered in the competitions—they might be willing to teach your class.

Many organizations, such as churches, schools, and social clubs, will hold craft bazaars as fund raisers, asking their members to bring in their work as a donation. Often, the crafter will be there to talk about the things he has made. This would be a good place to canvas for instructors, information, and perhaps prospective students. The local paper will tell you where and when these bazaars are being held and there are usually a lot of them. Craft booths also show up at street festivals, home shows, and art fairs. Check all of these places if you are serious about handicrafts and crafters for your library.

Teaming with Local Businesses

While you are in the super craft store or the small local shop, you might want to engage the manager or owner in a conversation concerning your vision of the library as a center of craft culture for the community (even if your dreams are not quite that grandiose). Let her know you are open to any sort of mutually beneficial arrangement. She might have someone in mind for an instructor if you need one (and her store doesn't hold classes of its own). It is, of course, to the store's advantage to hold classes on premises because the students will be primed to purchase after a session. Nevertheless, if the store is too small to comfortably hold classes, or if the store is a distance away from your community, they might welcome the opportunity to advertise themselves to a new set of potential customers.

Another deal you would love to make with these people is the donation of some or all the supplies for a project in return for your acknowledgement of their generosity in backing this fine endeavor in this great community, blah, blah, blah. Sounds familiar in some way, doesn't it? This is corporate underwriting in the grand Public Broadcasting System tradition. If PBS can keep itself on the air by running "noncommercials," then why shouldn't you? We take business donations all the time; just ask your children's librarian how she affords all those SRC prizes. You can also work with your local craft store to get insider information—no, not that kind of insider information, Ivan—the kind that will let you know about any new developments in your favorite craft. Crafts take new turns, use new products, gain even more in popularity, or fade quickly from memory. Just make certain that while you are busy publicizing their great generosity in underwriting your classes, they are just as busy telling all their customers about the library's fine programs for crafters.

Your Very Own Craft Bazaar
One way to treat your crafty patrons well is to let them display and/or sell their work at the library. Your regular attendees may, over time, build up quite a portfolio of finished crafts; a collection they might not have room to keep (the making is the thing) or be able to give to friends and relatives without straining relations. The best way for them to handle this potential house-busting problem is to sell the stuff off periodically, thus earning enough money to make more of the same things. If you have several crafts classes going on, why not schedule a room for a bazaar? A Saturday-morning event, with crafters selling their wares and demonstrating their skills to the public will not only be another feather for your programming cap, it might develop some more interest among your patrons for crafts and classes.

Not all crafts produce a surplus of product—quilting, for example—and not everyone wants to get rid of their work. Even those who crank out piece after piece will have some favorites they will want to keep. Keeping does not mean hiding away; arrange for your crafters to display their work in the library periodically. Again, not only are you giving other patrons a chance to see craftwork first hand, they might decide to take a closer look at doing it themselves.

The Popular Crafts

Hopefully, this section will deal with the more popular crafts around today because popularity does change over time, and probably according to place as well. What are presented here at some length are the preeminent crafts at the Peabody Public Library as of spring 2004. Some of these classes have been running for several years with no diminution of interest from the public. Some are newer, but still fill up their rosters on a monthly basis, which is the frequency with which we generally run our classes. Some individual projects garner so much interest that they are scheduled twice in a month, but that is generally up to the instructor. Fees for individual session range from $3 to $50, depending upon the craft. At this time, stamping is the most economical and stained glass the most costly.

If you have read and tried the suggestions in the previous section, you have already determined the most popular crafts in your community and perhaps they will match what follows. If not, bear in mind that they might be coming your way, or they could regain popularity if they have already passed through your town. All of them are mainstays of the handicraft world and will certainly have some adherents in your area.

Basketry

One of the oldest and, until recently, one of the most essential of human handiwork has been the making of wicker baskets. Outside of carrying things in animal skins (more important to use those to keep warm), our ancestors had no other way to transport their worldly goods during their nomadic period. When they finally began to settle into an agrarian existence, what better way to gather their crops than to toss them into the open top of a basket? There were no cardboard boxes, no metal storage bins, no cabinets, and no shelves for keeping possessions secure and out of the way, so they turned to baskets for this as well. The availability of natural materials in different habitats led to the assurance that most groups of humans would develop some form of basketry.

We are no longer tied to baskets, just as we are no longer tied to horses. We can travel with a suitcase, carry our "harvest" home from the store in sacks, and store our goods in plastic boxes. Even that old standby, the laundry basket, is now plastic. Compared to these modern conveniences, baskets just aren't very efficient; they don't hold liquids, they don't stack or collapse, nor are they airtight. Nevertheless, like horses, baskets are still with us. Why in the world is that the case?

When I married several years ago, I not only gained the love of my life, but her extensive basket collection as well. In the house, baskets hold remote controls, loose change, toilet tissue, hand towels, kitchen utensils, writing instruments, and much more. We use them for garden produce, holding bills (of the unpaid variety, mostly), for clean laundry, dirty laundry, flowers, food, and houseplants. They usually look better than metal, richer by far than plastic, and much more intricate than cardboard. They can be decorated, painted, stenciled, and patterned. They are art, craft, self-statement, and interior decoration. Is it any wonder that basketry is still one of the most popular of crafts?

The Basket Class

Because basket weaving is an intricate and not immediately intuitive art, easily learned, but difficult to master, your instructor will be relied upon to provide patterns, the proper materials and at least some specialty tools. As mentioned earlier, some craft classes run long and basketry happens to be one of them. Our classes last from 3 to 3.5 hours in length; ofttimes, the students end up taking the basket home, whether to finish on their own time or to haul back at the next session for help in completion. Because our classes are scheduled for Monday evenings, it is impossible to run them much longer; if your instructor has her Saturday afternoons available, it might be a better time to have a longer session (basket weavers get lost in time quite easily).

Basketry does not require a lot of specialized tools; most needed items can be found in the tool drawer at home. Long-nosed and side-cutting pliers, a flat-headed screwdriver, and spring-type clothes pins are the basics. There are also specialized clamps and weaving tools, but these are not very expensive and really not absolutely necessary. A plastic dish tub to soak the reed is all that is required to complete the beginner's tool kit.

A class in basketry will feature one pattern that might include several unique characteristics. A variety of weaves, handles, bottoms, and decorations keeps the student constantly learning new techniques, so no matter how many times she signs up for a class, it will always be a new experience. At the Peabody, we have offered over the years Easter baskets, video baskets, baskets for laundry, produce, and trinkets, as well as casserole carriers and even a basket lamp.

A certain negative stereotype still lingers over the craft of basket weaving, namely that it is something used in mental institutions to calm the nerves and occupy the hands of schizophrenic patients. While patently silly and cartoonish, a craft of any sort will pass the time—when there is time to pass—and take the mind away from the stress of everyday life. A good craft provides more than just busy work; it gives a true outlet to our innate creativity, produces something that is lovely to look at and, as a bonus, might even be functional. Your target audience will be looking for all of these traits (except the schizophrenia). Most basket aficionados are female; middle to late middle age; and either retired, at home, or with a part-time job. They are either empty nesters, or close to it, with a view toward redecorating the kids' room her way. On occasion, we have had younger people show up, but this is a craft best accompanied by the patience that is gained with age.

The Variety of Baskets

There are many ways to make a basket, although those of us who tend not to notice such things might be surprised by this, assuming that a basket is a basket. In the "stone age" of basketmaking, people had to make due with the materials that were close at hand—craft shops didn't deliver back then, apparently—and that led to vastly different styles of construction down through the ages. Many of these styles exist today at differing levels of popularity with crafters.

The most popular basket construction style, and the one usually taught to beginners, is the wood splint basket. These splints are usually white oak or some other hardwood shaved thin for maximum pliability. They can be a variety of widths, from less than ¼ of an inch to two or three inches. This variation gives wood splint baskets a wide range of appearances. Wood splints are also easily dyed, so that deep, consistent colors are possible. Splints are used for ribs as well as woven into the sides, and other materials can be worked in as well, giving yet more varied options for these baskets. The natural suppleness of the materials, along with its variety, makes these the easiest and most popular of all baskets for novices.

The rib or Appalachian-style basket does not have a distinct bottom, but is woven with reeds or wood splints around a hoop or hoops. It is difficult to describe this basket in print, but once you have seen one, you will recognize it immediately.

Wicker baskets use round materials, such as the small shoots or branches of willow species. You have probably seen these sturdy baskets holding plants, or as your child's Easter basket painted some garish shade of pink or blue. Like wood splint baskets, the material is initially woven as a bottom and then turned up or bent to create the ribs around which the sides are woven. A bit more difficult to weave because of the less supple material and the tight layering of each course, these rustic containers are still possible for the beginner.

Unlike most basket styles, the famous Nantucket Lightship basket can be traced back to its origins. In the 1850s, the seas around Nantucket Island in Massachusetts were served by a lightship—a moving lighthouse that could be anchored over dangerous rocks and shoals. The unfortunate souls who were stationed aboard this ship experienced long months of boredom, punctuated by the occasional violent storm. They relieved the monotony by weaving these unique containers. Unlike other baskets, Nantuckets are formed around molds, usually made of solid wood, but lately also of plastic. After the basket has been formed, the mold is reused. Because of the regular shape attained by the use of varied sizes of these molds, Nantucket baskets can be neatly stacked inside of each other, much like Russian nesting dolls. The materials of the baskets include a wooden bottom and thin round wicker. A cover with a scrimshaw inset is sometimes added. These baskets are very intricate and involve much work, and the molds tend to be very expensive (hardwood molds can costs hundreds of dollars), but a well-crafted Nantucket basket is an unparalleled work of art. Obviously not for the beginner, those who practice this form of the craft are not as easily found.

Coil basketry is an ancient art, but the resulting product is both uniquely attractive and highly functional. Using long strands of material, such as reeds, grasses, or straw worked into a rope, the baskets are built up in coils, which are held together with a glue-like binder. There are no ribs and no traditional warp and weave as in most baskets, resulting in a container so well made it can even hold liquids.

As your regular series of basket classes progress, you might want to try adding one of these more unusual styles occasionally, either as a treat for your regular students, or to see if you can spin off another class. Your instructor might know some of these other techniques herself, or at least know of someone who can teach them.

Quilting

Who among us has not slid under a warm, inviting quilt on a cold winter's night, snug and happy that grandma's handiwork has made all things right with the world? The unique beauty, elaborate patterns, and highly practical nature of this ancient craft have aided in keeping quilting at the forefront of leisure time activities. It also helps that a well-made quilt is an expensive item to purchase and, even though many hours are spent on its making, is more economical to make for oneself.

Despite more than a few claims that quilting is a uniquely American art form, the concept of putting cloth together in layers is a very old one, dating back to the ancient civilizations of Egypt, the Middle East, China, and Japan. These peoples used quilting mainly for clothing, however, not as the familiar large rectangle we now place on our beds for both beauty and warmth. This particular use of quilted fabric originated in the late Middle Ages in Europe, mainly in the homes of the wealthy, who stitched together (or had stitched for them) whole cloth to form their bed coverings. Use of this much whole cloth was an inordinately expensive undertaking, hardly open to the egalitarian connotations that quilting has achieved in this country.[1]

Piecework quilts, the form we most recognize today, are traceable back to England, which is obviously how they got to this country and became so identified with the United States and particularly its Westward movement in the 19th century. Because people of little means (and even those of modest fortune) could not afford to have large bolts of fabric shipped from Europe (and England controlled the amount of manufacturing allowed in the Colonies, for commercial reasons) simply to cover themselves at night, they found that piecing together strips, blocks, and scraps of fabric left over from the making of their clothes would work just as well as whole cloth for this utilitarian purpose. Of course, when a person is handed a pile of unrelated shapes and asked to put them together, she is going to use logic or creativity to render the whole as pleasing as possible. Thus, quilting became an individual artistic expression of the New World woman.

As the country burst out and population centers moved farther away from each other, women on farms and the frontier found themselves increasingly isolated; when they did gather for social occasions, it was often under the guise of cooperation in some large community project, much as the men would come together for barn raisings. The quilting bee was a chance to visit, exchange views and ideas, and catch up on whatever news they had heard, all the while working on a quilt. This quilt could be someone's personal project, or just as often, a community quilt used for fund raising, for use by the local church or town hall, or as a remembrance of some momentous event, either locally or nationally. (Such remembrances are still a common motivation for community quilting events.)

As America entered the "modern" post–World War II era of purchased goods, quilting went into decline as it passed from the list of necessary tasks; after all, couldn't a machine do it faster and better in the "jet age?" At about this same time, museums, galleries, and historical organizations began to recognize the importance of quilts as a part of our cultural, artistic, and historical heritage, and started collecting representative pieces, displaying them, or even mounting special exhibitions. Now quilts can be seen next to the great masters, in a museum sharing space with the artifacts of a former existence, and as a political statement. Likewise, what was once one of life's necessities became a popular leisure activity.[2]

Quilting Classes at the Library

Someone who can teach the basics of quilting should not be difficult to locate in most parts of the country, and neither should there be a problem finding people who will want to learn the craft. All the library really needs to do is to supply a room large enough to accommodate the crafters—quilters tend to take up a lot of space. Tables and some fairly comfortable chairs are the only other things necessary. The Peabody Public Library holds quilting classes, and if those classes were not listed on the schedule, we would not even know they were there most of the time. Quilters bring their work into the library in large plastic tubs, along with a tool box filled with sewing and cutting tools. Someone usually brings a portable sewing machine as well. Besides the sewing, quilters do a lot of exact cutting and need sharp implements and equipment that can make precise lines and curves. This will include scissors and rotary cutters, straight edges, curve templates, and protractors, as well as tape measures, needle and thread, and perhaps even an iron and board for pressing recalcitrant wrinkles from the fabric.

Our quilters display their finished work—and even their patches—on a regular basis at the library. This, as you can imagine, takes up a great deal of space because they do not exactly work in miniature. Quilts are best appreciated at their full unfolding because the patterns stretch across the entire surface. Usually, they are hung on quilt racks, which are folding frames of wood or metal over which can be draped the product, so that it can be seen by a walk around. If you have open floor space in your building that can accommodate several of these moveable supports, in a low-traffic area where the quilts will be safe, this is the best way to show them. Most quilters have their own racks, but they are easy to construct if the racks aren't available. The alternate method of displaying quilts is to hang them full from a wall. Probably not a library in existence has that kind of wall space.

Quilt Styles[3]

Quilt patterns are seemingly endless, and new ones are developed continually; styles however, reflect the era or group that first developed them, and remain pretty much constant to this day. Although some are more popular today than others, all of them use the same skills, if not the same outlook, and can be done by any competent quilt maker.

Whole cloth quilts. As mentioned, the first bed quilts were with a top layer of whole fabric, rather than pieces sewn together. This means the design and colors are in the purchased fabric, not in the creativity of the quilter; the skill and variation in this type of quilt comes rather from the elaborate patterns of stitchery, which could easily be lost in a fabric that is too ornate.

Strip quilts. Made of long strips of fabric, usually of differing patterns and running the width of the quilt, these items were a compromise on the cost of whole fabric quilts.

Block quilts. This is the type of quilt that most of us associate with quilting. Using uniform sized blocks rather than whole cloth or large strips, the block quilt is put together from these pieces to form the patterns on the finished quilt. Working with these smaller blocks is not only more cost efficient, it is also easier than trying to wrestle large pieces of fabric at one time. This may be one reason for its popularity today.

Amish quilts. As the name suggests, these quilts originated with the Mennonite religious sect. Northeastern Indiana has a large Amish community, and their quilt work can be seen on display and for sale in many local shops. A reflection of their ordered and simple lifestyle, the regular, geometric designs can be quite striking.

Mosaic quilts. Like their ceramic counterparts, these quilts use small pieces put together to form an overall design or picture. Mosaics can be made of many thousands of patches of fabric, which obviously means an incredible amount of work.

Foundation quilts. Small scraps of fabric are sewn onto a larger block, or foundation, fabric. These blocks are then joined to make the quilt. The popular crazy quilts, which can include pieces of ribbon and beads, are a type of foundation quilt, as are log cabin quilts, which employ geometric designs.

Other Quilts

Although the vast majority of quilters work in the traditional forms of square or rectangular bed coverings, quilting goes far beyond this single use. Items may be other utilitarian objects, or entirely fanciful creations. As mentioned earlier, the original use of quilting was for clothing: shirts, vests, robes, and coats are among the more common items of clothing that can be quilted. Quilt puppets are a popular and whimsical variation on the craft. Oven mitts, tea cozies, hot pads, and pot holders bring quilting into the kitchen, and are fast and easy projects. Art quilts are more traditional in their shape, but are wildly different in their content from more traditional quilts. They are meant to be hung on a wall and they are, as the name implies, fabric art.

No matter what sort of quilts are created as a result of the classes you schedule, you can be proud of the fact that you are helping to further one of the great historical crafts—one that not only serves as a staple of household efficiency, but one that reflects the personalities, emotions, and beliefs of the people who create them.

Scrapbooking and Related Paper Crafts

One of the first memories most of us have of school, or perhaps of Saturday mornings at the library, is of cutting up pieces of colored construction paper, gluing them into collages or masks, perhaps using paper towel tubes to make a tie rack for dad, or sticking lace on a red paper heart for mom. Like our love of sweets and our unbridled joy over holidays and vacations, paper crafts have been ingrained in us since youth, and often crop up again later in life as an unquenchable desire to cut and paste.

The idea of creating scrapbooks has proliferated in the last few years, seemingly as the Baby Boom generation begins to age into oblivion. As the author's generation—an admittedly self-centered bunch—starts to slip into the twilight years, they have come to realize that they will need something substantive to attest to their presence, if not their importance, in this world. In all fairness, there has been a shift in values as they begin to fill in their scrapbooks with what they finally begin to see as vital to them: children, grandchildren, family history, and community. The "me" generation has become the "us" generation, at least when it comes to memories. More than this generation is making scrapbooks, of course, but they did set the standard for importance of the individual and her need to leave some sort of mark. Beyond that pre-adolescent propensity to play with scissors and paste, scrapbook crafts give us the opportunity to document our passage through this vast, uncaring landscape, and reflect upon those people and events that have touched us in some way.

When the term *scrapbooking* was first used in front of me, the image it created was one of cardboard covers laced together and holding black construction paper filled with desultory photographs and yellowed newspaper clippings, with the occasional county fair ribbon or elementary school report card tossed in for a change of pace. Why in the wide world of crafts would someone want or need a class to learn that?

Scrapbooks have come a long way since this simplistic aggregation of memories and visions of faded Polaroids clinging tenuously to the page by a few corner mounts need to be banished from the mind. A well-made scrapbook today is a true work of collage art; it might be too busy and "cutesy" for some of us, but the sheer amount of detail, labor, and love that go into them is worthy of our admiration. Photos are still the backbone of the modern scrapbook, but their setting is much more elaborate, their narrative so complete, that we are no longer forced to flip to the back side in a usually vain attempt to discern the identity and provenance of the people in the photo. Tomorrow's archaeological dig, the scrapbook of today provides all the *in situ* evidence necessary to understand the social group depicted therein. For this reason alone, future genealogists will sing our praises for eons to come.

Scrapbook Speak
Like most avocations, scrapbooking has its own unique jargon, specialized equipment, and terminology designed to erase all chances of misunderstanding among its practitioners and befuddle the uninitiated. You would think that terms like *paper, glue,* and *stick* would suffice, but this is not the case with today's savvy scrapper. Perusing some of the terms in a scrapbooking glossary will make you think you have mistakenly opened a chemistry journal. Modern scrapbookers are building for the ages; little Khufus with their tombs of paper rather than stone, they expect their entries will be handed down to a family that will last into eternity. As such, the burial vault must be properly prepared. There will be no chance of the family's grand opening of a steamer trunk two centuries hence, only to find dust that was once paper and faded

squares that had contained precious photographs. Thus, today's scrapbookers toss around phrases that contain some incarnation of the words "archival" and "acid-free."

Like rare book librarians and historical archivists, scrapbookers are concerned with the permanence of a rather nonpermanent substance—paper. Acid is what makes paper turn yellow and disintegrate over time; cheap paper, like newsprint, is chock full of acid. Whether the acid comes from the paper's material, such as wood pulp, or some chemical used to treat, bind, or bleach, it will not only cause the paper itself to fall apart, it will also transfer this less-than-desirable trait to other items to which it comes in contact, even if those items are nonacidic. Therefore, scrapbookers pay good money for certified acid-free paper, chemicals that can "fix" the acid in news clippings, and for archival-quality bindings, protective sleeves, and mounting accessories. The same is true of glues and adhesives. In fact, glue is not used nearly as much as double-stick tape and adhesive tabs. Of course, no one can know how modern adhesives will stand up in the decades to come, but they can be no worse than the mucilage you find dried and crumbling in old photo albums and such.

Another set of scrapbooking terms revolve around what is known in the craft as embellishments—those little extras that decorate the space not filled by photos or text, or which help to draw attention to the main subject of a page. Die cuts, punches, stickers, and edges are all paper-based additions to the scrapbook.

Tools

Like materials, the tools of scrapbooking are familiar yet modified in some way or another for specialized usage. Scissors, for example, can be of the old straight-cut variety, or might have cutting surfaces that will produce a variety of fancy edges, much like grandma's pinking shears gone amok. Templates are used to crop photos and other papers into various shapes, create mounting surfaces or embellishments, or to emboss pages. Even pens, pencils, and markers come in special acid-free versions especially for scrapbooking. For a beginner's class, the instructor should have all the special tools and make them available to the class. Those students who wish to continue in the craft can then purchase their own over time.

Journaling

Considered the most important component of scrapbooking (after photographs), *journaling* simply refers to the text that accompanies and explicates the photos, clippings, and mementos in the book. These can be handwritten, typed, stenciled, cut out, or otherwise rendered. A serious scrapbooker will take some lessons in penmanship or calligraphy in order to produce the best handwritten text, giving it a more personal touch. However, the most common form of journaling involves the use of the many hundreds of fonts available on the computer, especially for long passages. No rule says that entries must be in typical linear fashion. Some creative crafters will enter their text in spirals, squares, waves, heart shapes, and other unusual patterns that can make a striking presentation or compliment the meaning of the text (for example, little Johnny's gridiron accomplishments could be heralded in the form of a football).

Altered Books

One lesser-known variation of scrapbooking is the altered book. A truly appropriate craft class for a library, this particular endeavor utilizes old hardbound books as the basis of the actual scrapbook. These books need not be old, rare, or particularly well bound. A simple novel that has been withdrawn from the collection will do nicely. The book's binding will be recovered, as will the interior pages, so that it will be impossible to determine what the book was in its former life. To form the actual pages of the scrapbook, several of the book's pages are glued or fastened together to increase their thickness and durability. The pages can be embellished with several of the same items used in regular scrapbooks, as well as more exotic items such as beads, ribbons, buttons, etc. Pages can be hollowed out to accommodate small three-dimensional items, such as rings, small bottles, toys, and whatever else is appropriate to the theme. As the decorated pages grow, extra pages from the old book are cut out in order to keep the altered book within the original size of the spine. No surface of the original book is left untouched, including the edges. Every page is a surprise, containing extras, such as cards, pop-ups, and cut-outs. It is difficult to describe these sometimes Daliesque concoctions, except to say that they are truly one of a kind.

The overall effect of an altered book is one of whimsy and playfulness; indeed, most altered books are not used for family memories and records, but for creating some personal statement, to observe a particular event, or to celebrate a favorite piece of music, literature, history, or popular culture. The first altered book I ever saw was in commemoration of the 75th anniversary of A.A. Milne's *Winnie the Pooh*. Any subject, personal or of a worldly nature, can make a wonderful altered book.

Stamping

As long as we are playing with paper, we might as well ink ourselves up and have a really fun time. Stamping comes in several forms and various techniques, but the main difference is whether you buy your stamps ready-made or make them yourself. Stamps have been used for a long time to create and decorate greeting cards, invitations, and stationery, but you would think that with the advent of high-quality computer printing, stamping designs and pictures onto paper would have gone the way of horseshoeing in the world of absolute necessities. Not so, as stamping continues unabated, not only on paper, but on anything that the avid stamper can find that will stay still long enough to be inked.

Stamping does use many surfaces besides paper; material such as glass, ceramic, fabric, metal, and wood are all fair game, though some take ink better than others. Stamped fabric can take the form of shirts, curtain, hats, and pot holders, among many others; glass and ceramic stamping can include windows, cups, kitchenware, sun catchers, and more. Stamped designs can be put on wooden or metal furniture, storage containers, luggage, walls, woodwork, and just about anything else the rabid stamper can get to before the family does an intervention. Many techniques can get a design onto a surface, and more than ink can be used: pastel chalks, charcoal, paint, watercolors, and dyes work as well. Applying the medium to the stamp with a brush can result in several colors on one stamped design.

For the involved stamper, the only way to go is to buy themed sets of stamps made of rubber and wood, similar to the old due date stamp of yesterday's library. This is where stamping differs from many other crafts, especially other paper crafts, because the cost of the tools—the stamps themselves—can far exceed the price one would pay for materials. A dedicated crafter can easily run her inventory of stamps into the thousands, as there is always one more design that needs to be bought to complete that current project. This can create quite a storage and transportation problem, as well as having to take care of so many items (rubber is not the most stable of materials). An instructor will probably bring to class only a small percentage of the stamps she has at her disposal; a complete collection shown to students might scare them off. Even though the cost of a single stamp is low, the prospect of addiction can run the budget into the ground after a while. The way around the large outlay of money for commercially manufactured stamps is to make them yourself. Children may carve potatoes and then use them for stamping, but grown-ups have more permanent alternatives with which to work. This end of the craft involves a bit more skill than simply pressing a stamp into ink, but the results would be much more satisfying than simply stamping with someone else's creation. If you can find an instructor who does this particular form of the craft, you might consider having her teach a session or two on homemade stamps.

Stained Glass

When the term *stained glass* is mentioned to most people, only one thing comes immediately to mind: church windows. Whatever youthful memories and emotions it might trigger, the vision of all those saints rendered in bright, primary colors, like a cubist's Technicolor dream, stays with us. While the sermon went on—and on and on—we could always entertain our immature selves by watching the play of lights and colors across the floor, stretching the images into expressionistic fiends. Or else we counted all the yellow panes in a window, or all the triangles. At least some of us probably did such things. No matter our individual deportment in the house of the Lord, we certainly all came away with a deep awe and appreciation of the majesty and craftsmanship involved in these beautiful celebrations of faith.

It should come as no surprise that many people have taken up stained glass as a hobby. There are specialty stores scattered across the country (not always in large cities) that supply the stained glass crafter, usually as a sideline for the proprietor's main business as stained glass artisan. Supplies and tools are also available on the web, but we are talking about shipping glass, so you might want to think about that before passing the suggestion on to patrons. What many people do not realize is that stained glass is not an especially expensive craft; square foot pieces of nicely colored glass can be had for four or five dollars. Nor is it a particularly difficult one, once you have learned the basics and developed some amount of dexterity and patience. The enormous cost of church glass and art stained glass lies in its size, complexity, and originality of design.

Tools

Although few tools are involved, it does take a bit of instruction to learn to use them properly and efficiently. The first is the simple glass cutter. We have all seen one of these, and probably even have one that has been handed down in hopes of it one day actually being used. It is the thing with a tiny carbide wheel on one end and a little club head on the other. I learned the trick to using one of these years ago when installing mirror wall tiles (that will tell you just how long ago). You make only one pass with the cutter, which makes a barely discernable line, and then snap off the unwanted pieces. You only get one pass with the tool, so it had better be a good one; thus the proliferation of straight edges, circle cutters, and curve and angle templates in the avid crafter's toolbox.

The other important—and even more formidable—piece of equipment is the soldering iron or gun. In order to join the metal and give it a finished look, lead-based solder wire is melted with the hot iron and made to flow into the open areas between the connecting channels. This device gets hot, but you can burn yourself as badly making candy, so simple safety lessons and respect for the tool will go a long way in making this as safe as any other craft in your library. In fact, the most frightening part about soldering is learning how to make the stuff flow where you want it to. At some point, the glass crafter will need to have grinders, polishers, and hole cutters. A Dremel tool is helpful, and even a glass saw can come in handy. Nippers are pliers-like tools that nibble away edges of the glass, and grinders and hand tools will make minor trims and adjustments for a perfect fit.

Materials
Some glass, some metal, and some stuff to make it all stay together should just about do it, right? Actually, yes, and no. Not meaning to obfuscate, but there are many styles, colors, and patterns of glass, and more than one kind of the metal "stuff." Traditional solid colored glass is what we think of when we picture stained glass, but the variety of stained and "art" glass available in sheets is almost endless. Besides subtle color shading similar to the thousands of paint chips the hardware store puts out to boggle our minds, glass can be made of several colors melted together and formed into patterns, shadings, swirls, and speckles. Special treatment of glass can render it crackled, opalescent, iridescent, and milky. That is a lot of glass from which to pick. Besides glass, other items used are Plexiglas, polished agate slabs, and bottoms of colored bottles. The channels of metal that hold the panes of glass are called *cames*, and they come in various sizes and styles, as well as in different metals, such as lead (traditional), zinc, and brass. Besides cames, there is also foil tape, which can be placed and formed around the edges of the glass pieces.[4]

Projects in stained glass feature just about any theme and include items that can be found in just about any room in the house, as well as outside the house. Stepping stones for the garden are a popular beginners' object, as are sun catchers. Planters, lamps, boxes for tissues, boxes for jewelry, trivets, and picture frames are also popular craft projects. Crafters use simple black-and-white lined pictures for templates, but as they progress, they can make original works.

Safety Issues
You now have a general overview of this craft and probably have decided that it is not quite as benign as stamping or scrapbooking. Boiling metals, toxic substances, and sharp edges are not the contents of a wizard's cauldron, but rather the substances of a lawsuit waiting to happen. If you want to offer stained glass classes to your patrons, you will need to be assured that certain safety issues are addressed. A concerned instructor will take care of these

things without being asked, but it doesn't hurt to double-check. Heavy gloves will protect the hands when working with hot solder, although the manipulation of the tool and the wire to make it flow into the proper places requires some hand dexterity. The edges of cut glass present real danger of severe injury. You could insist on pre-cut and beveled glass for your students, but this will detract from the full experience of the craft. Glass needs to be sanded so that the edges are safe as quickly as possible, and up until then, should be handled with the lightweight metallic gloves used by butchers and fishermen. Chipping off small pieces of glass, as well as grinding, drilling, and sanding will create flying shards, splinters, and dust that could cause eye damage; thus, good goggles are a must.

The most insidious dangers are those that we cannot see or anticipate. Lead poisoning is the unseen danger in stained glass work. Entering the body and building up over time, lead can cause brain damage, nervous system malfunction, and muscle breakdown. Because of its softness, lead can readily be absorbed through the skin; use of gloves when handling the cames, and caution against touching or scratching while using lead, will help to prevent subcutaneous absorption. Adequate ventilation is needed to remove fumes from hot solder and the lead with which it comes in contact. Open doors and windows if possible, and use a fan to vent the air outside. Fibrous dust masks can guard against large particles thrown up by grinding, but are inadequate for vapors. Full vapor masks with the proper filter canisters are the only useful breathing equipment in this situation, although probably not necessary in a well-aerated room. To be certain that all safety regulations are being met, consult an expert in the field or read some of the better books on stained glass, which deal with the problem in depth.

Food as a Craft

We could drink our milk from the carton, grab a slice of ham and drop it in our mouth, and ball up a slice of Wonder Bread and slide it down with another slug of milk; this would sustain our life as well as anything else. However, we (who are not thirteen-year-old boys) prefer to take the precious time at lunch hour to lay the meat between two slices of bread, spread the mayo or mustard evenly, perhaps even add a slice of cheese and some lettuce, and carefully fill a glass with our favorite beverage. This is more than the simple satisfying of a primal survival urge; we are creating something—even at the basic culinary level of a ham sandwich. Around the world, from the simplest homes to the fanciest of five-star restaurants, food is considered as much art as victual; thus, we are often forced to say, "That looks too good to eat!"

Beyond the physical appearance of the food, and the garnishes and arrangements on plate and table, the true crafting of food comes from taste. The blending of flavors, the contrast of textures, and the accents of herb and spice are what really makes us love food and seek out new and more wonderful dining experiences. We see and taste the food in our favorite eatery and ask for the recipe, much as we see a basket or a quilt and ask how can we do those ourselves.

The Wondrous and Weird Popularity of Food

A staff member at the Peabody Public Library is very much in opposition to any sort of food program in the library, and even against the serving of refreshments at other programs. Her concern is that we are contributing to the unhealthy situation in which we in the United State find ourselves, especially our children. She certainly makes a valid point, particularly in light of the fact that most of the library staff is overweight. Again, we need to look to our mission for guidance. We might wish to deny the value of romance novels to the intellectual development of our patrons, but we still supply them; denying their love of food will not change their eating habits. We can, of course, be more aware of what we are feeding our patrons at programs, and we should think in terms of food as a necessity that can function in a fun and interesting way, rather than the enemy. It is the kind of food and how much, not food itself, which is the enemy. Judicious planning of food programs can assist patrons with weight problems, rather than contribute to the increase of our collective waist size. Making all food unpalatable is not the answer to weight loss; creating flavor and delight in the right foods is what will turn us around. Don't schedule a class on how to make burgers, shakes, and fries; rather a program featuring some healthy Asian dishes, or low-carb delights, should be your aim.

The Food Channel

Nothing in the last ten years has changed the face of culinary art and its impact upon the nation as has the Food Network. Before food on TV, we had cookbooks; we have even more cookbooks now, but they exist because of the Food Network. In the 1960s, a few cooking shows appeared on PBS, and our knowledge of food expanded beyond our own family and community traditions, thanks to people like Julia Child and Martin Yan. The Food Network pushed cuisine-based media into overdrive; celebrity chefs multiplied in numbers and a world of culinary delights was paraded across our living rooms each evening. In areas of the country where food meant meat, potatoes, and gravy, and where "vegetable" was a dirty word, people were suddenly buying sushi mats and Cuisinarts. Of course, watching on television only serves to whet the appetite, so food classes are a popular way for would-be Paul Prud-hommes to learn the craft.

Finding "Hot" Food

Watching the Food Network—or at least scanning the listings for the coming week—will give you an idea of what people are interested in, just as watching *Trading Spaces* will tell you that everyone wants to trade rooms with their neighbors and decorate them (in disgustingly bad taste). We might like seeing it happen to someone else, but personally, no thanks. It is doubtful that the cult status of a program like Iron Chef has increased consumption of squid ink ice cream or stocked the nation's cupboards with bonito shavings; at best, most people look on in curiosity. To try some of these oddball—even for that particular cuisine—recipes, or even find the ingredients, is not a very likely scenario in most households.

If you truly want to find out what people are eating and cooking in your community, you have to check out the local establishments, both restaurants and food markets. It's best to start with the local supermarket, which is where the vast majority of the populace buys the bulk of its food each week. Check the meat and fish counters for variety and freshness (Do they even sell enough fish to keep it fresh, or is it all frozen, as in Northern Indiana?); look in the ethnic foods aisle for amounts and variety of items; check the bulk section to see if they have more than gummy worms and dog biscuits. Finally, a large wine selection (Mad Dog and Thunderbird don't count) indicates a wider appreciation of food than knowing the difference between a Big Mac and a Whopper.

Are specialty food stores in your community? If so, what do they sell and how much of it? Ask the proprietors about their best-selling items, and what people talk about recipe-wise when they come in the store. Go to area restaurants, not just the upscale ones, but the so-called family establishments as well; anything as long as you can sit down and be served will do. Look at the menus; ask the managers about the most popular items and what sort of specials they feature. Let the staff know what you are about and, for Emeril's sake, order something while you are there.

Your Own Celebrity Chefs

You don't need Bobby Flay or Mario Batali to lead your cooking classes; you don't even need a professional chef, although that might be a nice touch.

Any numbers of amateur cooks have immersed themselves in their chosen cuisine to the point of expertise and can probably cover any aspect of preparation, ingredients, cooking, and serving. They will also know where to buy needed items, and probably have a supply of the more esoteric herbs, spices, and condiments particular to their type of cooking. This is all essential to the student's future mastery of the cuisine. These local epicures might not have the artistic presentation down to perfection, but most people are concerned about taste, not appearance; by the time the family scrambles down to the table and serving spoons start flying, no one is going to remember that wonderful radish garnish or spun sugar lacework.

When you find people interested in doing a demonstration or teaching a class, you will need to be certain that they follow health and sanitation guidelines closely, especially if the food is to be eaten by program attendees (for that matter, you don't want the instructor to succumb to salmonella, either). It is best if you take over the storage and care of perishables after purchase (or purchase them yourself); you have much to be concerned about here and despite all good intentions, people do get careless with their food handling at home. That stomach ache you had last week was probably not the "stomach flu"; food poisoning is much more common than you think. Special care must be taken with poultry, not only in storage but in handling and preparation. Read the USDA purchase and safe handling guidelines for all perishable products at www.ams.usda.gov/howtobuy/index.htm.

You would also be wise to taste the flavor and quality of your would-be instructor's dishes before you permit him to be turned loose on your patrons. A really tough job, so you should not trust this to anyone else, especially if the menu contains items like lobster Newberg and beef Wellington. Seriously, you should have the prospective chef bring in a few samples of the items to be made in class and let you and members of the staff taste and rate them. Don't let them give you statements like "Ecchh!" or "great!"; have some sort of scoring system set up to rate the food. If a staff member states that she does not care for that particular dish or kind of food, do not rely on her to test it; rather, make certain that people with a taste for it rate it. Even though you won't have an instructor offering up mud pies, be certain that what is passed off as ethnic cuisine is truly that. Check the cookbooks and restaurants to make certain, if you are not an expert.

The Capacity to Do Food Programming

Every library has the ability to put on some manner of food program, even if it is just a lecture or a sampling of delivered or preserved items—a tea or coffee tasting, for example. Unfortunately, not all of us are equipped to do a true class or even a cooking demonstration. How satisfying it would be to simply hand out samples to your patrons is open to speculation. Still, if it is all you can do, by all means try it.

Cooking Demonstrations
A cooking demonstration is basically what you experience with such Food Network programming as *Emeril Live, Yan Can Cook,* or *Molto Mario:* a chef giving a step-by-step demonstration of a recipe or recipes, including ingredients, preparation, and perhaps some historical or social background. In the library, you would have your chef doing the cooking and explaining in front of an audience. The finished product will then be sent around the room for sampling—albeit the portions might be small if attendance is high. A copy of the recipe, with sources for the ingredients, will also be made available. To put on such a demonstration, it will be necessary to procure several items.

First and foremost, you will need some sort of a cooking surface. Unless the program is specifically about them, this does not include microwave ovens. Although many libraries have kitchens, few are fortunate to have them integrated into their programming rooms for demonstrations. I lobbied for this when the plans were being drawn for the new Peabody building, but to no avail. In lieu of such a serendipitous arrangement, several options are available to you.

Electric frying pans can be used for pan frying, sautéing, braising, and boiling. One of the deep, straight-sided types is best for these all-around tasks. Electric woks are not ideal for stir frying because they cannot adjust temperature as quickly as one sitting on a gas burner, but they will do when there is no other choice. Hot plates can function to heat other pots and pans, but if the particular pot is too large for the burner, the heat will not be even. These are best used for boiling. Many libraries have broiler ovens that toast, broil, and brown. These are useful for those particular functions.

Some home deep fryers can be used to make soup and stew as well; these fryers will have a temperature control on them. Convection ovens do the same work as a conventional oven, only they are portable and cook much faster. Electric griddles are handy for pancakes, crepes, and tortillas, and most have a reversible surface with a ridged grill on the other side. Electric rotisseries, roasters, rice cookers, and steamers are other table-top items that might have some use in your demonstration.

Finally, if you are not happy with the output of so much wattage, and the rather uneven cooking qualities of electricity, you might want to look into gas burners that can operate on a table or counter. Some of these items function as camp cookery and are relatively inexpensive, while others are made exclusively for restaurants and educational facilities and can cost several hundred dollars. Most run on propane or butane and can create a hotter, more even surface than an electric hot plate, as well as offer the immediate temperature control needed for so many types of cooking.

Unless you have a stage, you will do better with putting your chef behind a high counter rather than a table because the demonstration will be seen better and the chef can stand up straight and project to the back of the room, rather than be hunched over or sitting down. If you do not have such a platform, they can be fairly easily constructed; another job for the staff handy person.

The most important piece of equipment you can have at any cooking class or demo is the fire extinguisher. Be certain that it is filled and inspected on a regular basis, and is rated for both flammable liquids (grease and oil) and electrical equipment.

Cooking Classes

A cooking class will actually allow the patron to do some or all of the work involved in making a recipe. Like other true craft classes, the hands-on nature of such instruction limits the number of students, with ten or twelve being the usual maximum, depending upon the complexity of the dish and the students' familiarity with the techniques involved. This way, the instructor can move among the students helping them and making certain that everyone leaves with the same numbers of digits as when they arrived.

With a class of ten people, you will obviously need ten times the number of tools and cooking equipment as for a demonstration. This means either ten times the cost to the library or an increase in your resourceful nature. Some items can be shared, and you might be able to borrow some appliances from fellow employees or their families. Ask your prospective students to bring certain items that every kitchen has, such as pots, pans, place settings, knives, and cutting boards. If you are still limited in the number of cooking surfaces, you might want to have the instructor adjust the program for recipes that require short cooking time, therefore giving everyone a chance at the heat.

Using one's own, familiar utensils and appliances makes a lot of sense from the safety angle because working with the known quantity will cut down drastically on unpleasant surprises, such as, "I didn't realize this knife was sharp!" Make washing up an available option for the class; some people might not care to transport dirty dishes and cookware. Plastic leftover containers are cheap and a nice offering for those who will be taking food home.

Shortcuts can also be used to expedite certain processes and clear any potential bottlenecks. If a certain step or steps in the preparation is known to all cooks, such as peeling potatoes or slicing onions, it might be better to have them prepared, rather than forcing students to do busy work. If your chef has a special way of doing these things and his methods might profit the students, then a demonstration of that method should be included in the class. You need to have at least one serving of each finished dish on display during class to serve as a model.

If you plan on using a lot of tabletop electric heat sources, as well as mixers, food processors, etc., be certain that your room has sufficient electrical outlets and enough separate circuits to handle the load. Also be sure that all electrical cords are out of the way of foot traffic; tripping over an errant cord will not only result in a nasty fall, but in the possible spillage of hot liquids. Likewise, be certain that all pot handles are turned inward at all times and all sharp items are out of the way when not in use. An announcement of all safety procedures should be made before the class begins, and any violation of the stated rules should be rectified before class continues. Other considerations include the ever-present fire extinguishers, splatter protection, such as aprons and goggles, and a good first aid kit in case of cuts or burns. Long hair should be tucked under a cap, short sleeves encouraged, and loose-fitting clothing kept to a minimum around open flames to avoid potential trouble.

Other Food Programs

Besides cooking classes and demonstrations, which entail the following of a recipe from beginning to end, resulting in a finished dish—main course, dessert or appetizer—other aspects of the food world can be presented in a class. Condiments, gifts, snacks, etc., can be part of your food-centered programming.

Jellies and Preserves

Although home canning is a wonderful and satisfying pastime (one of the author's favorite) and a wise way to deal with excess produce, most of the recipes do not lend themselves to a class setting in the library. Much canning is very time-consuming, uses multiple pots (large ones), and most of the burners on the stove. All of these many quarts and gallons of liquid boiling away create much more steam than your library needs to have clinging to its walls and ceilings. There is a great deal of waiting around as well, and a boring class is a dead class. There are always concerns about contamination; although a good canner is a cautious canner, in a class setting, she could miss something that a student does or fails to do that might lead to problems. Students, despite all the lecturing and instructions might, six or eight months down the line, ignore the clear signs of botulism in their canned goods and consume the stuff anyway. That would be more than a lawsuit; we could be looking at negligent homicide.

Jellies and preserves are another matter altogether. The fastest and easiest of all canning, and a common item at fairs and craft bazaars, these spreads are made by many people who have never brined a pickle or sauced a tomato. There are several nice things about jellies and other "hard preserves" (as opposed to apple butter and its kin). You do not need fresh fruit to make them; frozen bags of supermarket fruits will do just as well. The cooking time is short—only a few minutes from boiling to ladling into the jars. Processing time is also short—ten minutes on the average. The jars are small—usually half-pints—so many of them can be processed at one time, avoiding a backlog. Best of all, some is always left over, which will cool and jell, and beg to be put on a cracker to be sampled. Because the jars are small and the contents probably won't last very long, there is little to worry about in the way of storage: just tell the students to keep the jars in the refrigerator.

Jams and preserves are easier than jelly because you are working with whole or chopped fruit; jelly, on the other hand, is made from the pressed and strained juice of the fruit. By using commercial pectin, either powdered or liquid, depending upon the recipe, the class members will be ensured of a good set, rather than depending upon precise temperatures held over a period of time.

Candy Making

Everyone eats candy, but not everyone makes it. Candy making is not one simple process, but rather many different techniques, some of which are easier than others. For the most part, candy making involves heat and time, and above all, sugar; lots and lots of sugar. Hard candies and gels are tricky because of the time and temperature variations needed; only a few degrees beyond the optimum point and your soft candy turns into a brittle mess. The easiest candies for neophytes to make in a class setting would be those poured or molded from the melting of other sweet ingredients, such as chocolate or marshmallows. Candies that require extensive cooking in the 300+ degree range can be very tricky and also rather dangerous; a hot lump of molten sugar will adhere like glue to your skin and keep on burning while you try to rip it off. Trust me on this one: I know first-hand.

Infused Oils, Vinegars, and Mustards

These highly flavored condiments are very popular at the moment, and the variations on them are endless. Luckily, most of the recipes are quite simple. For infused oils and vinegars, the main technique is to heat the liquid, boil it a while with the infusion, cool, and then bottle for a time before using. Oils and vinegars can be infused with fruits, herbs, spices, nuts, and other items.

These items, such as raspberry vinegar and chile oil, make attractive gifts and unique decorations when bottled in eye-catching containers.

Mustards have garnered a lot of attention because of their world-wide appeal and have assumed a sort of upscale snobbery, much like beer did a few years ago. No longer is mustard the yellow stuff that the working stiff slops on his hot dog at the ball game; rather it is haute cuisine, to be savored on the finest of cutlets and in the most sophisticated of sauces. A bit more work than infusions, they are still quite easy to make. There are large numbers of recipes, and the variety is quite impressive, from traditional brown mustards to fruit and vegetables varieties. They also keep well in the refrigerator, from six to eight months or more.

Food Gift Jars

Another craft that has received some attention in the past is food jars. These are usually quart or pint mason jars in which dry food ingredients are layered, sealed, and then decorated in some way. The dry ingredients are not desultory piles of stuff, but rather precisely measured spices, herbs, dried vegetables, beans, and other things that, when hydrated, will make a soup, salad dressing, sauce, or other edible dish. A recipe, or rather directions, is hung on the jar, water is added, along with additional ingredients, such as meat, and then enjoyed. The jars are usually modified by stamping, ribboning, and labeling in such a way as to increase eye appeal. Even the process of layering the ingredients is designed to appeal to the senses. The idea behind these gift jars is that it is an attractive gift of food, straight from the heart; in addition, after the recipe is made, the recipient gets a perfectly good canning jar.

Samplers

A sampler program is a bit like a church pot luck dinner, only slightly more organized. It doesn't require an instructor, and all the attendees are chefs. The food is set out and labeled buffet-style, everyone brings their own place setting, and they all line up to take samples of hopefully everything, but at least what they find appealing. Each cook will have copies of his recipe available for those who are sufficiently impressed by the creation to want to make it at home. You can have the cooks talk a bit about the background of their dish: where they found it, what attracted them to it, etc. Samplers should be given broad themes in order to keep from total culinary anarchy, but still provide enough leeway to have a large number from which to sample. Themes, such as desserts, appetizers, or salads, cast a wide net; to keep it a bit more focused, try theme ingredients, such as chicken or potatoes.

You will need very little planning and practically no equipment to hold a sampler. You will want to offer some liquid refreshments, such as coffee or tea, to go with the dishes. You might also want to maneuver your attendees into doing this on a regular basis—a sort of food club that can share recipes and techniques, and just meet to have a sort of culinary equivalent to the book discussion group.

Gardening

When people began leaving farms during the Industrial Revolution, they left behind thousands of years of working the land and, more importantly, the ingrained instinct to gather and save food for themselves and their tribe. Somehow, stopping at the Kwik Save on the way home from work to pick up milk and bread is not quite the same thing. Planting, growing, harvesting, and preserving have a feel that cannot be duplicated by purchase; thus the "I made this myself" attitude of so many crafts can be seen in gardening as well. After some 250 years of urbanization, things finally began to change after World War II and the rise of suburbia. Going from no yard, or a "postage stamp" lawn to a quarter of an acre or more stirred the long-dormant farmer in the concrete dweller, and thus was born the recreational gardener. Suddenly, garden plots began to appear, flower borders expanded, and garden centers sprang from the soil at every crossroads.

This might be somewhat of an exaggeration—after all, victory and other gardens existed before and during the war—but there is no doubt that gardening is a huge hobby in this country and, as a result, a big business; even supermarkets sell seeds, bedding plants, and fertilizer. If you think this is all a pleasant and harmless weekend diversion, try getting in the middle of a group of men arguing about whose tomatoes are the biggest, tastiest, and earliest. People are very proud of their garden achievements and will do anything and spend any amount to find the secrets to higher yields, bigger blooms, and sweeter fruits. Books and magazines are popular, and can teach much, but many gardeners want first-hand instruction from the masters—the guy who grows the five-pound tomato.

The Cooperative Extension

When most people think of the county extension office, they probably think in terms of the place you take your soil sample to be analyzed for mineral content or bring in that weird beetle with the two dots and three stripes to have it identified. In reality, these offices, administered by the state's land grant college, aid farmers, nursery professionals, and landscapers as well as the weekend sodbusters. They are charged with a great many outreach missions and their highly trained and educated staff will speak on a variety of topics.

The Master Gardener

Extension offices offer a series of classes to the general public called the *master gardener program*. Begun in Washington State in the early 1970s, these rather intensive courses, which include exams and practicums, turn the neophyte plant plunker into a green-thumbed expert in all facets of planting, feeding, and picking[5]. They learn to recognize nutrient deficiencies and how to deal with them, how to handle pests and diseases, and feeding and watering requirements. Part of the student's training is to go out into the community to teach others what they have learned. In fact the main purpose of the master gardener program is to provide trained amateurs to fill in for the all-too-few professionals available through extension. Perhaps you have heard of Jerry Baker, the television, radio, and print semi-celebrity, who touts the use of household cleaning and cooking products as garden cure-alls? He calls himself "America's master gardener," and although that might not be because of this program, he functions in the same manner. Most of the program graduates do not aspire to such lofty heights as Mr. Baker, but they will speak to community events and functions. They also attend fairs, gardening expositions, and work with the community in the beautification of streets, parks, and other public places.

Along with the professionals of the extension offices, master gardeners can be contacted to do a program or workshop at your library. If your local extension office does not have an expert in the topic you are interested in, you can either choose from the areas they do offer, or request that a speaker come from another office. This is not legal issue, but you do need to go through your home office as a matter of courtesy and territoriality.

The list of gardening topics is large, and you might consider any of them for your workshop, but some will be more popular in your area than others (citrus trees would not be a great choice for Wisconsin); still, there are some universal topics in gardening that would be essential for any series of programs at the library.

Vegetable Gardening[6]

Possibly the most popular of all garden endeavors, growing fresh vegetables for the table is not confined to the large suburban backyard; in fact, it need not be in a yard at all. Apartment dwellers with a patio or balcony can have tomatoes, peppers, cukes, and more, simply by planting them in large containers with good soil and adequate drainage. People with small plots of

land can multiply their yields with raised beds or plantings around buildings and fences. Vegetable gardening is seen as acceptable (indeed, almost
a right of passage) for guys, so you can tempt them into the library. Tomatoes are the most popular of all home garden crops because they don't take
up a lot of room when staked or caged, give large yields, and can be used in
a variety of dishes, either ripe or green. The increased popularity of
chiles—another container candidate—has made peppers a very popular
plant as well. With four species and hundreds of varieties, the interested
gardener can be kept busy for years to come. Pepper plants are also orna-
mental as well as functional.

Perennials and Bulbs
Unlike annual bedding plants, which are bought at the local greenhouse,
tossed in a hole with some fertilizer and water, then forgotten until killed by
frost, perennials take time and care. In turn, they will become a permanent
part of the landscape, and claim just a little piece of the gardener's heart. A
well-planned perennial garden will blend color, size, shape, and succession of
blooms into a harmonious work of seasonal art. There is much to learn about
these plants, and their initial expense makes it imperative that the gardener
be prepared to care for them in a knowledgeable fashion.

So, too, with bulbs, which are also pricey, promise years of blooms, and are
all different from each other in their care and storage. Some bulbs, such as
crocus and daffodil, can be planted and basically forgotten forever. Others,
like cannas and gladioli, must be removed from the garden each fall, stored
in a cool dry place, and replanted again in the spring. Still others are more
problematic: tulips grow differently in different climate zones, different soils,
and different light conditions; German irises must be dug up and separated
every three or four years; and some rhizomes will just not produce anything
but foliage, no matter what you try. So much to know, and a master gardener
just waiting to tell people about it.

Trees and Shrubs
Trees are among the most desirable of all plants for the homeowners (provided the roots stay out of the drainage tiles). For most of us, the long lives
of trees means that those there when we move into a home will be around
long after we have gone. Trees project a sort of spanning of the ages and
make us feel a part of things. Nevertheless, with so many new housing starts,
where the developer clears the land, names the subdivision after what used
to live there (Deer Run, Whispering Oaks), then sells the topsoil back to
the home buyer, people will need trees to hide behind, or whatever need

they have for them. These people will want to know what species are healthy, grow fastest and best in their area, and provide the desired traits, such as shade or the ability to shed all their leaves on the neighbor's side of the fence.

Shrubs are a similar product, faster growing and not as massive (usually), but still a long-term investment. Shrubs are most often used as borders, fencerows, and along the bases of buildings. Because of the difference in soil, light and moisture in these places, care is needed to select the proper plant for the proper spot. Shrubs also need to be pruned, and that is also a learned skill.

Pests and Diseases
Nothing is worse than happily buying your plants and seeds in the spring, putting them in the ground and watching them . . . destroyed. Hopping critters, flying, crawling and walking critters, and ones that come at them from underground are all waiting for your plants to get to that right size—not too small, but still tender—to begin their annual banquet. If you are lucky enough to avoid most of this brigade, there is still the disease corps to watch out for, not to mention drought and nutritional problems. What's a body to do? Well, for one, you can identify these bugs, animals, and viruses; you can know what to look for in your plants' behavior and appearance before fertilizing, and above all, you can know how to make these problems go away. Most of us do not want to spread poison onto our land, endangering pets, family, and wildlife, so we need to seek out alternatives that we can live with.

House Plants
Many of us can do a fairly decent job of growing marigolds or tomatoes in the backyard garden, but we haven't a clue about raising those strange, yet enticing, plants that grow indoors. For those brown thumbs who have succeeded in killing every houseplant they have ever touched—including the "unkillable" ones—the only recourse seems to be the purchase of silk plants. There must be a way to make these things flourish; some people have veritable jungles in their home. These people could be the ones you call for help. Everyone wants to grow a few plants in the house, apartment, or dorm room, but so very few of us succeed. A workshop on this topic could be a real winner.

Show and Tell
Another program that might draw some interest is a horticultural version of the food sampler mentioned earlier: people bring in their favorite blooms, plants, or produce in a kind of grown-up show and tell. They can discuss

planting and growing techniques, problems they had and solved, and favorite varieties. Perhaps a garden tool or a technique—composting, for example— can be discussed; seeds and cuttings can be exchanged. You don't need to do much to have your library act as a gardening information clearinghouse.

Birds and Other Critters

For many people, fauna are inseparable from flora in the world of gardening. This ecological approach means the holistic gardener expects to see animals and insects in constant touch with her garden, signifying that all is right with the world, or at least the backyard. For most of us, the animals most often associated with our peaceable kingdoms are birds. They come and go at will, some of them eat insects, they are lovely to look at, and they have wonderfully musical voices. We want them to stay and entertain us, so we need to know about them: what they eat, how they nest, and where they are the happiest. Thus, we can teach people how to make bird feeders (and what to put in them) and birdhouses (and where to place them for maximum use). They will want to have the "right" kind of birds in their yards, meaning finches rather than turkey vultures. Probably some people in your community spend a good deal of time doing these things and can speak with expertise. Try looking up local birding clubs, or check with the USDA Ag office or the extension service. Offering the animal equivalent of a soup kitchen and low-rent condos are the number one activity of gardeners who want to set themselves up in the critter business.

Another popular garden visitor is, surprisingly enough, an insect. Butterflies are very lovely creatures, and most people enjoy seeing them around the garden. Butterflies are usually associated with certain plants, both as adults and as caterpillars, so a knowledge of which plants attract which butterflies is essential to having them around. This is actually called "butterfly gardening." Again, the local extension or Ag office will help you out.

If you don't care much for birds waking you at five in the morning or having caterpillars munching what they shouldn't, how about a nice bevy of bats? Not all of us fall for the bad rap that bats have gotten over the years; we know that they don't get tangled in your hair, and they don't suck blood—at least not in North America. They do eat their weight or more each night in insects, and they do not bother us during the day, when we most want to be out in the yard anyway. In short, the good far outweighs the bad, and the only bad is that they are sinfully ugly little creatures. The thing a bat needs from you is a place to stay; in return it will eat its way through your mosquito problem. The same people who make birdhouses can probably show your patrons how to make bat houses as well.

No matter what sort of gardening programming you are doing, be certain to coordinate with the calendar year; gardening is very strictly regulated by the seasons, and people's knowledge needs to be in advance of the projected dates for planting, pruning, etc.

Men's Craft Programs

Of course, men can and do occasionally engage in the previously mentioned crafts, especially food and gardening, but there are hobbies and handicrafts that are more male-centric than others, and these need to be mentioned in some detail. In the Peabody Public Library, some of the so-called "men's crafts" have been our most popular of all programming. Much of what we would call crafts for men are actually part of an overall hobby, such as fly tying being a part of fishing. We will touch briefly on the hobbies as well as their attendant crafts. Some, such as tying trout flies, are as intricate and artistic as any handicraft, while others are on the more simplistic side, yet still popular because of their "necessity" as far as the crafter is concerned. Women can also enjoy these crafts, and you will probably draw several to your classes, but you are more likely to get the guys out for the night. If that is what you are aiming for with your programming, give a few of these a try.

Putting Food Up

Although canning and freezing are probably the most common methods to save your harvest or hunt, it goes way beyond those traditional methods, and today's guy is interested in most forms of preservation. Although some men, such as yours truly, learned canning at an early age, most saw it as something that mother or grandma did, and the younger ones among us probably see it as something that nobody does. If you take a trip to an outdoor store, or look through the catalogs sent out by major outfitters, like Cabelas or Gander Mountain, you will see the instruments and ingredients of what men view as their own exclusive food-preserving domain. More than likely, the idea that these are men's activities comes from the close association of guys with backyard barbeque. Some of these techniques do have a resemblance to barbeque and grilling, at least in their reliance on meat and heavy seasonings. Another connection is to camping, hiking, and other extended outdoor activities, in which preserved food plays a large role.

Sausage Making

No matter what your mind may tell you about the attraction between men and making long links of sausage, the real reason is that hunters like to use every bit of their kill, no matter how unappealing it might appear in its natural form. Please feel free to skip this section and the following one if you are a vegetarian, a member of PETA, or if you prefer not to think of the meat you buy in the plastic trays as having once been alive. You can resume your reading with *Beer and Wine*. Of course, very few hunters (of the nonpoaching variety) are successful enough to make very much sausage from wild game, so those with an interest in this form of food will spend most of their time using more traditional meats, such as beef, pork, and poultry.

Making fresh sausage (cured and smoked are not recommended for library classes) does not require nearly as many concerns as a regular cooking class. No cooking is involved, so the problem of heat does not exist; there is no need for extensive knife work because the meat is only cut into fairly large pieces to be fed into the grinder (real sausage makers don't use store-ground meat). There is still the safe-handling issue and prevention of cross-contamination from surface to surface, not to mention the fact that a meat grinder—even a hand-cranked model—can do some serious digital damage. In addition to someone who can teach sausage making, the meat grinder or, if that is not available, a food processor is the most important tool. A large mixing bowl for the meat and seasonings, a cutting board, and a sausage stuffer are the other necessities. Finally, you will need casings into which the mixture is stuffed. The process is simple, but the world of sausage is large, as almost every country has a "national" sausage and some, like Italy and Germany, have an incredible variety.

Jerky
Gnawing on dried animal flesh is just about as macho as it gets, so it stands to reason that guys would want to desiccate some of their own. Seriously, jerked meat is an excellent lightweight source of protein for backpackers, mountaineers, canoeists, and others who take to the wilderness for extended periods of time. Jerky can be made from any lean meat: poultry, wild game, some cuts of beef and pork, and fish. The problem with jerky is that it needs to be dried over low heat (140°–150°F) and this takes time, generally six to eight hours, depending upon the quality of the dehydrator. After cutting the meat into thin strips (no easy feat in itself), it is marinated in a liquid or cured with a dry rub for several hours or overnight. Jerky is a two-day job, so an actual class is probably not possible. A demonstration would be the best way to approach this topic. A wide variety of marinade recipes and rubs can be explained, and dehydrators are of sufficient variety that they, too, need some clarification. A selection of finished products can be passed around to satisfy the carnivore in your patrons.

Beer and Wine
Home brewing goes back to the beginning of agriculture, and winemaking probably even back farther, to our nomadic ancestors. Although people have always dabbled in home wine making, do-it-yourself beer went out of favor after prohibition was repealed, thanks to the bad reputation it received at that time (contrary to popular belief, the brewing and use of beer and wine in a private home were tacitly legal during this time). Recently, as imported and craft or microbrews have gained a following among the upper-middle class, making your own has enjoyed a resurgence. Home-brewing kits are sold in many outlets, and specialty brew shops have sprung up in malls and urban shopping districts. Like jerky, it takes time to make these potables, so a demonstration or lecture session would be more effective. Sampling may or may not be possible, based upon your library's policy on alcohol consumption on premises. For that matter, it might not be legal in your community if it is still dry.

Fishing Classes
Here is your chance to fulfill that old adage about teaching a man to fish. Actually, most of the people who come to a class will already know how to fish; they just want to know how to be better at it. The popularity of these programs will depend much upon where your library is situated; I grew up in Michigan, which has almost as much water as land, and where fishing is almost a religion. Children there and, more than likely, in Wisconsin and Minnesota, are placed in a boat with rod in hand as soon as they can flex their little fingers into a grip. The joy of that first experience never fades for the true angler, and is renewed in full with each trip to the water.

An angler's odyssey through life is a sort of evolution up the ladder of fishing's challenges. It begins with a bobber and some worms, moves on to casting artificial lures, then in some cases culminates with the placing of a hand-tied fly over a wily brown trout. In between, there is much from which to choose, and while some settle into one form of the pursuit, others will look for new challenges. What follows are only some of the highlights; a trip to that outdoor store's video section will help you to decide what people are looking for, as will a Saturday morning session with the cable television fishing shows (which are just a bit more exciting than televised golf).

Fly Tying
The height of any fishing experience is to catch a fish on a lure you have made yourself, thereby proving that you can fool Mother Nature. Or it might simply prove that you are smarter than a fish having a bad day. It really

doesn't matter which, because fly fishing and tying is one heck of a hobby (place personal opinion here). One of the things that fly tying does is extend the fishing season year around. For those of us who don't care for fishing through a hole in the ice, this is very important. For an angler there are two states of being: fishing and planning to go fishing. Fly tying takes those plans out of the dream world and puts them onto the workbench. A tier will look at each and every fly created, picture where it will be used, and what will be caught on it. It will be placed in a special fly box with expectations of using it at a certain time of the year on a certain piece of water for a predetermined species of fish.

Flies can be tied and used on just about any species of fish that eats insects, invertebrates, crustaceans, or other fish. That covers just about all fish, fresh and salt water. There are even flies that imitate fresh fruit (it seems certain species of carp are fond of eating ripe mulberries and other fruit that are blown into the water on windy days). Although most tiers start out following patterns found in books, they will eventually begin to alter these flies to better imitate the food found in and on local waters, and they can end up experimenting with entirely original designs. For our purposes, we need only to worry about a few "standard" patterns used to teach the craft to neophytes and intermediates. Your patrons will be a long way from original creations when they start classes; they will be a long way from it for several years.

Most of the crafts mentioned thus far have a relatively small variety of possible materials to buy; most of the variation comes from size and color. Also, these crafts do not rely heavily upon unique tools that have no other use in your life. None of this applies to fly tying; the tools are strange looking and can be rather expensive, and the materials are so numerous, a long-time tier could have several rooms filled with material and little of it redundant. Threads, furs, floss, chenille, yarn, plastic, cork, foam, Mylar, feathers, polypropylene, rubber, and more are used in the making of artificial flies. A tier's tool bench will resemble nothing so much as a surgeon's tray, except for the constantly floating bits of fluff and hair that makes it anything but a sterile environment.

Because students do not learn to tie in a few hours, a complete beginner's course of six to eight weeks will not produce anything that resembles a well-wrought piece; they can cobble together something that works to catch fish, but nothing they will really want to show to the family or fishing buddies. Their efforts compared to the teacher's work would be similar to setting a Precious Moments figurine next to Michelangelo's *David*. Finger dexterity and small size, not to mention working with unfamiliar tools and materials, is the problem with quality; the problem we have is trying to keep our patrons from getting discouraged at what they view as slow progress. Despite these drawbacks—and you should advertise them up front—there will still be many desperately interested in learning the craft. Perhaps only ten percent will continue, but that is why you have a class such as this: to let them know what is involved and let them decide whether it is worth it to continue.

The basic tools of fly tying are a vise to hold the hook, a pair of hackle pliers to wind materials (usually feathers) onto the shank, small pointed scissors with large finger holes, and perhaps tools with such enigmatic names as a *whip finisher* and a *dubbing twister*. With the exception of the vise, all of these tools are inexpensive. The vise, however, is a problem. The most essential piece of equipment, cheap ones can be had for $15–20, but they will not hold a hook very well, and like most cheap tools, will dissuade the student from further pursuing the craft. Although the best hand-machined vises can cost anywhere from $300–500, a decent working model can be had in the $50 range. A kit that contains all the essential tools can be purchased for $60–75 dollars. Most experienced fly tiers have so much material that they probably would not mind sharing the relatively small amount needed for a class with the students. The only really expensive materials are the genetic rooster hackles, and beginners do not need to use those to learn. The only other expense is the cost of a few dozen hooks for each student, a cost of $3–4 per person.

Will you get people putting out $50–75 for a class in a difficult craft they may not want to continue? What about dedicating six or eight nights of their busy lives to the class? Without a doubt; people who want to tie and fish will find the time, and they have probably paid out more money for a rod or reel than they would to learn how to tie a fly. Most classes fill up immediately upon advertisement, and you will get a long waiting list as well.

The intensive individual instruction necessitates a small class, about eight at the maximum. To find an instructor, contact the local chapters of Trout Unlimited or The Federation of Fly Fishers; all of their members probably are adepts at the craft, and one will jump at the opportunity to pass his knowledge on to others.

Other Lure Crafting

Fly fishermen are not the only ones who make their own baits; spin and bait casting enthusiasts also enjoy creating lures. These lures encompass a much wider range of materials and styles than fly tying; they are usually much larger; and a credible product can be turned out by anyone who can cut, paint, melt plastic, and use a screwdriver. These lures were once called "plugs" by old-timers, but now go by a variety of evocative names given them by bass fisherman who want to appear as sophisticated as fly anglers. Made from wood, metal, molded plastic, and closed-cell foam, they fit into several broad groups: spoons, so called because of their shape, are made of metal that is painted or plated, with designs, feathers and hair often added; spinners consist of a blade that rotates on a wire shaft; soft-bodied lures are molded from a vinyl plastic and resemble worms, lizards, grubs, bait fish, and aliens from the planet Grzmikfyk VI; jigs are lead-headed hooks dressed with furs, feathers, or the above-mentioned aliens.

Several lure building techniques—especially spoons and jigs—require painting and may generate some undesirable odors. The new epoxy paints are generally not as noxious, but it is still a good idea to have outside ventilation. Other styles of lures, such as jigs and soft plastics require heat; jig making also means lead, a problem dealt with in the section on stained glass. Spinners are probably the most benign of the lot, requiring only the twisting of stiff wire with a special (inexpensive) machine. Most of these lures require treble (three-pointed) hooks in relatively large sizes, making them more hazardous than a small single hook safely held in a vise. Working with barbless hooks will reduce the chance of serious injury; the hook will still stick you, but it won't tear flesh on the way back out.

Rod Building

One other fishing craft that might be of interest to some of your patron/ anglers is rod building. Starting with blank, tapered graphite, fiberglass, or bamboo shafts, crafters use thread to wrap on guides and tops, glue on cork for handles, and apply a protective finish to the overall product. Besides being roughly half the cost of a ready-made rod, the angler can create personal combinations of weight, length, handle styles, and guide sizes and colors not normally available on factory models.

Rod building materials vary in cost, with blanks being the greatest expenditure. Fiberglass blanks are the cheapest, and thus probably best for learning. Few fishermen, however, would build rods in the quantity in which they would tie flies or make lures. A dedicated fly angler, like me, only has nine fly rods collected over about thirty years.

Flies, however, are another matter. It is nothing to make hundreds or even thousands in a winter's work. You never seem to have enough colors, styles, or sizes. This can be the same with spinning and casting lures. When booking a class, remember that there are many times more spin and casting fishermen than fly fishers, so gear your events to their interests. Find instructors in lure making by contacting local fishing clubs (other than the two mentioned for fly tying), or call the nearest chapter of the Bass Angler's Sportsman Society (B.A.S.S.).

Casting Clinics

Learning to cast a lure or a fly is not strictly a craft, but it is part of the hobby—the most important part, obviously—so why not schedule one in your quest to bring the guys to the library? The Peabody Public Library has conducted several fly-casting clinics, with good turnout. We are still asked (after two years) if we will be doing another. Fly casting is relatively simple, once a person has been shown the process and had it explained to them; otherwise, they will spend their time whipping the water and themselves with the line. By teaching them correctly from the start, they can avoid slipping into bad habits, much like a golfer and her swing.

Lure casters also need to learn a variety of techniques which have been given odd names such as pitching, flipping, dead sticking, and drop shotting (although, to be authentic, you need to drop the final "g" off each of these and replace it with an apostrophe). The Peabody has water on its property in the form of several ponds, so such clinics are easily held; nevertheless, a fair-sized lawn will work if you avoid using hooks on your lures. Steer clear of parking lots because pavement is tough on lines.

Model Making

Women will often grow up to collect the items they played with as a child; witness the cost of an old Barbie doll in its original box. Men, however, are different; they collect their youthful playthings, but they continue to play with them as adults, under the grown-up cover name of "hobby." The items aren't the originals, but updated, more sophisticated, and much more expensive versions of what existed in the past. Because they have finally broken the spell of parental guilt ("we can't afford that; there isn't enough room"), adult males buy big and buy lavish when it comes to hobbies. If you go to a hobby store—not to be confused with a craft store—you will likely see a greater percentage of grown men to boys, although guys will often bring their sons along as camouflage. If you think children's toys are expensive, wait until you get a gander at the adult versions. Remember that Revell plastic model of a WWII airplane your brother put together (badly) one weekend? What cost a few dollars and had only a few pieces then has risen to 100 or more dollars with literally hundreds of parts. What guy could resist plunking down a large portion of his paycheck for the chance to sniff glue and lose tiny pieces of plastic in the carpet? At least you will know where he is on the weekend.

Model Railroads

This century-old hobby is nothing like you remember it; you picture the happy toy train going around in a circle under the Christmas tree. Nothing is further from actuality; these hobbyists are building entire civilizations in their basements and play rooms. This realistic re-creation of cities, towns, countryside, and wilderness is the setting for an elaborate layout of train tracks, sidings, and yards. The entire system might even operate on a schedule, and the trains had best run on time! There is, in the ultimate grasp at virtual reality, a tiny camera available that can be mounted to the locomotive that sends an engineer's-eye view of the landscape to a video monitor.

Model railroading is actually several crafts in one, and will keep the average putterer occupied well into retirement. A model railroad is always a work in progress, just like a real community, with demolition and new growth; it just wouldn't be as much fun if they couldn't play with it. Creating trees, grass, mountains, and other natural features is one part of the creation of this world, but there is also traditional model making, with buildings, homes, factories and other structures made of plastic or wood, painted and weathered to look real (but 87 times smaller). The model railroader also has to be a fairly competent electrician to wire all the tracks, buildings, etc., and make them work correctly. Mostly, the serious model railroader will want to have a thorough background in real railroads, so as to be familiar with rolling stock, locomotives, the operation of freight liners, and even history.

A program could consist of information for those interested in getting into model railroads, talks about layouts, wiring, creating realistic scenery, and more. You might have a model railroading club in town; if so, some of the members might be happy to do a program. If not, a railroader is probably just waiting to be discovered; like many "guy" things, modelers are just dying to tell people what they know about the hobby.

Radio-Controlled Models

The other hugely popular—and expensive—area of the model world is radio-controlled devices. Usually automobiles or airplanes, they also include helicopters, military vehicles, and boats. Many years ago, you could go to the park and follow the high-pitched scream of a model airplane engine to find someone with a wire-controlled model. These planes basically flew in circles, with the "pilot" making them do a limited number of aerial tricks. Because of the wire, the person in control also went around in circles, making great entertainment for the kids waiting to see him fall over. With the dawn of radio controllers, interest in a hobby that no longer involved dizziness and nausea skyrocketed.

Although we do not have any library-sponsored RC modeler's programs, the local model airplane club does meet monthly at the Peabody Public Library—not to fly, but to hold their general meeting. Fortuitously, the public park is across the street in case the urge hits them, and the library itself has enough ground without wires overhead to make flights possible as well. Most RC airplane enthusiasts build their own models from scratch, and are probably excellent engine mechanics; a program introducing these aspects of the craft to the general public might prove popular, as would a demonstration of the abilities of these and other radio-controlled vehicles. If you don't have room at the library, see if you can plan to meet at the local park or ball field.

Do-It-Yourself

Hardly an all-male activity, interest in home repair and improvement is at an all-time high. At least a half a dozen cable television networks are devoted in part or entirely to this craze. Home improvement superstores like Lowe's and Home Depot are springing up everywhere. The original guru of the home handyman, Bob Vila, has been joined by a raft of other tool-toting celebrities and even that insidious pop culture creature, the reality series, has invaded the do-it-yourself world. Although you can't let patrons build a new kitchen in your program room, there are many informative themes on which you could base a series of programs. If you don't mind a little sawdust now and again (and who doesn't?), you could even have some demonstrations of small projects and techniques.

Shop Skills

"Measure twice, cut once" is an old carpenter's caveat that, unfortunately, many of us amateurs do not heed as often as we should. Among the basic skills any tool user should have mastered is the fractional arithmetic of the tape measure. A local carpenter, more so than the math teacher at the middle school, is the person to lead a workshop on this subject. Although a math teacher will give a person rules and formulae, a carpenter will give tips and shortcuts, and an easy way to think about the entire process, thanks to years of experience and more than one short board.

"The right tool for the job" is yet another saying you probably heard your father say at some time or another. Sage advice, except that most of us don't know our forstner bits from our spade drills, or when to use one instead of the other. A short course in tools and how and when to use them could be a very interesting program; you might even get some men to show up. Check your local hardware store (the real one, not the help-yourself version) for experts in this field.

What are the dimensions of a two by four? If you said two inches by four inches, you and many others would be wrong. Lumber, for some inexplicable reason, is measured nominally, usually in the rough before it is planed to smoothness, which takes roughly a half inch off of each dimension (except length, which is fairly accurate). Bad news for your room addition, if you didn't know that. While we are at it, what is the difference between a carriage bolt and a stove bolt, and why in the heck do they have such archaic names? One look at the plethora of the hardware aisles or the lumber yard will convince you of the importance of teaching people to understand building materials; the wrong thing in the wrong place will not only make an embarrassing mess, it could be a disaster for the home handy person.

The most important of all shop skills to be learned is that of safety. Power tools can make our work so much easier and faster (like a calculator vs. your fingers), but they demand a respect that is lacking in our handling of such things as screwdrivers and hacksaws. What is kick back and how dangerous is it to life and limb? Did you know that a router motor can turn at speeds of up to 25,000 RPM? How fast will that accelerate a wood splinter into an unprotected eye? Tool company representatives, of which there is at least one undoubtedly plying your district, can speak about the dangers as well as the advantages of their products; they do not want you severing limbs and then suing the company. Major tool companies include Black and Decker, Skil, Milwaukee, DeWalt, Porter Cable, Makita, and Craftsman (Sears). If they can't help you, it's back to the helpful hardware man.

Although this section is aimed at drawing more men to the library, you might wonder if any would actually show up for a shop skills class, thus advertising to the world that they don't know basic "guy stuff"; there are a lot of men who don't know these things, and those who do are always happy to learn more, so don't worry. Needless to say, such classes will also draw from the female side of your patronage.

Furniture

One thing needs to be stated up front: do not let anyone hold a class at your facility that involves the stripping and refinishing of old pieces of wooden furniture. There are basically two ways to strips the finish off of wood: by chemicals or by abrasion. The chemicals are highly toxic, can burn skin, and smell terrible, while what is peeled off is a sticky mess; abrasion simply means sawdust filling every inch of breathing space. It may be best to leave this surprisingly popular pastime to the garage or the back yard. There are minor projects and repair on furniture of this type that can be demonstrated in the library: sticking drawers, dysfunctional casters, broken legs, peeling veneer.

Perhaps the quintessential furniture repair project is reupholstering. People bring in their favorite chair and learn how to re-stuff and re-cover it. This is actually a fairly easy pursuit, once you know a few basic procedures. A job on a chair can usually be finished in one evening, and the techniques can transfer themselves to other items in the home, such as sofas.

Basic Home Repairs

Plunging out a stopped-up toilet is no one's idea of a fun handicraft, but a few lessons in basic plumbing repair and maintenance will save the average homeowner hundreds, if not thousands, of dollars over the years. Besides unclogging drains, fixing leaky faucets, and replacing broken pipes, a plumbing workshop can explain the basics of plumber's tools, the different types of pipe and their uses, and when and when not to call in a professional. Plumbers don't really like being called out for minor problems, and would be happy to show your patrons how to do these things.

Electricity is not something you want to let your unwired patrons fool with in a class setting, for obvious reasons. That does not mean that you shouldn't have some demonstration programs to show them some of the simpler things about house wiring. How to change fuses, reset circuit breakers, and perhaps even putting in a new switch or outlet can be discussed, along with basic safety precautions that should be observed both when working with electrical wiring or just using an appliance.

Auto Basics

The Peabody Public Library has held a basic auto maintenance class for those who don't have a clue about what's under the hood. Because that includes a lot of men, as well as women, we avoided using cute stereotyped titles, such as "powder-puff mechanics." For those less than enthralled by the smell of gas and grease, the class included an overview of the engine and how it works, the changing of oil, filters, and spark plugs, as well as the location of fuses and the replacement of head and tail lights. Just about anyone who works on their own vehicles on a regular basis can do this class; we had the teenaged daughter of a staff member conduct ours. Class size can vary, depending upon the size of your library's parking lot.

Hunters' Workshops

Depending upon your location, you may have many avid hunters among your patron base. Holding some workshops of interest to them can be a way of showing that the library cares about them as well. Not as many ancillary crafts relate to hunting as to fishing, but some of them might be possible for the library to sponsor. There are also a couple that you should probably avoid. Reloading is a fairly simple process by which spent shell casings are refilled and sealed using a special press; this is more economical than purchasing new shells each time, and the hunter can vary the strength of the charge to personal preferences. Because what is being refilled into the casings is gunpowder, you might want to pass on this one. Another is the scent workshop.

Hunters believe they can make themselves invisible to their prey by masking their scent with certain natural chemicals. Without going into too much detail, these chemicals are derived from the animals themselves, and do not exactly smell fresh as a spring breeze. It is better not to have your program room full of people sampling such fare.

A safer workshop might entail the learning and use of various game calls, which are designed to make an animal believe another of their species is close at hand and making either threatening or amorous vocalizations. The most common of these calls are duck, geese, wild turkey, crow, deer, and elk. These calls are either manipulated by blowing, striking, or scratching them. Hunters learn the different calls and their meanings ("Go away or I'll claw your eyeballs out" is probably the wrong message to send if you want a squirrel to get closer to you). If you do schedule such a class, be sure it is in a fairly soundproof room, as a dozen or more of these cacophonous noisemakers working in unison is a rather daunting noise. Patrons should not be led to believe that the library is possessed.

Decoys
Finally, the making of decoys is an ages-old craft of the hunter. Some incredibly realistic renderings of birds are truly art; there are more stylistic and easier-to-construct decoys made of wood, plastic, canvas, reed, and other materials. Check local wood-carving and hunting clubs for potential instructors in these crafts.

A World of Crafts

We might have given you a great deal of craft possibilities to think about, but in reality we have hardly touched the surface of this large, diverse world. Many more crafts, with many variations on each, are to be explored. You will not know if any of them will be of interest to your patrons until you can find an instructor and schedule a class or two. A few years ago, the Peabody Public Library offered a course in scrapbooking, and not one person signed up for it; today, we have to put them on waiting lists. We have tried a number of these "lesser" craft classes with varying degrees of success; we do not offer any of them on a regular basis, but will repeat some of the more popular ones from time to time. Scheduling craft classes is similar in some respects to collection development in that it is driven by patron wishes. We always make note of what our patrons are requesting, and if enough seem to have an interest in a particular craft, we will attempt to schedule a program. At times, people cannot get to a class if it is in conflict with other engagements, so it pays to try more than one session if the turnout is low for the first one. You need to be sure you don't have a programming gem before you toss it out.

Interior and Exterior Decorating

Really a part of the home do-it-yourself craze, designing and decorating your own living spaces has become a very popular pursuit. Painting or papering walls and hanging a few pictures were once enough for our grandparents, who, for the most part, felt lucky just to have a home. Now, however, we seem possessed with the notion of possession and must surround ourselves with all manner of stuff. Once upon a time in the Cold War, people built underground bunkers to guard against the end of the world; now, our bunkers are our homes, and we are guarding ourselves from the outside world.

House Staging

House • Staging. *v.t.* That branch of interior design that takes a person's personal statement in home decor and turns it into a bland, generic pile of walls and floors in order to make the home saleable to a bland, generic general populace.

Perhaps this harsh definition is more fitting of Bierce than Webster, but it does convey the general idea behind this enterprise: you can't sell your house to someone else if it looks too much like you. Neutral colors, well-lighted rooms arranged for maximum flow, and an uncluttered, open feel will allow a prospective buyer to envisage the many possibilities of a room, rather than just one—yours. Like the title says, you are creating an empty stage on which the buyer can strut her own imagination.

A design consultant recently approached me with the idea of holding a staging seminar at the library. Having never heard the term, but still interested in all manner of programming, we scheduled the event, advertised it, and, to our surprise, found out just how many patrons were trying to sell their homes without success. We quickly held another session to accommodate those who were unable to attend the first one. If you aren't lucky enough to have a designer walk up to you and offer to do a program, check with your local real estate offices to see if they can recommend someone.

Painting Techniques

Just putting one color of paint on the wall won't cut it in today's design world; faux painting techniques, intended to make your plaster walls look like something else, continue to be the rage. These include sponge daubing, dry brushing, rag rolling, marbling, stenciling, and texturing. Most of these methods can be taught at table top with pieces of wallboard, so a program can be held at the library—with tarps.

Redecorating

The variety of floors, wall coverings, paint, fabric, window treatments, and color combinations have all burgeoned in the past few years; putting this all together into a room that doesn't resemble Picasso's worst nightmare is a daunting task. The redecorating seminars at the Peabody Public Library are taught by the same designer who does our home staging workshops. A designer that has her own retail shop will probably be glad to give an introductory seminar, no doubt hoping to gain some sales from the students.

Landscape Design

Landscaping is much more than gardening; in fact, it has little to do with gardening in the traditional sense. Landscapers are not interested in growing so much as they are in placing plants. Placement of flowers, trees, and shrubs, construction of such human elements as walks, fences, and gazebos, and the integration of existing structures are all part of landscape architecture. You can check with the county extension office or local landscapers for presenters.

Flower Crafts

Many people enjoy flowers—their color, aroma, and freshness—but some want to do more than simply admire them in the garden or a vase; they would rather turn them into a craft. Flower arranging consists of making the most pleasing arrays of fresh-cut flowers possible, using size, shape, color, and fill as a guide. The problem with a course like this is the supply of fresh-cut flowers. It could probably be done with silks, but the individuality of each piece would be missing. The best thing to do is try and get a local florist involved, either as supplier or instructor. Florists will usually throw out flowers that are a few days old, but these would certainly be good enough for learning purposes. Wreath making is popular in the autumn and at Christmas time; again, the local florist is the person to contact. We have had several such classes (they are mainly demonstrations) at the Peabody, usually during the holidays.

Dried flowers are also an important part of the craft world. Potpourri is mainly made from dried petals, flower heads, and seed pods, although they are mainly for looks, not aroma. Dried baby's breath and various leaves and pods, such as teasel and eucalyptus, are also filler in fresh-flower arrangements. Some people even dry their own flowers, either wild or domestic, and would appreciate tips on more successful methods. Check with craft stores and herbal shops to locate instructors.

Needle Crafts

Needle crafts use yarn and thread, and usually some sort of needle, whether it is a standard-eye sewing needle, or some variation such as a crochet hook. There are a wide variety of needle crafts: some are very popular while others have sort of fallen by the wayside over the years. Some are coming back into style and some are declining. Most needle crafts that are popular today have their own magazines and pattern books. While quilting is a type of needle craft, most are more personal and solitary endeavors, and can be transported and practiced in a variety of public places.

Knitting

One of the most familiar of the yarn crafts, knitting uses two long, straight, and formidable-looking needles to work wool or other types of yarn together into loosely constructed items of apparel and household goods. Although the stereotype of the knitter is a grandmother in a rocking chair, the truth is that knitting is a relaxing pastime of interest to a wide range of people. In the past, knitting was one of those crafts handed down in the family from generation to generation, but that is less the case in today's world, so curious individuals will be looking for instructors.

Crocheting

Using fine yarn or thread available in many vivid and subdued colors, both solid and variegated, crocheters make table covering, doilies, potholders, afghans, and even rugs. The author's mother was a crochet addict, spending time in front of the television making one piece after another; much of the time subdued cursing and fuming could be heard coming from her corner of the room as she pulled apart her work looking for the latest mistake. Older crocheted pieces are collectible and can be quite valuable. Although not nearly as popular as it once was (doilies are a vanishing species), and not as quickly learned as some crafts, there might still be some interest in it in your area.

Needlepoint

Along with cross-stitch, this is another popular needle craft, and you will find much craft store space devoted to the two pursuits. A wide range of advocates will be found in a given area, and there are probably quite a few around you. You might recall that football player turned actor Roosevelt Grier did needlepoint as a way of relaxing, so don't rule out anyone as a potential student.

Other Yarn and Thread Crafts
Weaving, an ancient craft, still has adherents across the country. Because it requires a loom—a large, intricate device, costing hundreds of dollars—it can be a relatively expensive craft to enter into initially. It is doubtful that an instructor would have enough looms of her own to furnish them to even a small class. The Peabody Public Library is at present planning to hold a weaving demonstration, with a local weaver providing commentary and showing the various styles of weave possible. Tatting (lace making) is hardly the most popular of needlework, but we have had classes in the past, with some success—at least the few people who attended were interested enough to kept coming back. Other crafts in this genre include embroidery, ribbon crafting, sewing, and macramé.

Candlemaking
A few years ago, everyone seemed interested in candles. Requests for books at the library surpassed most of the other crafts put together. Booths in the mall made and sold candles on the spot; and you could not go into a gift, card, or stationery store without being floored by the conflicting aromas of scented candles. This was before we had built our new facility, and were unable at that time to hold any programming, let alone crafts, so we never knew just how popular it could have been for us. Critical mass must have been reached at some point; perhaps people actually took inventory of their candle supply and found that they had enough to cover power outages for the next two millennia. Maybe the late 1990s brought an end to romanticism among Americans, and the result was a sharp decline in candlelit dinners, bubble baths, and other intimate moments. Perhaps I just don't know what I'm talking about, but I certainly have noticed less candles floating about my own abode.

Candlemaking, although it requires heat, is not a hard class to hold at the library, nor are there many tools involved in most types of candle craft: a pot to melt the wax is paramount and, depending upon the type of candle, some molds. Luckily, wax melts at a fairly low temperature (140°–150°F), so pouring and dipping are not quite as dangerous as some other "hot" crafts. As with other plugged-in classes, be certain to have enough circuits to keep from plunging the library into darkness and enough outlets so that cords are not snaked all over the floor, multiplying the chances of spillage. Melted wax is hot enough to hurt, and wax is a terrible thing to get out of carpets.

Types of Candles
All candles need wax (except gel candles), and they all need wicks; beyond this, materials and tools will vary according to the style of candle being made.

Tapers are the old-efashioned candles you see being made at colonial or frontier re-enactments. They are usually connected in pairs by the wicks, which are used for dipping in the vat of wax or tallow (do not agree to the use of tallow in your library). When several wicks are draped over a stick and then repeatedly dipped into the wax, it forms the familiar tapered shape.

Scented candles are usually, but not exclusively, poured into apothecary or other lidded jars to preserve their aroma. Probably the most popular of all candles, they can be scented with just about any aroma or combination of aromas available. They are usually dyed to a bright color that the maker feels is a match to the scent. Because hot liquids are being poured into glass, breakage is a possibility. Only the best-quality jars should be used and they should be placed in large pans during the pouring. Hot essential oils are quite volatile, so it is advisable to provide sufficient ventilation to help prevent strawberry/papaya asphyxiation.

Gel candles are relatively new to the candle-making scene. They look like they are made of the same stuff as sterno, and are transparent. The gel is also melted and poured like wax; unlike wax, gel melts at a higher temperature (above 250°F).

Carved or ribboned candles are possibly the most beautiful of all candles. A core candle is molded, and then further built up by dipping in contrasting colors. While still warm, the candle is carved with blades, peeling down ribbons of multi-colored wax to form folded and spiraled ribbons. The result is a piece that is almost too beautiful to burn.

Collectibles

Collecting is not really a craft—or is it? It takes some skill, it involves putting a lot of stuff on your shelves that is not really necessary, and it creates a steady drain on the wallet. Sounds a lot like all the crafts we've been discussing. Actually, collectors do much more than just find and buy things; they inventory, arrange, display, learn about, and even repair the objects they collect.

eBay has totally changed the collectibles game. In the past, a person had to go on an extensive hunt to fill in the gaps in a collection. The hunt was the thing, and it could take years to locate those elusive and rare pieces. Now, however, everything is on the Internet for the bidding. People still search through the shops and attend conventions, but it has to be different, knowing that anything is within a few mouse clicks. The dynamics of what people collect has also been changed by connectivity. At one time, some things just weren't available to collect in certain areas, such as surf boards in Kansas. Now that the limits are off, our jobs become even harder. If you have ever worked a reference desk, you know how frustrating it can be when someone asks for price guides to things you never even knew could be collected ("What do you mean, you don't have a price guide to Victorian fire extinguishers?"). You can go to area antique stores, ask the owners what sells the most, or check into collector's clubs in your area. Then there are always the old standbys: stamps, coins, toys, baseball cards, glassware, etc.

Contact a collector—those are the people always wanting to put their stuff in your display cases—to see if they would be willing to do a program about their passion. A series of programs on introductory collecting of several different items might prove to be popular. A typical class for beginners might include a history of the collectible, how much is out there, who is collecting, what the cost is to start a collection and what is involved in getting in deep, a list of sources, dealer, price guides, and contacts. The speaker would also bring a representative sampling of her collection to pass around or, if too expensive or fragile, to be observed reverently from a distance. Always be certain to have a good number of up-to-date price guides for any class.

Conclusion

These are only a few of the many handicrafts that occupy peoples' minds and empty their bank accounts. If you want to research the potential of some other crafts, check the appendix for a fuller—but by no means complete—list. Reading up on them, in books or online, might convince you to schedule a few—if you can find an instructor. Good luck.

Notes

1. The Artist's Palette. A *Brief History of Quilting*. artistspalette.com/coffee/history.html

2. A *Brief History of Quilting*.

3. Carroll, Laurette. *American Quilts of the 19th Century*. www.fabrics.net/Laurette19thCentury.asp. The descriptions throughout this section.

4. Isenberg, Anita, and Seymour Isenberg. *How to Work in Stained Glass*, 2nd Edition. (Radnor, PA: Chilton Book Company, 1983), 18–52.

5. *Purdue University Extension*. *Master Gardener Program*. http://www.hort.purdue.edu/mg/about.html

6. University of Illinois Extension Service. *Watch Your Garden Grow*. http://www.urbanext.uiuc.edu/veggies/index.html

~

CHAPTER SEVEN

The Ubiquitous Book Group

When most people think of adult library programs—if they think of them at all—it is usually that ubiquitous oldie but goodie, the book discussion group that comes to mind. Long before Oprah, people have been getting together to talk about books they find fascinating, either for content, or because they are bestsellers and the need to be "in the loop." Although book groups can and do form in many places—homes, work, school—the library seems to be the most sensible setting for such an event. Patrons and librarians alike see this as the natural order of things and, indeed, in the past life of libraries, when their main function was the dissemination of printed matter, it might have been the only natural adult programming option.

Of course, today's public library still functions as a book place, and many still see that as the main function (in reality, it usually is). However, the view has changed sufficiently to widen our scope a good deal. Nevertheless, the book discussion group remains one of the most popular programs offered by libraries, as seen in both the ALA and the NCES studies.

It not only conforms nicely to the perceived notions of the library as a "book place," but it can also be a constant on the calendar, filling a regular spot, and adding to the perception of the library as a dynamic, happening place.

It is not the purpose of this chapter to discuss the dynamics of actually operating a discussion group: setting goals, facilitating, choosing titles, themes, etc. Many good books have been written on the subject (see the reading list), and these can be used, either by library staff or the group members, to conduct the ongoing management of the group. Rather, it is the forming of a group that can get together, stay together, and prosper for years to come that is our goal.

At first thought, starting a book-discussion group would seem to be a "no-brainer," consisting mostly of advertising an organizational meeting and letting them go at it. This might be so for some lucky libraries with a motivated, self-starting clientele, but in the majority of cases, much prodding and coddling will be necessary to bring together and, more importantly, keep together, the disparate elements of a book discussion group, commonly known as individual personalities.

The Politics of the Group

So, you have posted flyers and put announcements in the local paper and the library newsletter. There is an organizational meeting for the library's brand new book group and you have a dozen or so people show up, if you are lucky. If you aren't so lucky, you have two or three people show up or, worse, thirty or forty. What do you do? Maybe you need to rethink your advertising. Maybe, if too many people came, you should have narrowed the focus of the meeting to certain interests. If there are too few people, you need to get the word out more, and for a longer time. Perhaps you haven't targeted the right people: those who have the time and the inclination to make reading more than a solo activity.

Certainly, you can do any and all of these things, but first, it is best to work with what providence and your advertising skills and budget have brought to you. If you have but a few people at the meeting, it is a start. If these people have an interest—a real interest—in starting a group, then they will find more people to join. Book lovers of that sort rarely exist in their own vacuum, and probably have been sharing good reads, and their insights on them, for a long time. If the few people you have seem to be intent upon forming a group, encourage them to ask around for more prospective members and assure them that you will do the same. If you are not in direct contact with the reading public of your library, enlist the help of reference or reader's advisory: it is almost certain that they know several people who would be glad to look into a book group.

You might also suffer from an embarrassment of riches at that first meeting. What do you do if several dozen prospective members show up? Much has been written on the subject of the "proper" size for a discussion group and, surprise! There is little consensus on the matter. A small group (less than 10–12) might offer comfort, spontaneity, and the chance for all to participate, but the

Table 7.1. Average Group Size

Group Members	# of Libraries	% of Libraries with Book Groups
1–9	229	31.0%
10–19	358	48.3%
20–29	108	14.5%
30 or more	46	6.2%

Source: American Library Association. 1999. *Survey of Cultural Programs for Adults in Public Libraries 1998* [computer file]. Urbana-Champaign, IL: American Library Association/University of Illinois at Urbana-Champaign [producer and distributor].

dynamics of a really good discussion will be lost if all manage to fall silent at the same time. A larger group would help to forestall such a possibility. A large group, however, would be intimidating to less-gregarious personalities, prone to the forming of cliques, and could implode from its lack of similar goals. Table 7.1 shows that most libraries have opted for the small group.

If you do happen to have a large response to your "cattle call," you might want to offer the possibility of several distinct groups to those assembled. Dividing by preferred time of meeting would be the first step. This is usually the biggest sticking point at the beginning. Once that is established, the groups can work within themselves if they feel further refinement is necessary. One thing to remember: do not end up creating more groups than you can handle at your facility.

Group Dynamics

Mixed vs. Homogeneous Groups
Sameness is often safeness; sometimes it is not. If your group is all professional women, it can be assumed that they share a somewhat common worldview. Being successful people, however, might mean that so many strong personalities will lead to instability. Many involved in the formation of discussion groups advocate the mixed group—age, gender, etc., as a more viable endeavor. Married couples, father and son, or mother and daughter, are all possibilities. Laskin and Hughes say of married couples, "it gives them a worthwhile social occasion at least once a month. And it gives them a shared intellectual interest, reviving those old bonds that drew them to each other in the first place."[1] With book groups around, who needs a marriage counselor?

Gender
It is apparent to any public librarian that their largest group of adult readers is female. Men certainly use the library, but they much more often are

"looking for things," such as information, a how-to book, or their kids. It therefore should come as no surprise that most book groups are composed of women. It might fall upon you, as creator of the group, to deal with gender makeup.

Men are, by nature, loners. Coming together for anything, even the Super Bowl, is more on the line of a truce rather than a social event. Competitiveness, plus the ingrained idea that men "stand on their own," are natural deterrents to the success of a good book group. Now that an entire gender has been impugned with that stereotype, you need to know that these are only things that can happen, not what will happen. Most men— at least those to whom reading is important—can probably function quite well in a civilized setting. I, for example, have never even watched a Super Bowl, let alone cared who won (growing up in Detroit can sour one for pro football). I have also been privy to some incredible displays of competitiveness among females. The point being made, of course, is that we deal with people as individuals, not pre-label them as the worst illustration of their particular group.

Although gender differences are not the only thing that can disrupt a group, it is a consideration when planning. Some might feel inhibited around members of the opposite sex, no matter how well-bred, well-spoken, and understanding they are. Likewise, in a mixed group, literary comment can more easily descend into arguments over perceived gender topics that may or may not even be an ingredient of the book in question. When discussion is sidetracked into such channels, it is not productive to the continued health of the group.

Age

Another factor that can lead to nonproductiveness in discussion, as well as feelings of mistrust and/or misunderstanding is the relative ages of the participants. As a certified Baby Boomer, I feel an immediate affinity with those who have shared my world. At the same time, I have come to an understanding, and in several cases, true friendship with, Gen-Xers. But looking in both directions from there, I find the "Greatest Generation" much too removed, however admirable they might be, and those in their twenties undoubtedly hail from another solar system. On this last count, I believe that this is certainly the rule more than the exception.

Just as men and women might see things so differently as to be totally incomprehensible to each other, the culture of age certainly divides us even more—especially in this rapidly changing era. We don't just lack a common understanding; we might not even speak a similar language.

If one wishes to form a rule (which, again, can be broken as needs be), a twenty-year range is about the limit. That is actually quite a large range when you look at it, both in experience and outlook. Because we are concerned with adult programming, let us examine the possibilities for groups that consist of those over twenty years of age. If the median age is thirty, then members can range from twenty to forty. Likewise, a median of forty means a range of thirty to fifty (it is probable that the older the median range, the more comfortable the group will be stretching the upper range boundary). True, a twenty-year old may be missing the wisdom of old age in such a group, but if said twenty-year old desires such wisdom in the first place, she will easily find herself fitting into an older group.

Because we are speaking of people who have the common denominator of book-love to begin with, differences in language, outlook, and style have automatically shrunk. In fact, disparity of age may be welcomed in many groups. If a group of all twenties is reading *The Electric Kool-Aid Acid Test*, just who is going to explain some of the terms to them, not to mention why people in the 1960s would even drive around in a psychedelic bus offering LSD to strangers. Likewise, a sixty-year old reading something like William Gibson's *Neuromancer* might really be up the cyber-creek without a motherboard.

Economic and Social Background

By now, you should be feeling rather uncomfortable. After all, isn't this sort of labeling antithetical to the egalitarian nature of libraries and their celebration of diversity? True, but it might also be crucial to the continued health and life of your book group. Reality is, no matter how much a person wants to be in a group, if that group does not want him, he will end up as a party of one.

Thus said, we will move on to something even more distasteful: economic and social class. Say what you will, this country very much delineates its citizens along the lines of economic status, which, in turn, leads to social status. Although the public library may be a great leveler of class in one way, tossing such differences together in a book group might be a way to foment class warfare, not to mention derailing your precious project.

Often, problems arise in this area indirectly and in some surprising forms. Take the example of the group of adults that gets together on their lunch hour, looking for a break from work. They are professionals or retirees who either have no children or who have recently emptied the nest. Into that group comes someone with several young children, whom she watches during the day so her husband can do the same in the evening when she works.

If she insists on bringing the children along, the group dynamic is ruined. The entire group might share the exact income, the same jobs, the same political and social views, and the same neighborhood; that can all be overridden by the presence of what the others might view as a disruptive force ruining their day, but a mom might just see this as a normal attachment to her life that she has long ago learned to block out when the need arises.

What of a group of confirmed vegetarians who meet for discussion during lunch, then discover that one of their number is an incorrigible carnivore? What if it were the other way around? Confrontation and social ostracism, and we haven't even gotten to the book yet.

These examples of group dynamics might not arise for you, or if they do, it might happen within the workings of the group, after it has gotten off its feet. Nevertheless, you do need to be aware of them, to be aware of ways they can be resolved, and be ready to pass that knowledge on to the group or its leader. It is, after all, your love child, and you need to continue nurturing it.

Goal Setting

Setting goals might seem an odd exercise for a book group, which is a continuing entity that really doesn't have a defined target. Nevertheless, being certain that everyone understands what the group is about—what is expected and what will not be tolerated—is a desirable effort. If nothing else, it will make certain that all members are on the same track. As a sort of charter or constitution, it can be used when things threaten to get off track. "We are about reading fiction, not self-help," might be an answer to one such problem. If the goals are to be changed somewhere along the line (and this is something to consider if the group is floundering), then this can be done by the members as a whole.

The One vs. the Many—the Problems of Personality

If dealing with group differences promises you any number of future headaches, then so should the problem of individual personalities. We all want to shine in a group and feel that we have something to contribute to this world and this society. The difficulty comes when we tend to move from the position of one of many lights in the heavens with a role to play to the Ptolemaic idea that we are the center of all things. Casting a shadow on the group in a variety of ways is the individual who, often unknowingly, pushes her own agenda before that of the group. Often, simply pointing out the problem is enough to correct it. First, however, you need to know what to look for.

The Natural-Born Leader
Natural-born leaders are good, aren't they? Yes, of course. In the hierarchical scheme of things, they are much sought after. Even in the more egalitarian world of the group, they are often necessary to move things out of the stagnating center ground. Their main pitfall, however, is when they become unaware of those times when they need to be a peer rather than an overseer. A true leadership personality can easily be taken aside, have the problem of unneeded supervision pointed out, and they will rectify the situation without animosity. If they do not do so, they actually fall into the next category.

The Bully
This is a much more difficult person with which to reason. He or she actually enjoys being in control and will not easily step aside when confronted. Luckily, such a person is easy to spot and can be dealt with at the time the group is formed. If not, ignoring the person (their demands, not their legitimate discussion input) seems the best way to deal with the situation.

The Book Hog
This person is described by Rollene Sall as, "The first in and the last out of the discussion. Feverishly eager to let everyone else know exactly how much he/she loved/hated the book."[2] Unbridled enthusiasm such as this just needs to be reined in, and such a person is usually happy to let the next person talk, if just reminded that the next person is there. You might need to do this any number of times, but it is certainly better than dead air.

The Variety of the Book Group

Possibilities—that is what the book group presents to its members and to you, the librarian. It is a many-faceted gem that can be mined in a variety of ways. If you do it correctly, the reward could be several groups, all alive and well in your library. It extends beyond fiction—even beyond the written word—and the variety is what will keep people coming back and make others join. If you can't find a theme from the following list that will work as a viable discussion group, then you will just have to invent one of your own—which is what people have been doing since book groups have existed.

General Fiction
This is probably the most common of discussion groups, and allows the members to pick from a wide variety of fiction types. The reader is exposed to a great deal of variety, and people are able to suggest some of their favorite tomes. The only thing that limits the possible choices here is the word *fiction*.

If the group is adventurous, nothing under that banner will be taboo. If one month's pick is a disappointment, well, c'est la vie and on to next month. This is where the mixed gender and/or age group belongs.

Genre Fiction

Habits are hard to break, and this is just as true for the inveterate reader as it is for anyone else. We know that certain types of fiction circulate better than others in our libraries. We can make generalizations across the board, but it is really best if you study your circulation statistics to determine what the preferences are in your area. If you don't keep statistics by genre, then you probably need to start.

Many genres, or rather subgenres, are being added to the vocabulary all the time, from ice-age fiction to cyber-punk. Some are so narrow that you could conceivably exhaust the category in less than a year. We will deal with the traditional categories. As a rule, if someone is interested in these main genres, they will not be shy about exploring some of its outer limits.

A genre book group might not appeal to all, but for those who are attracted, the bonds will be much stronger than merely a love for reading. After all, Cubs fans are all human (for the most part), but not all humans are Cubs fans. So let us raise our glass and toast our favorite team!

Mystery

The mystery novel may be the uncontested champion of genre fiction. Not only are its numbers high in published works and library circulation, it is a varied, yet easily identified area of fiction. It has a venerable past, dating to Edgar Allen Poe and Wilkie Collins, and many memorable and endearing characters. It lends itself well to the series, featuring several recurring characters, thus making it both familiar and safe. We know that Hercule Poirot will solve the puzzle, and do it with a minimum of violence and tawdry sex.

The main drawback to the genre is the many subgenres that exist, and the loyalty that many readers give to them. It might be difficult for a cozy reader to get into a hard-boiled PI or a police procedural. One fast-growing area of the mystery field is the historical mystery, which could take place "anywhen" from ancient Mesopotamia to Victorian London. Most people are naturally drawn to history—even more so when it is presented in an entertaining manner, so this may be a possibility.

Romance

Like mystery, the romance field is divided into many subgenres. However, the differences are not as wide, at least for the most part. Barring the occasional aficionado of sci-fi or time travel romance, the Regency is not going to differ a great deal in content from the Scottish Highland or the American West novel (love, after all, is still love). The main stumbling point here is language and explicitness. Many patrons object to the more steamy romances, and this can cause a problem within a group. If the group is agreeable to reading more tame romance, a series such as Heartsong, Love Inspired, HeartQuest, and others inspirational romances can be a good source.

It probably goes without saying that this sort of group is going to attract female members almost exclusively.

Historical

Historical fiction can include the above-mentioned mysteries, as well as such off-beat areas as alternate histories (rightfully placed in sci-fi/fantasy). It ranges from the Ice Age novels of Jean Auel and the Gears up to the events of the 1960s and 1970s, such as James Ellroy's *Cold Six Thousand*. Good historical fiction is well researched in regards to people and events, and often mingles fictional characters with actual figures of the period. It can be a learning experience beyond the mere literary, and appeals to men a great deal more than the aforementioned genres. The main drawback is that such novels are often massive in size and scope, such as the works of Edward Rutherford. Reading and discussing such material in the usually short times allotted can be daunting. If such books are chosen, it is wise to suggest to the group that they give themselves extra time.

Sci-fi/Fantasy

One of the great library myths of our age is that only young boys (and men who refuse to grow up) read science fiction. Any library staffer who has paid the least amount of attention to what patrons check out will realize that many women do read the genre. This is especially true of the fantasy co-genre, which we usually, but often mistakenly, append to science fiction. Many female authors present a woman's point of view in these alternate worlds, and some, such as Ursula K. LeGuin, rise to heights of true literary excellence. Readers in this genre tend to be of all ages and economic backgrounds, but their affection for the subject is deep and genuine, and can result in some startlingly original and involved discussion. They are linked by their love of the future and its possibilities, and often make for the most lasting of groups.

If you still do not believe that women can be science fiction fans, take home a copy of the film *Trekkies* and watch it; you will see as many Klingonettes as Klingons.

Themed Fiction

Unlike genre fiction, what holds themed fiction together is not the subject matter or style, but rather a more artificial mortar. Books that have been made into films are one such example. The novels can be varied in plot, style, and structure, but they all hold the common theme of having been viewed by someone in the film industry as being adaptable to the screen. With theme fiction, your group is more likely to find a wide variety of reading matter without the added job of searching far and wide for it.

Literary Fiction/Classics

For those who enjoy the *New York Times Book Review* or would like to relive their days at college, this is the group they will form.

Books into Films

A group can do much with this theme, including classics made into films, genre novels made into films, and even—for the adventurous—novelizations of films. The group can stay mainly with a literary discussion, do a critique and comparison of the novel and the film, or even include a group viewing of the film as part of the meeting.

Local Authors

The definition of "local" depends upon where you happen to be located. If you are in New York City or Chicago, local need not extend beyond the city limits. If you are in northern Minnesota, it would probably include the entire state; for some states, it would probably mean an entire region. Nevertheless, the binding theme here is an author who understands the lifestyles and problems unique to where you live. The authors might be living or deceased, widely acclaimed, or virtually unknown. One advantage of a group reading local authors is the chance that they might actually visit your library.

Bestsellers

Ready-made lists are the main feature here. As a sponsoring librarian, however, you might want to have your group shy away from current bestsellers because it might be difficult to supply them with product. Unless, of course, you can convince them to buy their own copies and then donate them to the library when finished.

Nonfiction

Book groups reading nonfiction are an entirely different sort of animal. They might be more serious in their intent, and resemble not so much a literary club as a debate society. Although any book of fiction might present controversial or topical ideas, but the straightforward presentation of these ideas as fact makes nonfiction a much hotter button. Don't be lulled into thinking that certain subject areas will be devoid of turbulence, and thus safe for a group. Any time you get two people together for coffee and a donut, you run the risk of a full-blown battle over jelly or cream-filled.

This doesn't mean you should discourage your patrons from forming such a group. Indeed, encourage the process, but just let them know that things might get hot. David Laskin and Holly Hughes, in their work, *The Reading Group Book*, make a strong case against psychology and self-help books. This is the work of a support group, not a book-discussion group and, "they lead people to expose themselves. This can get dangerous—or tedious."[3] To that subject list, we might add religion, because tampering with belief systems is not a good idea, and logical argument and faith are often mutually exclusive.

Poetry

Although poetry might feed the soul and make the spirits soar, it probably will not fuel a book group indefinitely. A nice change of pace from time to time (if all the members are agreed), a strictly poetical reading group should probably be avoided. A group of poets, however—now that's another matter and another chapter.

Bestsellers

Like bestselling fiction, this comes with ready-made lists. Beware though, most lists are rather heavy with pop psychology and self-improvement books. If they could just pick in between these bones of contention, they would have some prime meat. As with fiction, supply can be a problem.

Subject-Oriented Nonfiction

The best stories of successful nonfiction groups center on the subject or topic group. These groups might feature one subject exclusively (history is a favorite), change occasionally, or change constantly. Rather than reading one single work, the members are encouraged to seek out different works on the current topic. If, for example, the subject is the American Civil War, members could all read an overall history of their choice, or choose or be assigned certain aspects within the conflict, such as individual battles, politics, or civilian life.

By having a fresh and ever-changing outlook, these groups can avoid the problem of stagnation that plagues some groups. Choosing a topic and assigning readings can be almost as stimulating a process as the actual discussion session.

Mixed Literature Groups

If you have a mixed group of people, it stands to reason that you can have mixed literature groups as well. Although a great many people will read nothing but fiction or nonfiction, there are also those who simply read—be it novels, history, poetry, or the lifestyle page of the Sunday paper. Reading is the thing for them, and they are ready to tackle anything. If your group decides upon this course, be sure they know enough to draw up some specific plans for their future picks, e.g., fiction this month, poetry next, a history book after that, etc.

While you are at it, if you feel brave enough, why not suggest a mixed-media group, incorporating books, articles, film, music, and just about anything else that might conceivably fit into a group that can still be called a "book discussion." If the library can supply it, let them know that they can go there.

Some Pitfalls on the Road to Success

Finding the Right Books

If you work in the stacks or do reader's advisory, you will undoubtedly have run across the befuddled bibliophile. When faced with the selection available in even the smallest of small libraries, they go into panic mode and are unable to pick anything to read. Patrons have been known to intercept pages taking carts of returned books to check-in stations on the premise that if someone else has read it recently, it must be worthwhile. We have all been asked, to our horror, to suggest something that we ourselves have recently read. This can get rather touchy, for example, if the requestor is the retired minister's wife and your usual reading matter includes such titles as, *I Brake for Bad Boys* and *The Sheik and the Virgin Princess* (actual book titles).

Rest assured that at some point in the history of your discussion group, you will be asked for input and concrete suggestions. When this occurs—and it will be sooner rather than later—you have two choices: your knowledge or someone else's. Refusal is not an option.

If you work in reader's advisory or at the reference desk, you will probably have some handle on the problem. You know of many resources to advise people on their reading life, and you have probably read a large enough variety of reviews (if not the books themselves), to give something resembling a cogent answer. If not, the following is for you.

Reach Out and Touch Your Co-Workers

No matter how small your library, someone is working there, "because I love to read." If it isn't their job to keep on top of books, it is their passion to do so. Find that person if you don't have a reader's advisor. A true book lover can't wait to tell you her last dozen or so reads and just how wonderful they were. Of course, you might want to follow that up with a bit more objective research, just to see if it really is what the group wants.

If you do have a reader's advisor, or someone in collection development who spends his days staring at *Booklist* and *Publisher's Weekly*, then it is suggested that you become the most steadfast of friends, if you aren't already.

Review Journals

If you don't already look at review journals, you should. In addition to planning programming, I also select all the materials for the adult patrons of the library. A dozen years of reading *Booklist* and *Paperback Advance* has made me one of the most knowledgeable people in the community on books I have never had the least desire to open, let alone read.

Many of the vendor announcement magazines contain thumbnail summations (they aren't reviewing what they are selling) of books, if you don't care to immerse yourself in full-length and often disparaging reviews. Just gather up several months' worth, check the bestseller lists, and compare the two to come up with some instant background on the best-known authors.

Reference Books

Of course, if it were as easy as stated, then we wouldn't need to pay for the expertise of real reader's advisors. It isn't and we do (easy and need to pay, respectively). However, even the best of reader's advisors know when to stop relying on their own vast amount of knowledge and go to the reference shelf. Just like the good librarian who will look up the spelling of a word for a patron no matter how certain she is of it, we need to give even our superior brains a reality check from time to time and use the books.

Perhaps the mother of all reader's advisory tools is called, appropriately enough, *The Reader's Adviser*. The last edition of this six-volume work was, unfortunately, published in 1994. The heir apparent at this time appears to be Gale's *What do I Read Next?*, a two-volume set that seems to be updated on a regular basis. Another standard available in most libraries and regularly updated is H.W. Wilson's *Fiction Catalog*.

At a more economical level, ALA has published a recent (2002) series of works dealing with specific genres of fiction. Thus far, the Readers' Advisory Series includes mystery, romance, sci-fi/fantasy, and horror.

Moreover, any number of excellent annotated subject and genre fiction bibliographies are available from such publishers as Scarecrow, Greenwood, and McFarland.

If you have the time, peruse these volumes and learn; otherwise, give them to the group and let them wallow in book heaven for awhile. They will undoubtedly find something to read.

Online Options

If the Internet had done nothing else for the librarian, the mere proliferation of readers' advisory sites on the Web would have endeared the little cyber darling to us for all eternity. Just as there are a thousand sites for each role-playing game, and a hundred more for each pop star, readers and librarians have flocked to the keyboard and sent their lists out over the ether.

There are readers' advisory pages on many libraries' home pages, as well as sites dedicated to reading in general and genres in particular. Sequels pages are often quite helpful to the reference librarian who finds herself befuddled by the light-speed proliferation of series titles these days. Some of the genre sites have taken a laser scalpel to their favorite reading and subdivided it into sub-subgenres, so there can be no doubt that the retired-art-dealer-turned-international-spy title the patron has in his hands will be have a read-alike to be discovered.

Some of the more comprehensive sites that will yield a gold mine of titles are:

- Kent District Library's Books and Reading Page (http://www.kdl.org/books)
  Includes author pages, awards lists, new and notable fiction and nonfiction, staff picks, and the popular What's Next? search for books in series.
- Overbooked, a site run by Ann Chambers Theis of the Chesterfield County (VA) Public Library, is a large website that includes links to other sites, lists, and a discussion forum. The lists include new books, starred reviews from journals, such as *Kirkus* and *PW*, and themed fiction. Access is at http://www.overbooked.org/.
- Reader's Robot is a genre fiction site from the Thompson Nicola Regional District Library System of Kamloops, British Columbia. It delivers short patron reviews for more than 5000 titles. The URL is http://www.tnrdlib.bc.ca/rr.html.
- Morton Grove Public Library's Webrary (http://www.webrary.org/rs/rs-menu.html) is a readers' advisory service that includes lists of all the books that its discussion groups have tackled for the last several years. It also has extensive links to review and list sites.
- On the fee-based side of the online world is the web version of Gale's *What Do I Read Next?*, as well as *Novelist*, an Ebsco product that con-

tains more than 100,000 titles and 1,200 ready-made lists. It also has a read-alikes feature, endearing it to haggard librarians everywhere.

These sites are only a small sampling. Many fine web pages deal with just about every type of reading and every fiction genre you might think of. Probably the best way to find some of these pages is to go to Genreflecting (http://www.genreflecting.com/). This online version of the popular readers' advisory book contains enough links to keep you and your discussion groups busy for a long, long time.

Other Reading Groups
One last, but by no means least, source for ideas is other reading groups. They might be nearby, or across the country, but they are only a phone call or a URL away.

Finding Enough Books
One of the most important factors for people joining a library-sponsored book group, rather than forming outside, is that a library can supply the needed product (i.e., books). Even if you do not have a programming budget, you should be able to procure the needed volumes for your group or groups. Several methods and combinations thereof will ensure an adequate supply— even if your group has fifteen to twenty people in it.

You need to plan early to be certain you have the items in hand in plenty of time for the group to do their reading, and to have them through the discussion. This will entail working with the group to plan ahead on their selections, either six months or a year. It could also mean limiting the actual selections to those that can be easily had, depending upon the library's circumstances.

Interlibrary Loan
The obvious place to get enough books for a group is interlibrary loan. This, however, has some just as obvious drawbacks. Time is one factor that works against ILL. Even getting the requests out early, you might not get all of them back in a timely fashion, and because each library has its own policy for loan periods, due dates will often be staggered. Of course, it goes without saying that this author would never advocate ignoring those dates so as to have all copies available through the discussion period.

Another problem that can be faced by some libraries is finding enough libraries to lend the books. Many small- and medium-sized libraries do not belong to OCLC, or can do so on a limited basis, so that avenue might be closed. If it is an option, one must send out multiple requests, ideally at least twice as many as needed to cover unfilled requests. These requests should be made to only one library, rather than a string, as is normal, or else you will run into a time factor.

Depending upon circumstances, you might be near many small libraries, which may or may not carry that particular book; you might be near a large library that has multiple copies of the book; or you might have a regional or statewide system for interlibrary loan. You will need to determine which method yields the best results. Library consortiums can handle the multiple requests, but remember that they, too, will probably be using OCLC, with its built-in possibilities of delay and refusal.

Purchase

There are two likely scenarios to library involvement in purchasing books for the group. First, the library can use its materials budget, purchase all copies, and add them to the collection after the discussion. Second, the library can make its discount available to the group members, who would then purchase the book at a reduced rate and keep it for themselves. This second option might not be legal in all states, so check your library laws carefully.

Depending upon the currency of the book, purchase might be the only option. If the book is available in paperback version, it can be purchased if the group doesn't mind handling this sort of binding. There might also be a problem with vendor stocks on some older, but still in print, books.

Extra copies purchased by the library can also be resold at book sales, if it is determined that they should not be added to the collection. Purchasing might seem like a problem best done without, but the option can create a lot of goodwill between the group and the library, and not lead members to wondering just what the attraction is to continued meetings at the library.

Shared Book Group Databases

The Peabody Public Library adult services department belongs to a rather loose group of area libraries that exchange ideas and information on adult-related themes. One of the group's members had come up with a novel way to recycle the book group books she had purchased, or at least to extend their useful lives. She keeps a list of all past book discussion books and the number of copies she has, and makes it available to the other libraries. The group is attempting (remember, this is a loose group) to create a more complete, up-to-date, and streamlined database for all of the participating libraries to share.

Creating such a shared resource would certainly make book procurement easier for librarians, and would actually create another suggested reading list for the group—one that could be gently urged upon members because it offers a guaranteed source of material.

Readers' Guides

No, we aren't talking about the old periodical indexes, but rather a helpful little pamphlet usually issued by the publisher to sum up the book and give readers thoughtful questions for discussions. Most of the major publishers have an archive of these guides on their websites. Simply go to their home page and look for something like "readers' services," "for book lovers," etc. Making these mini-*Cliff Notes* available to your group will further endear you to them.

In addition to publisher's sites, many book group sites also list discussion questions for books. Reading Group Choices (http://www.readinggroupchoices.com) and Reading Group Guides (http://www.readinggroupguides.com) are two such sites. Individual authors' websites often have similar guides on them. Both authors and publishers are very attentive to their readers, and will do whatever it takes to make them happy. Take advantage of their good nature.

Keeping the Group Together

Even if every member of your group is a perfect match, and would never think of criticizing each other's opinions, they are still individuals with their own lives and personalities, and their needs must be dealt with to keep the group alive and going.

Vacations

Some people view vacation time as punishment and only take it if forced to; the sane amongst us relish our two, three, four, or more weeks away from the monotony of making a living. Summer and the December holidays are peak times for vacations, and the wise group is the one that cancels meetings when it appears that several of its members will be gone. Most working people have an idea of their vacation schedule well in advance during the course of the year, and planning can be done early on to determine if the group wants to "skip" a session or two.

Another aspect of the vacation problem arises in groups that have senior members, who spend as much time as six months away from their primary home. It might be healthy for the group to only meet during the "off season," whether that is winter or summer, depending upon your location. Because nothing is simple, the opposite might also be true. Suspending meetings because of the absence of a small percentage of members could cause resentment in others, and might (gasp!) send them to some other, nonlibrary sponsored, group. As you might have gathered, this is probably in part a result of the afore-mentioned age dilemma, and is best dealt with during the actual formation of the group. If everyone goes away for several months, then so does this problem.

Dropouts and Drop-ins

Once a group hits its stride, and people know what to expect of each other and the discussion session, it would seem that there would be no further problems. In the world of everything's cozy, however, a sudden change can spell disaster. For many reasons, people drop out of groups. They may move away, or have health or personal problems, and their leaving could throw off the dynamics of a group, at least for a while. However, if someone leaves for no apparent reason, and gives no explanation, the effect on the group could be profound. If possible, find out why the person is leaving, so as to clear the air. A sudden dropout could send signals to the others that they are to blame, and that can only lead to bad things.

Likewise, adding a new member to an existing group, especially one that has been together for a long while, can prove just as traumatic. Upsetting the longstanding dynamic can leave people who are used to constancy a bit ill at ease, if not downright unreceptive. Of course, the group itself should have final say on whom, if anyone, is added to their numbers. Usually, members will suggest a friend as member, but if the request comes from out-side the group—even from you—it is best to tread lightly. If the group is amenable to the idea, arrange an informal, "getting to know you" meeting apart from the regular discussion.

Burnout

As comfortable as most people are with the familiar, most things do get old after time. This can happen to the best of groups, and when it does, they ei-ther attempt some drastic changes or they bid each other a fond adieu and go their separate ways. Where you come in is helping with the drastic change. We have already discussed the wide variety of book discussion groups avail-able, and perhaps changing from, for example, literary fiction to a genre, or even a subject-oriented group will rescue the group. Readers are usually open-minded people and will at least give it a try. If they don't like the change, the worst that can happen is the end of that group, and the beginning of your ef-forts to start another.

To Feed or Not to Feed

At the Peabody Public Library, we have created a programming monster; people will call about our programs simply to see if we are serving refreshments. We originally felt that "if you feed them, they will come," or alternately, "anything to get them to the program." Unfortunately, the more you do, the more they expect.

When it comes to feeding a book discussion group, you have a bit more control over things. A specific number of people, whose tastes you know, make it easier to plan, and not be stuck with leftovers (which never really happens, if you have a staff as perpetually famished as ours). Of course, you are going to need some sort of a budget to feed them at library expense, but even if you don't have that budget, you can volunteer to shop (with their money, of course) and set up for the group.

The most obvious situation in which to offer food is the afternoon discussion, during which the group would be happy to have a light lunch of sandwiches, salads, or fruit and veggies. After, all, everyone is on a diet, at least in public. Snacks are an option at an afternoon or evening discussion, and coffee and dessert for the dinner group can be an affordable offering. Goodwill doesn't have to cost more than you can afford, but the rewards are greater than you could ever imagine.

One Community/One Book: The Discussion Group on Steroids

There has been no shortage of press on the concept of "one community/one book, " or "(place name here) reads." Begun by Seattle librarian Nancy Pearl, the idea has spread across the nation, as states, cities, town, counties, and other assorted communities scramble to join the popular function.

And why not? As a way to bring our oft-divided communities together, it is a useful tool for government and social organizations. For those concerned with literacy, it is a way to spotlight the positive points of reading and make those who don't a little more likely to join those who do. This, of course, is not always the case, as we have seen with the diversity of people and their ideas. New York City had a large problem trying to settle on a single title. "Some felt that the city was simply too diverse to be united by a single title, proposing that the whole concept was offensive."[4] The committee in New York finally chose *Native Speaker*, a first novel by Chang-Rae Lee. It is the story of a first-generation Korean American and, although generally praised by critics, it can hardly be seen as addressing the problem of diversity in a place like New York City.

It is not the purpose of this book to delve into the mechanics of organizing and running such a wide-ranging program; the popularity of the subject has spawned a great deal of interest on the subject. ALA has produced a CD/planning guide entitled *One Book One Community*, and gave a workshop on the topic at a recent Mid-Winter conference. Information can be had from the Library of Congress's Center for the Book (http://www.loc.gov/loc/ cfbook), which also has links to centers in individual states.

When and if your community develops a "Reads" program, the library will somehow be involved, either in making copies available, hosting discussion groups or special events, and more. Providing copies from acquisitions can play havoc with a library's budget, and not having enough can do the same with its goodwill in the community. Hosting is another matter, and perhaps a chance to form other (or your first) discussion groups.

One Community's Initiative
In Whitley County, Indiana, the Peabody Public Library's home, the initiative for the One Book/One Community project came from several organizations. The county literacy council, the friends of the library, and the three libraries in the county all contributed to the work, and a grant was procured for purchase of the final choice.

Choosing the book to read was a community affair in itself (Whitley is a small county—pop. 30,000). Ballots were placed at several locations, asking people to write in the book they most wanted to see as a county-wide selection. From these ballots, the top ten titles were selected and a new ballot printed, asking once again for the community's input. The final book chosen was *To Kill a Mockingbird*. Using the grant, the committee was able to enlist the Peabody Public Library in the purchase of a large number of paperback copies, which were put in tubs for distribution at the county's libraries. The Peabody's book discussion group promptly latched onto the title as one of its monthly books.

No matter what your involvement in a One Book/One Community initiative, it is going to be a winner for the library, and for your programming.

Adult Reading Clubs

One final variation of a book discussion group is the adult version of the Summer Reading Club. Reading clubs for adults—summer, winter, or whenever—have been gaining in popularity. They are easy to set up and administer; there are no discussions or meetings, and it requires no effort on the part of a patron beyond signing up and reading a book she would normally not have read without incentives. A few visits or calls to area businesses—especially restaurants—will procure prizes, and in the end, all will end up happy.

If you don't have a clue about summer reading clubs, simply pay a visit to your colleague in the children's department. She has the experience, and will probably be happy to share it with you. Remember, SRCs are the reason children's programming numbers are so high.

Notes

1. Laskin, David, and Holly Hughes. *The Reading Group Book*. (New York: Plume, 1995), 26.

2. Saal, Rollene. *The New York Public Library Guide to Reading Groups*. (New York: Crown Publishers, 1995), 39.

3. Laskin, et al. *The Reading Group Book*, 39, 66.

4. McFann, Jane. "One City, One Book: Creating Community through Reading." *Reading Today*, 20, no. 2 (Oct./Nov. 2002), 24.

CHAPTER EIGHT

~

Selling Your Programming

Finding speakers, arranging dates, surveying patrons, begging for budgets, and dealing with the stickiest bundles of red tape imaginable; tough stuff, all of this, but you've made it through the worst of adult programming, right? Pish! You haven't even begun your fight. You need to advertise them, market them, push them until their little bottoms are frayed, and then start all over again, at a higher energy level. You need flyers, calendars, newspaper announcements, ads, radio and television PSAs, newsletters, mailings, word of mouth, bulletin boards, road signs, and anything else that will politely scream, "Come to our programs; you'll enjoy them!" to the community.

It is well known to librarians, and probably to all those who work with the public, that people do not read signs. You can drop a five-foot high neon in front of them proclaiming "Closed Friday!" and it is certain you will incur their wrath on Saturday for not telling them. We make our patrons read our Internet usage policy right in front of us, and they will then proceed to ask us every question just answered in the handout they were just force fed. There are two variables within your control to explain why people don't read your advertising: it either is not there to be read or it has competed for their very limited attention spans, and lost. There is not much we can do if they read it and don't comprehend, but we can certainly ensure it is there for them to read. The best remedies are getting the word out and getting it out in such a manner that it will be irresistible. When we are faced with patrons who have seen our solicitations, understood what is expected of them (come to the program), and still refuse to obey, we must convince them of the ineluctable nature of our product; this is what is known as marketing. Getting a person to pay for something that is normally free, like water and television, is the consummate form of the art; all you must do is convince them that they want something for free that they would normally have to pay for. It isn't very logical, but it's what we have to do.

The People You Need

You rely on your co-workers, friends, and outsiders when putting together programs; you will need to rely on them even more when it comes time to get the word out about those programs. In a small library like ours, I am often forced to take people from their "regular" tasks when there is an important program upcoming. Preparing publicity is as time-consuming as any aspect of library work: while it can be very interesting, it never seems to get done, especially in a library that offers several programs each week. Because few, if any of us, have been trained in marketing, the job can become very frustrating. "I didn't go to school for this!" is the most common cry of anguish to be heard. We didn't go to school to be procurers of programs, either, but we seem to be working our way around that obstacle. Unfortunately, the idea of being even a bit like the prototypical Madison Avenue shark is anathema to the artistic sensibilities of the typical librarian, and we are much more comfortable creating programs. Selling ourselves and acting as spin doctors for our products smacks of crass commercialism, yet we would be nowhere in today's commercial-driven world without it.

Librarians as Marketers

When we moved to our new facility in 1999, my director stated her dream to me: a program a week. If your director is like mine, her dreams will sooner or later translate into your job. Sure enough, we found ourselves pushing for and finally surpassing that goal. Although I never believed that my job security was tied to the number of programs I could schedule, I took the mandate seriously. No one has, to my knowledge, had a dream about program attendance, and I doubt that the board will be paying us by head count anytime soon, but whenever attendance is low, I look at all those empty seats and shudder, feeling that I have somehow failed in my job. This is the impact that marketing has upon us.

What specifically can we do as nonspecialists? Certainly we can attend some workshops on the subject, if there are any. Like adult programming, instruction on marketing for librarians is lacking, to say the least. You can take some general business workshops, but somehow they do not translate well to our particular form of business. Much of marketing and advertising is in the understanding of human nature and the way information is assimilated. I have hinted at this earlier, in mentioning peoples' short attention spans and the need to make our message correspond to how our patrons actually see and hear.

As professor Harold Hill stated concerning the art of selling, "You gotta know the territory." For us, the territory is the library's district and its patrons. Studies have probably been done on that community by local business in an effort to identify its buying public and their proclivities. These studies may have information of import to your situation. Check with the local chamber of commerce to see if they know of any such work that has been done. The U.S. Census Bureau has information down to the city and county level on education level, employment, ethnic background, and other economic and social factors. Although much of what you find will seem apparent to you, it is always best to have the actual facts.

Having the facts, both from these outside sources and your own data, can help you in scheduling programs that will be of interest to the most people. However, more factors are at work in the success or failure of your planning than finding the right events. Anyone who has ever heard a patron bemoan missing a program by beginning with, "I wanted to come, but" and ending with such sundry statements as "it was May Day and I was parading my missiles at Lenin's Tomb," knows that having good programs is only one part of the equation. Day, time, other events in the area, and sometimes just rotten weather can all by tossed in to make a shambles of the most careful of plans. These variables work to either bring people to your library or keep them away; at some point you will have to make yourself intimately familiar with all of them.

Public Relations Professionals

Then again, if your library is part of a growing trend, you might not have to worry about any variables. Many libraries, even the smaller ones, are hiring people with marketing experience. These people often come from the media or business. They know their way around marketing intimately and, if they are local, they will have made important area contacts that you would never dream of making—all to the benefit of the library. I have spoken to several directors who have recently hired such people and they uniformly wonder how they ever got along without one for so long. The smaller library can afford public relations professionals by finding people who are retired or raising a family and want only part-time work. Because library publicity is not a constant demand, twenty hours a week can suffice in most cases. If we had twenty hours a week to devote to only one task, we could get a tremendous amount accomplished. Of course, you will have to share this person with the other departments in the library, even though it is obvious that your consid-erations should be foremost.

Some libraries have combined program planning and publicity into one position, though I frankly don't have any idea what sort of credentials would make a person excel at both jobs. If you don't have a publicist on staff, you may want to consider one. Of course, funding is always a problem. When I asked my director about the possibility of hiring such a person, she simply asked me who I would like her to fire in order to hire one. Given what we gladly toss our funds at these days, something as substantial as pos-itive publicity might be worth holding back on the latest techno-toy or passing AV format.

The Artists Among Us

If we were all to hire public relations staff, this chapter could end effectively now; but we won't and it doesn't. We will go on assuming that you and your staff will work to get the word out about your programs. Your will need to have someone who can write creative copy—clever and original, but factual and to the point—and someone who can fashion visually pleasing and eye-catching designs. This might be one person or two; or it could involve the entire staff, in turn. You can study all the rules of advertising, even get a mar-keting MBA, but if your ad copy is incoherent or just plain and ugly, it won't matter: people will ignore you and all your work.

Whether you are creating a flyer, a newspaper ad, or a highway billboard, your work needs to attract attention in the first moment it is seen, and it must do it with both words and images. Highway billboards are a good ex-ample of the rule (although not all follow it); next time you are driving 60 (or whatever speed you crazy librarians drive), try reading and grasping the message of the billboards that pass you by. You have perhaps three or four seconds to see it, read it, and understand it. This is why billboards are simple and highly graphical—even when they only contain words. Although we are not all in an auto on the highway, we all are barreling along at high speed in our society.

The person who does our flyers came to us via elementary education, a graphic line of work if ever there was one. Having to get the point across to those developing little minds meant that she was more than capable of put-ting across a point to library patrons. The combination that works in her ads are a single, evocative graphic, a large eye-grabbing headline of two or three words, and some smaller informational sentences that are short and to the point, all tied together with border and background colors that blend pleasingly but never overwhelm. A perfectionist, she at times agonizes over things that I don't see, but the end product is always outstanding.

The writer of descriptive paragraphs is also to be treasured, once you have found him. Putting together the necessary factual information in a clever and attention-retaining manner is an art form in itself, and will pique the curiosity of many who might otherwise have passed on your event. Whenever you have more than one person working on an advertising project (we usually have two), be certain that they share a similar vision of the statement being made and the ideas to be conveyed by the finished product. Your copy needs to blend its elements seamlessly rather than pull the viewer in opposite directions. Much like a songwriting team, we write the descriptions first and the graphics are developed around them, with a good deal of back-and-forth consultation until the final product is agreed upon.

Products to Help your Artists
You probably do not have a commercial artist on your staff and even if you do, you will not want them spending all their time doing original artwork for what is essentially a throwaway piece. The person doing your graphics does not really even have to know how to draw, but only how to blend design elements, use a computer, and have some creativity; the rest is simply high-tech cut and paste. Our semi-official ad person (actually head of circulation, but who does only one thing in a library?) uses a program called Print Master for the vast majority of her work. It is a fairly common application, and is often used by children's departments for greeting cards, banners, and other highly visual jobs. An inexpensive product, it has more than a dozen CDs containing literally tens of thousands of design elements, with even more downloadable from its website.

Many libraries have opted to purchase the full Microsoft Office suite for their network of computers. This suite contains Publisher, another large program that can do newsletters and brochures as well as flyers. Like Print Master, it is graphics-loaded, with much more available from Microsoft online (these programs usually have a built-in link to their graphics site). Publisher has the advantage of working with other components of the suite, such as Word and Access. These files can easily be imported and integrated with the Publisher elements. It is also common enough that you can send your files out for use by newspapers, printers, or other places that need more than just a printed copy of the work.

In addition to the graphics that come with such programs and that can be downloaded from the company's web site, many thousands of online sites offer clip art and graphics, as well as type fonts. Some of these sites offer general graphics, while others are specific in nature. Some are free, but the largest of them usually have some sort of fee for downloading. Beware of using a search engine's image search; while it will return much that is very specific to your needs, it will also return a great deal of copyrighted material.

One of the best purchases your library can make is a decent digital camera. Easy to use (with some practice), it has the advantage of showing you what the picture looks like immediately after taking it, and the ability to delete it on the spot. They can also be taken to the computer and downloaded at any time, and the editing software that comes with the camera (or any other photo-editing program) can manipulate the photos to offer a variety of effects, cropping, and color variations. Use pictures of past programs in your newsletter to show others what they missed, or archive them for reuse if a similar program is offered in the future.

Friends of the Library

Your friends group can do more than sell used books; they can help in many informal ways to get the word out about the library and its offerings. Many members of a volunteer organization, such as friends of the library, have deep community roots, and they can spread the word (and maybe supply some friendly pressure) concerning your programming. They can contact the media, put flyers up around town, and even work the programs themselves, as goodwill greeters. Quite often, a friends group will be better received by the community than library staff—especially the professionals who might be seen as outsiders in a small community. Friends members, like most volunteers, will often belong to more than one community organization, and they will be able to talk to members of these other groups about the library—something you might not be able to do, or do as effectively.

Rallying the Troops

It has been stated many times in this book that programming is not a solo effort; it rides on your staff and their willingness to buy into your vision. Selling the programs to the public is no different. The front-line staff—those at the public desks—can generate more publicity for your library than most any other form of advertising. For them to do that depends upon two factors: their knowledge of your programs and a desire to see it succeed. Work hard with your staff to keep them informed of all the programs; send e-mails, post messages at the desks, verbally remind them of upcoming events. Better still, be sure they are a part of your planning process, which will then give them a vested interested in the success of adult programming. Morale is the secret to all successes and failures at a library or any other form of business; if your people do not believe in the product, how will the public be convinced that it is right for them? The clerks at the Peabody regularly mention programs to the patrons, even as they are stuffing their books full of program bookmarks and their bags full of inserts. Most clerks enjoy bantering with the customers, and can get rather adept at working their commercials into their regular exchanges. Often patrons will agree to come to a program just to seem agreeable and get away from the commercial behind the desk, but our program surveys tell us that these conversations pay real benefits.

In-House Advertising

In-house advertising for your events is the only form of marketing over which you have total control. Unless your budget precludes even the purchase of paper, you can give your patrons a steady dose of announcements in a variety of forms. This might at first seem a bit like preaching to the choir, but a large number of regular library users not only don't attend your programs, they might not even be aware that your library offers programs to adults. This stuff is, after all, rather new, and the people who come in and get books and leave have a preconceived notion of what a library does, and programs are not it. After five years of intensive programming, we still run across such people, so we firmly believe in the value of homegrown advertising, be it flyer, bookmark, or newsletter. Patron education never ceases.

For the most part, in-house advertising has little or no cost involved, except the time it takes for its creation. As they say, all we have that is free is our time. The time we use on in-house advertising should include flyers, bookmarks, posters, newsletters, and calendars. Each of these have their advantages and disadvantages, and each needs to be used in proper context.

Flyers and Posters

Flyers are the most commonly used form of advertising at the Peabody Public Library, and for good reason. Creation of a good-looking flyer, one that imparts its information at a glance, is the basis for all of our other forms of advertising and, with modification, can be used for other applications, such as newspaper ads and calendars. I mentioned some of the aesthetics of flyers earlier in this chapter. They need to catch the eye (and attention) from some distance—at least twenty feet, even if they are placed closer than that—in order to bring the casual passerby close enough to gather all the information contained in them. Ideally, they should be placed close to where the majority of your patrons will be (i.e., the circulation and reference desks). Such a thing is not always feasible, given the normal amount of crowding at such areas and the number of programs you might want to publicize. Modern graphics software and word processing have a myriad of text fonts, from such standards as Courier to such inexplicable doodles as Wing Dings. Sometimes a font can be used to reflect a certain mood inherent to the event, but, for the most part, you should stay with something simple and readable. You do not want people to ignore your hard work because an "f" appears to be an "s", or because some fancy script font resembles decorative scrollwork from a distance.

When designing the flyer, a headline of as few words as possible should be able to sum up the program. If the patron is interested, she will be drawn in to read the rest of the copy, consisting of two or three sentences telling such details as date and time, fees, speaker information, and any one or two things you might find unique and attendance-worthy about the subject. Keep the copy together and horizontal, rather than spreading it out across the sheet or getting into such frills as running text around the edges or spiraling it outward. People go to a flyer for information and to a gallery for artistic expression. Graphics should accompany, rather than dominate, and the picture is best kept simple: a photo of the presenter, clip art echoing the subject, or a rendition of the craft or artwork being made. A silhouette of a saxophone will reinforce an ad for a jazz band, but a picture of Coleman Hawkins might be lost on people. We use several types of printer paper for our flyers, mostly in soft pastel hues or off-whites. Hot colors distract from the information and are best left to brochures and mailings, where they will stand out among their duller brethren.

Posters should be larger versions of your flyers and can be neatly printed, cut, and taped together from multiple sheets printed from your computer. Despite the fact that they are at least four times as large and easily seen, posters are not as useful as flyers because of this large size. Most wall and window space is at a premium in a library, and too many large signs not only give a sloppy, cluttered look, the sheer in-your-face-commonness of them will teach people to ignore, rather than be drawn to, them.

Placing flyers and posters for optimum exposure is almost an art form in itself. Bulletin boards are a natural place to put an announcement, but they are not always in a direct sight line along the path of our patrons, meaning that they will have to want to go out of their way to read the board, if they even know where it is. Most bulletin boards seem to be a concession to public service rather than a commitment to it. What I propose, and what our library has, is an inescapable sight line to our flyers when you come in the front door and head any place in the building. This is not a built-in feature of our facility; architects don't think in such mundane terms as ad place-ment; rather, we have a message board on an easel, and our most imminent events are posted there. People are at least forced to glance at the signs; nevertheless, it is better than the informational bulletin board that is out-side the building, about ten feet to the right of the doors (did I mention that the parking lot requires that you approach the doors from the left?). Other places to put your flyers include the aforementioned public desks, the ends of stacks, restroom doors, elevator, and near computer signup stations or OPAC terminals. When posting signs, try to keep them at what was for-merly known as eye level, somewhere around five to five and a half feet. This will accommodate the majority of adults, forcing them to neither bend nor stretch excessively.

Bookmarks

Everyone makes bookmarks available to their patrons at the checkout station. We might buy them from ALA or some library supply company; we might get them gratis from some organization or from our state or regional library dis-tricts; we might also make them ourselves. The interesting thing about book-marks is that they stay with the average patron longer than just about any-thing else they get from the library (except knowledge, of course). How often do you open and close your book during the course of reading it: dozens of times, most likely. In the course of two or three weeks, a bookmark can be handled and viewed many times. By giving patrons bookmarks with program information on them, we can avoid the avoidance of signage that can happen with flyers and posters. Bookmarks should be made on cardstock—as heavy as your printer can handle—in order to have them stand up to repeated use, and should be changed every month. The same design rules apply for book-marks as for flyers and remember: you can use both sides.

Bag Inserts

This is a favorite item of retail stores. They put some of their ads or flyers from other organizations or businesses (not those in competition, obviously) into your store sack. When you get home, it either falls out or you have to take it out before you can fold or crumple the sacks for storage or disposal. You can use one of your flyers, but that is more than is called for in a situa-tion where it might not be read. A simple sheet or half-sheet explicating your programs for the week or month should suffice. Also, a noncolor version of your calendar can be used. This is not high-tech marketing, and although it has adherents, we prefer the bookmark route for our patrons, even the ones who are only checking out videos.

Newsletters

A major form of library advertising is the newsletter. At the Peabody, we do a monthly letter and, by the director's wishes, it is focuses upon our programming, both adult- and youth-oriented. Very rarely will you see book lists or staff reviews of a favorite film or novel. Although a monthly newsletter is quite labor-intensive, and it seems that no sooner is one issue sent out than the next deadline has arrived, we chose that option because we are constantly adding programs to our schedule. In fact, one of the major factors in setting dates for events is that they will be in the newsletter and in patron hands in plenty of time for them to be able to plan on attending. If you time your newsletter to come out on the first day of the month, the first program of that month—if not previously scheduled and mentioned in an earlier issue—should not occur until a week later.

Newsletter design is extremely important if you want people to do more than glance at the pictures. Like flyers, newsletters should be eye-catching and to the point. They should not be dense with text, but rather contain enough "white space" so that each article stands out in its own field of emptiness and immediately draws the eye towards it. Each article should basically be a mini-version of your flyer, without the graphics and visual embellishments; save the embellishments for the text instead. Photographs and other graphics should be kept small and to a minimum, also used as a way to break up the sameness of text and draw attention to specific parts of the page.

No matter how often or how thoroughly you may mention your events in the text of articles, you need to have a separate listing for them in a prominent place, being the front page of the newsletter. They should be set off to one side in a box or sidebar of a color contrasting that of the paper stock. We run ours down the left side of the first page on a blue background and, when the schedule is very full, it is continued on page two. We actually list the current month and what is known of the coming month's schedules. The information for each program includes the title, date and time, fees and registration, and a very short description.

Calendars

A monthly calendar of the date block variety is also a good idea and should be available for pick up at the circulation desk. Many people prefer to have such visuals, which can be easily displayed and even used by the patron for other appointments. We put our programs on a separate calendar than that of the children's department because their many crafts and story times tend to dominate the space. Our calendar features small versions of our flyer graphics (why reinvent the wheel?), and we will also add graphics for major holidays or whimsical events from Chase's, especially if the schedule is rather sparse that month. Small refrigerator magnets printed with the library's name and phone number can be purchased cheaply and given with the calendars so that the patron will feel compelled to stick the thing on the refrigerator when they get home.

In-House, Out-House

Some of these ideas can easily be used beyond your facility as well as inside. Flyers can be posted (with permission) on public boards in such community establishments as supermarkets and laundromats. If you do so, keep a list of each flyer and where it goes so that you can send someone to remove them after the event, as a courtesy. Bookmarks can be placed at such public places as the post office or banks. Newsletters are often mailed to patrons. As a show of its commitment to programming and marketing the library, the board of trustees of the Peabody Public Library has made available a budget to print and send a newsletter to each registered family (not individual) in our district. This is quite an expense, but is probably the best form of advertising we have. If you cannot do this, you can always create a list of patrons by asking them if they would like to receive a newsletter at home.

Perhaps the best form of in-house created advertising that can reach outside the library is your web page. Among the many things it already does, it can display calendars (there are programs available for online registration for your events), make available extended articles on special events, keep blogs, and even house a copy of your newsletter. With home connectedness increasing every day, and the speed of DSL and satellite feed, you can be sure that in the future, most of your advertising will be aimed at this medium.

Using the Media

No matter what we say or whom we hire to say it, we will never be as effective with our in-house advertising methods as one well-placed announcement in the current dominant forms of media. Newspapers, television, and radio reach more people than we can ever hope to do. That is the good news. The bad news is that absolutely everyone with something to sell also knows this. When you try to get your message out, you will be sharing a very limited amount of print space or airtime for your public service spots, which means that you could very well lose out if you do not know how to play the game. Remember, too, that all media are not equal for all things, so you will have to do some homework to decide which works best for your needs in your community. The local Fox affiliate might not be the best place to announce an upcoming classical concert, but public radio might not be the place to shill your latest basket class, either.

Working with the Local Newspaper

When I hear other librarians talking about the wonderful relations they have with their local newspaper, I must admit to being overcome with jealousy. At times I feel that we are the only library in the world with a local "paper problem." When I attend conferences and workshops centered around marketing, however, I am reminded that good relations with any media is more the exception than the rule—at least from our point of view. Groans and grumbling will fill the room when the topic of newspaper relations is brought up. The solution most presenters—be they librarians or marketers—give to this problem is a proactive one on our part: one that can be easily learned.

Learning the Newspaper's Style

Do you send program information to your local paper, only to feel that it is lost in some bureaucratic black hole or sent directly to recycling? Perhaps it is impossible for you to find the reporter responsible for community affairs. A typical newspaper has certain ways to handle all the information that comes into their offices each day, and if it isn't in the proper form, it won't stand much of a chance. Most papers have specific forms for news releases, and it will behoove you to find out what the form looks like. They also prefer news releases as factual, no-nonsense documents that will afford them the greatest latitude in using the information. If they would prefer you to write copy for them rather than provide mere facts, you need to find that out, also. Do not waste your time providing any headlines because not even the reporters with bylines get to do that; it is a purely editorial function.

Most newspapers have a particular mission, just as you do. This can include almost exclusive local coverage, it might be mixed with a portion of area and state news, or it might lean heavily to national news. Those that deal heavily in local coverage will usually have the means to hire a fairly large staff of reporters who can cover the local scene and be on call for breaking stories. Others, with more limited resources, rely almost solely upon wire service reports to fill their editions. It will not take much work to decide which type of paper you have in your town. Even so, a paper that carries a lot of local news might not consider your announcements as news. A bond issue or a board member caught dipping into the company till might be considered newsworthy, but a craft workshop probably will not. Likewise, a paper relying on outside sources for its stories might be happy to have your little tidbits, or they might view them as extra work for people they don't have or who cannot be spared. You need to check the actual amount of community news that any newspaper does to see just how difficult it will be to get your information considered before others.

Selling Your Story

No news, as the saying goes, is good news, but in the media game, good news isn't really news at all. Why should a newspaper—or a television station, for that matter—tell a story that really doesn't matter one way or another? A story that doesn't grab the reader, make them angry, relieved, or glad doesn't sell newspapers and, ultimately, advertising space is not going to make it. Sure, most newspapers have the obligatory front-page human-interest photo of the mushroom hunter who finds a morel that resembles Richard Nixon's head, but a steady diet of that will not only bore the readers, but probably drive the reporting staff to seek more meaningful employment. Let's face it: no reporter is going to want to pad her resume for that job at the *Times* with that sort of stuff. Like obituaries, we are just an unfortunate part of life that has to be dealt with somewhere on page thirteen.

Recently, while my program announcements were conspicuously missing from the local paper, it ran a front-page story in which a county councilman likened our library to a "sexually oriented store" for refusing to filter our Internet stations. Sometimes what we need to do is make our anemic little announcements into similarly lustful potboilers that any reporter would be proud to slather across the front page. Let's tell them that we aren't just offering programs, but are changing lives, teaching skills, and entertaining in a way others in the community have not done; in other words, we make a difference. Any bit of information can be woven into a moving piece of news if you word it just right, and getting spin on an otherwise dull topic is what will often put us into the paper. It doesn't matter if the generally held view of the library is that of an unexciting, if necessary, place; your job is to make it sound as if that view is old, outdated, and just plain wrong. When you finish, the public should get the feeling that the crew for Speed 3 is filming chase scenes through your stacks. This might sound slightly silly, but it could be the story that works.

Overkill

One of the problems we face at the Peabody is the large number of programs we schedule, both in the adult and the children's departments. At first it might have seemed a novelty that we had programs at all, and the paper took our information, no matter how dull, as a sort of news feature in itself ("local library has more than old books!"), but it quickly became old news and then no news at all, just more free notices to squeeze into the community section. At present, we are having more luck putting our program notices into the larger Fort Wayne paper (one county to the east) than in the local paper. Part of the problem is that our local paper strives to be a county rather than a city news source—it has neither the city nor the county mentioned in its title. Two other libraries are in the county, neither of which do as much as we do because they are much smaller, and trying to be equitable to them means we are cut out of the publicity loop many times. If you have a similar problem, the best way to effectively deal with it is to decide which events are important or novel enough to be sent to the paper for exposure. If your craft classes fill up on their own—as they often do—you probably do not need to bother the paper with them. The only other option is to take out paid advertisements for heavily scheduled times, if you have the budget.

Radio and Television

If you are lucky enough to have a radio or television station in your community, you should attempt to work with them as well. People get more information from such passive forms of media than they do from newspaper, and it is free, compared to paying for a subscription. Even if the broadcast media are not in your immediate area, they might still be willing to get your announcements on the air. Some libraries produce their own spots, and I have seen some very good ones. However, low production values may turn your attempt into something resembling the local used car ads, and that can destroy any credibility you are attempting to gain. If you don't feel comfortable with doing your own, or paying to have them professionally done, the best way is to simply fill in a PSA form similar to a news release and let your copy be read on air. Such forms can be had from the station in printed form or as a fill-in form on their website. Most stations have regular times when such announcements are read, hopefully not at 3 A.M. A regular community calendar will be the most stable place for your announcements, if the station has one; it will air at the same time or times every day, and might even broadcast your events several days in advance.

A somewhat natural partnership will exist between the library and the local public radio station (NPR), rather than the purely commercial broadcasters, who are required by law to do a certain amount of public service announcements, but rarely are inclined to move beyond the minimum. A public station has more inclination and more time to devote to community affairs because they buy their programming individually and might do a lot of local production to fill in when the budget is low. Northeast Indiana Public Radio, which covers our area, plays its public service ads twice a day, at mid-morning and again at mid-afternoon, and has a separate broadcast for children's events in the area, which is usually dominated by local public libraries. They also will display the announcements on their website for several weeks prior to the event, if you get it in to them early.

If you have a community cable access station in your community, and are feeling ambitious, you might try your hand at a regular program that encompasses all things library. You probably won't be reaching a large audience, but if you publicize your presence on air, there might be some interest in it, especially if it is well done and involves your patrons in some way, such as reviewing books. We all like to see people we know on the telly.

Scheduling with the Community

In a smaller community competition for event attendance can be quite fierce. Everyone—rightly—feels that their particular cause is important, and even a relatively small number of organizations scheduling at the same time can spread the prospective audience so thin that all will end up losers. It is really a simple task to sit down with these groups and work out some form of community calendar, to which all can contribute and at the same time view and correct any scheduling conflicts. Considering the number of internal conflicts we run into when trying to find a room and a date, it might seem like an immense effort to work around outside schedules, but it is really in everyone's best interest to do so. With access to such a tool, you can place your advance schedule there in order to allow others to work around it while you can do the same when you have a more immediate program to book. Some events, such as high school sports, are fairly well fixed year in and year out, and you will always avoid such conflicts (few libraries that I know of schedule programs on Friday evening). At times, events can work in a complimentary fashion and should be scheduled together. A town festival or county fair, for example, can bring people into the area who are looking for more entertainment than that one event can provide.

One problem we have run into is that many well-advertised speakers attract the attention of several organizations wishing to book him for an event. This actually happened to us when we had a speaker appear the week before another group also scheduled him for a public appearance. This caused a great deal of ill will, despite the fact that it was the speaker, not us, who knew that the conflict existed. A community-accessible calendar would have solved the problem.

The best place for this calendar is on a community website, where it cannot only be altered by a community organization, but can also be viewed by the general public.

Targeting your Advertising

Sometimes the best advertising is the least advertising. Look at your program schedule for the coming month or two: are all of the programs of such a generic nature that you can't think of anyone who wouldn't want to attend, or can they be classified by subject and sold to those with more narrow interests? It takes a lot of work, much of it wasted, to get your message out on such a broad scale—especially when the results might not reflect the labor invested. By targeting that segment of your patron base that has a natural affinity to a particular program, you can avoid spending time and money sowing unfertile fields.

Mailing Lists

Mailing lists are one of the oldest marketing tools around, and businesses have been buying or creating targeted lists for many years. They are sold by the thousands of names, specific to just about any pursuit you can imagine, by companies that gather such information. The typical retail list is, of course, no use to us, but we can easily develop our own for program advertising.

Developing Mailing Lists

When I talk about lists, I don't expect that you would go out and collect thousands of names with which to overwhelm the post office; rather, these should be selective lists, probably less than 200 individuals and less than 50 organizations and businesses. The best way to place an individual onto a subject-specific list is to use the statistics available on your circulation system. Look for patrons who check out a lot of one kind of book, be it genre fiction, home repair, or American history. Create your subjects by studying your typical programs, such as author visits, lectures, etc. Patrons also use our circulation system to receive e-mail notification for new materials that arrive at the library. They will enter a profile in the database, and will be automatically sent word when their choices come in. Why not use this method to let them know about our programs as well?

"No-Send" Lists

A lot of press has been devoted lately to the menace of the telemarketer and his dinnertime/bedtime/all-the-time sales calls. Several years ago, Indiana enacted a very comprehensive law against this form of harassment and surprisingly, the federal government has recently followed suit. It would seem that people are quite capable of wasting their money on needless things without help from outside phone calls. The very same rebellion is going on with regards to e-mail and pop-up ads on the Internet. We might want to believe that we are above such low-level commercial activities and that the message we have to sell is more important than vinyl-clad storm windows. Unfortunately, not everyone sees us as the benevolent bringers of culture that we view ourselves to be; to many, we are bad enough as a tax drain, without appearing in their mailboxes every other day. At the Peabody, we get calls every so often—some quite irate—from people who want to be removed from our lists. Whether they think they are saving us money, or simply want to vent against "junk" mail by haranguing one of the few institutions that will listen, I have yet to figure out. Nevertheless, when we do get such a call, we will immediately—don't take the name and set it aside to do later—remove them from our lists. I usually just throw away mail I don't want, but those who need to act against it are people who might begin a crusade if not given satisfaction. Rather than court future public relations problems, the best course is compliance.

Mailing to Groups
We do not normally send targeted mailing to individuals, relying rather on our newsletter, but we do find that mailings to community organizations and businesses are effective. These mailings consist of current flyers and a calendar; thus, we try to confine ourselves to organizations that have bulletin boards or other ways to disseminate what we send them. For businesses, we confine our postings to those events that will be of interest to the business and their employees, such as seminars and workshops (we recently had a seminar on how to get along with your co-workers). We do send a monthly calendar to the chamber of commerce, which graciously inserts a list of our programs in its monthly newsletter. Service clubs and civic organizations, such as Optimists, Rotary, and Kiwanis, receive mailings from many groups and pass them around to their members at meetings. They usually get requests for donations or involvement at some level, so it might be nice to get something relatively benign.

Friends of the Library—Again
One final note concerning your friends group, which you should by now realize is an invaluable asset. Because most of them will be highly esteemed in the community, taken as a group they will have even more respect. A group such as the friends of the library will seem philanthropic and benevolent, working toward a higher goal; they will be the right people to approach businesses and groups via mailings, even if you do it and use their heading (with permission, of course). Rather than us begging for recognition, if it comes from the friends, it might be seen as a request from peers and, therefore, a worthy charitable undertaking.

APPENDIX A

∿

Works Cited

American Library Association. 1999. *Survey of Cultural Programs for Adults in Public Libraries 1998* [computer file]. Urbana-Champaign, IL: American Library Association/University of Illinois at Urbana-Champaign [producer and distributor].

Carroll, Laurette. *American Quilts of the 19th Century*. www.fabrics.net/ Laurette19th-Century.asp

Harris Interactive, *Attitudes and Beliefs about the Use of Over-the-Counter Medicines: A Dose of Reality*. Prepared for: National Council on Patient Information and Education (NCPIE), 2002.

Holt, Glen E., Donald Elliott, and Amonia Moore. *Placing a Value on Public Library Service*. http://www.slpl.lib.mo.us/libsrc/resurp.htm

Isenberg, Anita & Seymour. *How to Work in Stained Glass, 2nd Edition*. Radnor, PA: Chilton Book Company, 1983.

Laskin, David, and Holly Hughes, *The Reading Group Book*. New York: Plume, 1995.

McFann, Jane. "One City, One Book: Creating Community through Reading." *Reading Today*, 20, no. 2 (Oct./Nov. 2002).

Purdue University Extension. *Master Gardener Program*. http://www.hort.purdue.edu/ mg/about.html

Subject Matter and Scope of Copyright (2000). Title 17 *U.S. Code*, Ch. 101 ON-LINE. GPO Access. Available: http://www.access.gpo.gov/congress/cong013.html

The Artist's Palette. A *Brief History of Quilting*. http://artistspalette.com/coffee/ history.html

U.S. Department of Education, National Center for Education Statistics. *Programs for Adults in Public Library Outlets*, NCES 2003-010, by Laurie Lewis and Elizabeth Farris. Project Officer: Bernard Greene. Washington, DC: 2002.

U.S. Department of Education. National Center for Education Statistics. *Profile of Undergraduates in U.S. Postsecondary Institutions, 1999–2000*, NCES 2002-168 by Laura Horn, Katharin Peter, and Kathyrn Rooney. Project Officer Andrew G. Malizio. Washington, DC: 2002.

United States Census Bureau. *Statistical Abstract of the United States 2002*. Washington, DC: Government Printing Office, 2003

University of Illinois Extension Service. *Watch Your Garden Grow*. http://www.urbanext.uiuc.edu/veggies/index.html

~

Websites

FirstGov, The U.S. Government's Official Web Portal
www.firstgov.gov
The starting place to find anything federal, including agencies with speakers.

NASA Speakers Bureau Home Page
www.nasa.gov/about/speakers
The starting point to find speakers from individual NASA facilities.

American Library Association Public Programs Office
www.ala.org/ala/ppo/progresources/authors/authorsyour.htm
Authors@Your Library online database

St. Louis Public Library
www.slpl.lib.mo.us/libsrc/restoc.htm
Cost-Benefit Analysis, Placing a Value on Public Library Services.

National Center for Education Statistics
nces.ed.gov/pubsearch/pubsinfo.asp?pubid=2003010
Programs for Adults in Public Library Outlets. 2002 survey

Cultural Policy and the Arts National Data Archives
www.cpanda.org/data/a00081/a00081.html
The ALA survey of adult cultural programs in public libraries.

The Columbia City Village Idiots
village-idiots.cjb.net
See the people who do our theater for us and be very afraid. Check out the Murder at Ill-brede Manor *page to see the first of our mystery plays.*

Samuel French
www.samuelfrench.com
One of the largest dealers in theatrical performance rights. They also have interactive mystery plays.

Broadway Play Publishing
www.broadwayplaypubl.com
Another large publisher/performance rights house in NYC.

Dramatist's Play Service
www.dramatists.com
Rounding out the big three of play publishers.

Websites Mentioned in the Text

Film Licensing and Distribution
Motion Picture Licensing Corporation
www.mplc.com

Movie Licensing USA
www.movlic.com

Kino Video
www.kino.com

Criterion
www.criterionco.com

Facets
www.facets.org

New Yorker Films
www.newyorkerfilms.com

Filmsite
www.filmsite.org

Musicians
American Federation of Musicians
www.afm.org

Theater
Samuel French
www.samuelfrench.com
Play scripts, interactive mysteries, and royalties

Dramatist's Play Service
www.dramatists.com
Play scripts and royalties

Broadway Play Publishing
www.broadwayplaypubl.com
Play scripts and royalties

Eldredge Plays
www.histage.com
Interactive murder mysteries

Haley Productions
www.haleyproductions.com
Interactive murder mysteries

PlayDead.com
www.play-dead.com
Interactive murder mysteries

Mysteries by Vincent
pages.prodigy.net/jeff.ludwig/mystery/game_vincent.htm
Interactive murder mysteries

The Columbia City Village Idiots
village-idiots.cjb.net
See the people who do our theater for us and be very afraid. Check out the Murder at Ill-
brede Manor *page to see the first of our mystery plays.*

Government Sites

FirstGov, The U.S. Government's Official Web Portal
www.firstgov.gov
The starting place to find anything federal, including agencies with speakers.

NASA Speakers Bureau Home Page
www.nasa.gov/about/speakers
The starting point to find speakers from individual NASA facilities.

United States Code
www.access.gpo.gov/congress/cong013.html

Educational Programs

American Red Cross
www.redcross.org

Herb Society of America
www.herbsociety.org

National Center for Complementary and Alternative Medicine
nccam.nih.gov

United States Department of Agriculture
www.ams.usda.gov/howtobuy/index.htm
How to buy vegetables, fruits, and meats

Craft Programs

Brief History of Quilting
www.finequilting.com/coffee/justjava/ history.html

American Quilts of the Nineteenth Century
www.fabrics.net/Laurette19thCentury.asp

Purdue University Extension
www.hort.purdue.edu

University of Illinois Extension
www.urbanext.uiuc.edu

Finding Authors

American Library Association Public Programs Office
www.ala.org/ala/ppo/progresources/authors/authorsyour.htm
Authors@Your Library online database

Mystery Writers of America
www.mwa.org

Romance Writers of America
www.rwanational.org

Horror Writers Association
www.horror.org/librarians.htm

The Authors Guild
www.authorsguild.org

Novelists, Inc.
www.ninc.com

Poets and Writers
www.pw.org

Western Writers of America
www.westernwriters.org

Sisters in Crime
www.sistersincrime.org

Science Fiction and Fantasy Writers of America
www.sffwa.org

Book Discussion Groups

Kent District Library Books and Reading
www.kdl.org/books

Overbooked
www.overbooked.org

Reader's Robot
www.tnrdlib.bc.ca/rr.html

Webrary—Morton Grove Public Library
www.webrary.org/rs/rsmenu.html
A good source for book group choices

Genreflecting
www.genreflecting.com
The Web version of the famous book of all things genre fiction

Reading Group Choices
www.readinggroupchoices.com
Read what others have been reading. Includes plot summaries and discussion questions

Reading Group Guides
www.readinggroupguides.com
Like above, but even more choices

Library of Congress—Center for the Book
www.loc.gov/loc/cfbook
Information on one community/one book

Studies and Surveys

St. Louis Public Library
www.slpl.lib.mo.us/libsrc/restoc.htm
Cost-benefit analysis, Placing a Value on Public Library Services

National Center for Education Statistics
nces.ed.gov/pubsearch/pubsinfo.asp?pubid=2003010
Programs for Adults in Public Library Outlets. 2002 survey

Cultural Policy and the Arts National Data Archives
www.cpanda.org/data/a00081/a00081.html
The ALA survey of adult cultural programs in public libraries

APPENDIX C

~

Some Further Reading

Book Discussion Groups

Fineman, Marcia. *Talking About Books: A Step-by-Step Guide for Participating in a Book Discussion Group*. Rockville, MD: Talking About Books, 1998.

Saal, Rollene. *The New York Public Library Guide to Reading Groups*. New York: Crown Publishers, 1995.

Slezak, Ellen, ed. *The Book Group Book: A Thoughtful Guide to Forming and Enjoying a Stimulating Book Discussion Group*. Chicago: Chicago Review Press, 1993.

Crafts

Golden Hands Encyclopedia of Crafts. 24 vols. London: Marshall Cavendish, 1980.

Rose, Grace Berne. *The Illustrated Encyclopedia of Crafts and How to Master Them*. Garden City, NY: Doubleday, 1978.

Music

The Marshall Cavendish Encyclopedia of Popular Music. 21 vols. New York: Marshall Cavendish, 1989.

Sadie, Stanley, ed. *The New Grove Dictionary of Music and Musicians*. 20 vols. Washington, DC: Grove's. 1980.

Stambler, Irwin. *Encyclopedia of Pop, Rock, and Soul*. New York: St. Martin's Press, 1989.

Whittall, Arnold. *Musical Composition in the Twentieth Century*. New York: Oxford University Press, 1999.

Theater

Cassin-Scott, Jack. *Amateur Dramatics*. London: Cassell; New York: Distributed in the United States by Sterling Publishing Co., 1992.

Litherland, Janet. *Broadway Costumes on a Budget: Big-Time Ideas for Amateur Producers*. Colorado Springs, CO: Meriwether Publishers, 1996.

Film
Ebert, Roger, ed. *Roger Ebert's Book of Film*. New York: W.W. Norton, 1996.

Katz, Ephraim. *The Film Encyclopedia*. New York: HarperCollins, 1998.

Keaney, Michael F. *Film Noir Guide: 745 Films of the Classic Era*. Jefferson, NC: McFarland, 2003.

Richie, Donald. *A Hundred Years of Japanese Film: A Concise History*. Tokyo; New York: Kodansha International, 2001.

Weldon, Michael. *The Psychotronic Video Guide*. New York: St. Martin's Griffin, 1996.

APPENDIX D

Policy Statements

Program Policy

Appleton Public Library, Appleton Wisconsin
Adopted January 11, 1999

Rationale:

The library sponsors programs to further its mission by serving groups. Programs consistent with the library's purpose may include those intended to educate and inform the public, to promote community discussion, or to present cultural events or entertainment.

Policy:

1. Library programs will generally be free and open to the public, except as noted below.
2. The library may co-sponsor programs with other organizations. Policy restrictions on library programming shall apply to programs held on library premises.
3. Staff plans library programs and makes them available to the community as a whole, but some programs, such as tours, may be given to designated groups on request.

4. There are several types of library programs:

   a. General programs and regularly offered classes are free and open to the public.
   b. Advance ticketed programs are special events with limited seating.
   c. Ongoing program series or classes may restrict participation and be limited in enrollment. Examples include story hour series, book discussion groups, and similar groups.
   d. Private programs for library meetings or library support groups may include invitation-only attendance, an admission charge, or fundraising, with approval of the director.
   e. Public programs planned for library fund-raising may include an admission charge in exceptional cases and with approval of the director.
   f. The library provides group tours or library orientations on request. Some aspects of these programs may be planned jointly with the requesting group.

Approved by the Library Board, 1/11/99

Policy Statement for Adult Programs

The Jackson County Public Library will present programs that are informational, educational, cultural, and recreational to the citizens of Jackson County. These programs will often be presented in cooperation with other agencies and institutions, as well as other public and private resources.

The Jackson County Public Library and its board of trustees endorse and support the Library Bill of Rights and the American Library Association interpretation resulting in Library Initiated Programs as a Resource.

Programs will be planned to meet the interests and needs of community members and will represent the wide range of ideas and views contained in our materials collection. They will represent the library's philosophy of free access to information. The ultimate responsibility for selection of library programs rests with the library director who operates within the framework of the policies determined by the board of trustees.

Most library-sponsored programs will be free. There may occasionally be a materials fee requested by the co-sponsoring agency when these materials cannot be reproduced by the library due to copyright or other restrictions. However, when there is a fee for materials, this fee will be stated up front, and should not exceed actual material costs to the presenter. All classes will be open to the public. All materials to be used by a co-sponsoring body must be approved by the library before the scheduled program.

No individual or organization who presents a program at the library for public attendance is allowed to sell their product or services or collect names, addresses, and phone numbers of attendees during their presentation or during their time at the library. Exempt from this are authors or performers who come to speak about books they have authored or perform songs they have written or performed on video or audio. Before or after the presentation, the author, performer, or his/her representative may unobtrusively sell copies of the published or recorded work. Presentation at the library of any specific idea, strategy, financial plan, or investment does not constitute library endorsement. Organizations or business affiliation will be used by the library in our promotion of programs. This also does not constitute endorsement, merely acknowledgment.

Adopted October 20, 1998, Revised May 16, 2000
Source: Jackson County Public Library, Seymour, Indiana.

PUBLIC PROGRAM POLICY: Peabody Public Library

Purpose of programming
In support of the library's overall mission to provide educational, informational, and recreational material and opportunities to the public, the Peabody Public Library supports community programming that fits these criteria.

Program Themes
- Arts and crafts instruction
- Musical performances
- Author visits
- Lectures on historical and literary themes
- Live performances of a historical or literary nature
- Storytellers
- Programs of an informational nature from community leaders, professionals, and/or business persons.
- Teleconferencing and distance learning utilizing the library's state-of-the-art equipment
- Programs involving the wetlands located on library property. These include:

1. ecological workshops
2. nature study
3. nature art classes

Program Parameters

The library sponsors programs of a noncommercial nature. Commercial enterprises that disseminate generic information pertaining to their enterprise, but which may be used in a general manner by the public (e.g., a lawyer speaking on estates), will be considered as program subjects.

Product selling is discouraged at any library-sponsored event. The exception to this rule is an author signing his/her work, or a performer offering audio or video versions of their performances.

Although the Peabody Public Library does not shy away from topics of a controversial or debatable nature, it will take assurances to schedule only speakers and information that show integrity, expertise, and a fact-based view of the topic.

Program Particulars

Scheduling

Library-sponsored programs that are scheduled for the physical facilities of the Peabody Public Library (i.e., the community rooms, board room, study room, Indiana Room, or similar venue), must be scheduled through administration in the same manner as scheduling by patrons and individuals.

The library staff persons scheduling such programs shall consult the event schedule and inform potential lecturers, performers, etc., of available dates. In certain cases, in event that an important program can be given only at a certain date and time, library needs will supercede public reservations of facilities. In such cases, the library director shall be consulted and a final determination made.

Other Venues

In addition to in-building facilities, library-sponsored programs may be held outside on library property (especially those pertaining to the wetland), or in other local venues, if it is determined that the library cannot provide sufficient space, services, or equipment for a particular event.

Publicity

Peabody Public Library–sponsored events shall be publicized by the staff of the library department originating the program. This includes, but is not limited to:

- on-premise posters and flyers
- flyers placed on (and subsequently removed from) community bulletin boards

- newspaper announcements
- purchased advertising space in newspapers
- library website listings
- circulation desk handouts and bookmarks

Library staff may develop original publicity and marketing copy, or make use of information (biographies, photos, testimonial, etc.) provided by presenters. Program presenters and participants shall be told of the level of library publicity, and if more is desired, the participants may engage in their own supplemental publicity, provided it does not misrepresent the Peabody Public Library and its positions on programming.

Refreshments
At the discretion of the head of the department scheduling the event (and the presence of sufficient funds), light refreshments may be served at an afterglow following the program. This time may be used by staff to meet patrons and gauge their feel for the program and any possible future events that might be of interest to them.

Setup & Cleanup
Program setup (equipment, seating, tables, refreshments, ect.) will be provided by library staff, except in the case of equipment or items brought by the presenter. Assistance with these will be provided by staff upon request. Likewise, library staff will clean the program room or area immediately after the program. This includes, but is not limited to, storing tables and chairs, washing up dishes, emptying trash, and turning off lights or other electrical equipment.

Financing Programs
Admittance to all Peabody Public Library–sponsored programs is open to the general public. Generally, the only charges applied to any program are for materials or instruction books or sheets related to arts-and-crafts programs. On occasion, admission may be charged to cover the costs of presenters or performers.

The Peabody Public Library will finance programs and related costs (advertising, refreshments, etc.) through budget, grants, gifts, and partnerships with sponsoring entities.

Source: Peabody Public Library, Columbia City, Indiana.

APPENDIX E

~

Program Evaluation Forms

Please take a moment to fill out this survey. CHECK ALL THAT APPLY:

Program Name: _____

How did you hear about this program?
1. ____Newsletter
2. ____Newspaper announcement
3. ____Flyer in the library
4. ____Flyer at an area business
5. ____Peabody Public Library web page
6. ____Bookmarks or bag inserts
7. ____Heard it from staff
8. ____Other: _____

What did you enjoy about the program?
1. ____Expertise/knowledge of presenters
2. ____Entertainment factor
3. ____Information obtained
4. ____Atmosphere of library
5. ____Refreshments
6. ____Other: _____

In which areas might we improve our programs?
1. ____Choice of topics (e.g.): _____
2. ____Scheduled times
3. ____Refreshments
4. ____Other: _____

Which program topics would you like to see in the future?
1. ____Music
2. ____Theater/plays
3. ____Business/finance
4. ____Author visits
5. ____History
6. ____Storytelling/humor
7. ____Hobbies
8. ____Crafts
9. ____Other: _____

Which times would be best for scheduling future programs?
1. ____Weekday (Monday–Thursday) evenings
2. ____Weekday afternoons
3. ____Friday evening
4. ____Saturday afternoon
5. ____Saturday evening
6. ____Sunday afternoon

Source: Peabody Public Library, Columbia City, Indiana.

Thanks for Coming!

PLEASE TAKE A MOMENT TO FILL OUT

… …

How did you hear about our program? (circle all that apply)

Newspaper   A friend

Community calendar   Radio   Library newsletter   Library website

other _____

What was your favorite part of this program?

_____

_____

What suggestions would you make?

_____

_____

May we ask your age? _____   **Do you have a library card?** _____

What other programs have you attended?

_____

What are some of your interests (to help us plan future programs)?

_____

_____

May we have your name and address?

_____

_____

Source: Wells County Public Library, Indiana

APPENDIX F

~

Sample Contracts

Sample Contract #1

* We, the undersigned, are in agreement to have (NAME OF SPEAKER/PER-FORMER) speak/perform on (DATE) from (START TIME) to (END TIME) at (LOCATION).

* The amount of agreed-upon compensation, to be given after successful completion of the program, is ($xxx).

* The organization should include a clause stating that it will not be obligated to give any payment unless all points in the contract have been satisfactorily fulfilled. In addition, if the speaker/performer does not show up at the specified time, the contract is null and void.

* If the performer has special needs regarding setup configuration, sound equipment or other special arrangements, it should be spelled out in the contract who will see that these needs are met.

* The contract should include the signatures of all those involved.

* After the contract has been signed, copies should be made and distributed to all those concerned.

* Attach all pertinent information that will expand on the nature of the program.

* Head Speaker/Performer:

(Signature of head speaker/performer) _____
Date: _____ (Printed name) _____

* Director of Library:

(Signature of director) _____
Date: _____ (Printed name) _____

* Library staff person responsible (if not the director):

(Signature of staff person) _____
Date: _____ (Printed name) _____

Source: Mid-Hudson Library System, http://www.midhudson.org/program/PerformersContracts.htm

Sample Contract #2

This contract is made (date) _____ by and between the board of trustees of the _____ Public Library (hereafter referred to as Sponsor) and _____ (hereafter referred to as Speaker) in connection with an engagement sponsored by _____ Public Library, upon the following terms and conditions:

Type of
Engagement: _____

Compensation: _____

Terms of Payment: payment in full after last presentation at the _____ on
_____

Additional Terms:

1. In the event that the engagement covered by this contract shall be prevented by weather, physical disability, or any other cause beyond the control of the parties, the Speaker and the Sponsor shall respectively be relieved of their obligations stated in the contract.

2. The Sponsor reserves the right to cancel this engagement for any reason at any time prior to 30 days preceding the engagement, voiding this contract and excusing the Sponsor from any payment or other compensation. If this contract is canceled by the Speaker less than 30 days prior to the scheduled engagement, the Speaker will reimburse the Sponsor the amount of $_____ to help defray the production, promotion and labor costs that are incurred up to the date of the cancellation.

3. The Speaker shall indemnify and hold the Sponsor harmless from any claims or damages that arise from the Speaker's negligent or intentional acts or omissions.

4. The Sponsor reserves the right to audio or videotape record any lecture, reading, or speaking engagement. The Sponsor may retain the tape in its files, may replay the tape for its employees, and may make the tape available to Sponsor's customers. Sponsor shall make no more than three copies of the tape. Sponsor shall not sell the tape. The Sponsor shall provide a copy of the tape to the Speaker, upon the Speaker's request.

5. In the event expense reimbursement is included as compensation, the Speaker shall provide the Sponsor with receipts or similar documentation adequate to confirm the expenses incurred.

6. This Contract is a personal services contract, and is not assignable by either party absent the prior consent of the other party.

7. This Contract represents the entire agreement of the parties hereto, and may not be amended except in writing signed by the parties.

Sponsor: Board of trustees of the _____ Public Library,

_____

Mailing address:

_____

_____

Library director's signature: _____

Date: _____

Speaker name: _____

Signature: _____

Mailing address:

_____

_____

Date: _____

Source: Mid-Hudson Library System, http://www.midhudson.org/program/PerformersContracts.htm

Index

~

About the Author

A native of Detroit, Michigan, **Raymond Ranier** came late to the library world, working as a bartender in his twenties and a fishing lure manufacturer in his thirties. After receiving degrees from the University of Michigan and Indiana University, he settled into library life in the small town of Columbia City, Indiana, within striking distance of Fort Wayne.

Ray is married, has three children, five grandchildren, two dogs, assorted fish, and whatever wanders into his yard to raid his vegetable garden. In his off hours, he enjoys traveling, camping, canoeing, and fly fishing. He enjoys programming for his library, and really enjoys it when people actually attend. His pet peeves include the high price of oil, mean people, and Republicans (or is that a redundancy?).